African Policy Innovation and the Political Economy of Public-Private Policy Partnerships

Fred Olayele
Sprott School of Business, Carleton University, Canada

A volume in the Advances in Public Policy and Administration (APPA) Book Series

IGI Global
PUBLISHER of TIMELY KNOWLEDGE

Published in the United States of America by
IGI Global
Information Science Reference (an imprint of IGI Global)
701 E. Chocolate Avenue
Hershey PA, USA 17033
Tel: 717-533-8845
Fax: 717-533-8661
E-mail: cust@igi-global.com
Web site: http://www.igi-global.com

Library of Congress Cataloging-in-Publication Data

Names: Olayele, Fred, DATE- author.
Title: African policy innovation and the political economy of public-private policy partnerships / by Fred Olayele.
Description: Hershey : Information Science Reference, 2021. | Includes bibliographical references and index. | Summary: "This book focuses on a broad range of reforms capable of driving competitiveness and economic growth in Africa, including trade, fiscal federalism, redistribution, factor endowments, economic resilience and diversification, resources, welfare and innovation capacity"-- Provided by publisher.
Identifiers: LCCN 2021040432 (print) | LCCN 2021040433 (ebook) | ISBN 9781799873839 (hardcover) | ISBN 9781799873846 (paperback) | ISBN 9781799873853 (ebook)
Subjects: LCSH: Economic development--Africa, Sub-Saharan. | Public-private sector cooperation--Africa, Sub-Saharan. | Africa, Sub-Saharan--Economic policy--21st century. | Africa, Sub-Saharan--Economic conditions--1960-
Classification: LCC HC800.Z9 E44655 2021 (print) | LCC HC800.Z9 (ebook) | DDC 338.960905--dc23
LC record available at https://lccn.loc.gov/2021040432
LC ebook record available at https://lccn.loc.gov/2021040433

This book is published in the IGI Global book series Advances in Public Policy and Administration (APPA) (ISSN: 2475-6644; eISSN: 2475-6652)

British Cataloguing in Publication Data
A Cataloguing in Publication record for this book is available from the British Library.

Advances in Public Policy and Administration (APPA) Book Series

ISSN:2475-6644
EISSN:2475-6652

MISSION

Proper management of the public sphere is necessary in order to maintain order in modern society. Research developments in the field of public policy and administration can assist in uncovering the latest tools, practices, and methodologies for governing societies around the world.

The **Advances in Public Policy and Administration (APPA) Book Series** aims to publish scholarly publications focused on topics pertaining to the governance of the public domain. APPA's focus on timely topics relating to government, public funding, politics, public safety, policy, and law enforcement is particularly relevant to academicians, government officials, and upper-level students seeking the most up-to-date research in their field.

COVERAGE

- Government
- Law Enforcement
- Political Economy
- Politics
- Public Administration
- Public Funding
- Public Policy
- Resource Allocation
- Urban Planning

IGI Global is currently accepting manuscripts for publication within this series. To submit a proposal for a volume in this series, please contact our Acquisition Editors at Acquisitions@igi-global.com or visit: http://www.igi-global.com/publish/.

The Advances in Public Policy and Administration (APPA) Book Series (ISSN 2475-6644) is published by IGI Global, 701 E. Chocolate Avenue, Hershey, PA 17033-1240, USA, www.igi-global.com. This series is composed of titles available for purchase individually; each title is edited to be contextually exclusive from any other title within the series. For pricing and ordering information please visit http://www.igi-global.com/book-series/advances-public-policy-administration/97862. Postmaster: Send all address changes to above address.

Titles in this Series

For a list of additional titles in this series, please visit:
http://www.igi-global.com/book-series/advances-public-policy-administration/97862

Transforming Government, Nonprofits, and Healthcare in a Post-Pandemic Era
Joanne E. Howard (Illinois Institute of Technology, USA)
Information Science Reference • © 2022 • 310pp • H/C (ISBN: 9781668423141) • US $250.00

Interdisciplinary Approaches to the Future of Africa and Policy Development
Icarbord Tshabangu (Leeds Trinity University, UK)
Information Science Reference • © 2022 • 375pp • H/C (ISBN: 9781799887713) • US $215.00

Direct Democracy Practices at the Local Level
Christophe Emmanuel Premat (Stockholm University, Sweden)
Information Science Reference • © 2022 • 325pp • H/C (ISBN: 9781799873044) • US $215.00

Handbook of Research on Interdisciplinary Studies on Healthcare, Culture, and the Environment
Mika Markus Merviö (Kibi International University, Japan)
Information Science Reference • © 2022 • 365pp • H/C (ISBN: 9781799889960) • US $270.00

Challenges and Barriers to the European Union Expansion to the Balkan Region
Bruno Ferreira Costa (University of Beira Interior, Portugal)
Information Science Reference • © 2022 • 372pp • H/C (ISBN: 9781799890553) • US $215.00

Smart Cities, Citizen Welfare, and the Implementation of Sustainable Development Goals
Ana Cristina Pego (Nova University, Portugal)
Information Science Reference • © 2022 • 402pp • H/C (ISBN: 9781799877851) • US $215.00

For an entire list of titles in this series, please visit:
http://www.igi-global.com/book-series/advances-public-policy-administration/97862

IGI Global
PUBLISHER of TIMELY KNOWLEDGE

701 East Chocolate Avenue, Hershey, PA 17033, USA
Tel: 717-533-8845 x100 • Fax: 717-533-8661
E-Mail: cust@igi-global.com • www.igi-global.com

"Fred Olayele understands policy, markets, and society – and he makes a compelling case for leveraging the private sector to spread socially beneficial innovations. This is an indispensable guide for anyone interested in understanding our continent's journey towards sustainable development, particularly the political economy of policy innovation."

Her Excellency Ameenah Gurib-Fakim
Distinguished Professor and Former
President of the Republic of Mauritius.

"Drawing on multiple case studies, Professor Olayele has written a provocative analysis on how Africa's public and private sectors can collaborate on a range of issues, including trade, climate, and technology. His monograph is a trumpet call to African policymakers, business leaders, civil society groups, and key stakeholders to build an African economy that transforms adversity into opportunity, and barriers into stepping stones for inclusive and sustainable growth."

Dr. Witney Schneidman
Former Deputy Assistant Secretary of State for African Affairs, United States Department of State.

For my wife Titi and children, Feran and Fisola.

My late mother, Comfort Adefisola, for the many sacrifices and without whom none of my success would be possible.

And the many policy change agents out there working day and night towards the African Renaissance.

Table of Contents

Foreword ix

Preface... xii

Acknowledgment xvii

Section 1
Introduction

Chapter 1
Unpacking African Development Dynamics: A Political Economy Perspective ..1

Section 2
Africa in the Context of Policy Innovation

Chapter 2
Policy Innovation in Africa: Problems and Promises 16

Chapter 3
Policy Change: Theories, Evidence, and Implications 35

Chapter 4
Policymaking and the African Renaissance..73

Section 3
The Political Economy of Policy Innovation

Chapter 5
The Political Economy of Modern Capitalism 103

Chapter 6
State Structures and Economic Modernization...134

Chapter 7
Structural Shifts and the Race to Net Zero: A Policy Diffusion Analysis 157

Section 4
Public-Private Policy Partnerships

Chapter 8
Public-Private Policy Partnerships: A Policy Innovation Paradigm 179

Chapter 9
Development Finance and Venture Capital: A Policy Diffusion Model 205

Chapter 10
Tax Policy Innovation and Financial Inclusion 221

Chapter 11
Trade Policy Innovation and the AfCFTA Imperative 239

Chapter 12
Regional Innovation Engines for Development 255

Section 5
Conclusion

Chapter 13
No Foot-Dragging: Let's Transform Africa 274

About the Author 290

Index 292

Foreword

Fred Olayele's *African Policy Innovation and the Political Economy of Public-Private Policy Partnerships* explores varying economic, social, and political contexts – under a pan-African framework – to offer real-world insights into the highly complex, dynamic, and regionally differentiated innovation economies on the continent.

The author recognizes the often complex and non-linear nature of policymaking and offers a fresh perspective for situating the political economy nuances of African countries over an extended period. Through the lens of history, he looks at the period prior to 1870 and the 'scramble' for Africa, into the era when African countries started their journey towards self-determination.

Clearly, the public policy development process from immediate post-independence Africa till date has been informed by various biases. Leftist ideologies became popular in many countries across the continent immediately after independence – partly as a resentment against the evil of colonialism and imperialism – while neoliberal capitalist tendencies staged a comeback after the dismal performance of socialist doctrines. Therefore, as the author argues, harnessing the policy-market nexus to increase aggregate economic welfare and increase social mobility is long overdue.

The author alludes to the implications of the knowledge economy for the innovation discourse in the African context. Research remains the cornerstone of innovation, and African governments must refine existing policy design and implementation frameworks to ensure the positive externalities from the outputs of research and development (R & D) activities in the ivory towers are maximized. Given the pace at which the digital revolution is driving intellectual property (IP) enforcement and monetization, the need for rethinking incremental policy innovations around IP in the African context has never been more important. When technology transfers dominate spillovers, a sound public policy approach that can help guarantee the enforcement of IP becomes critical. To the extent that the private and social returns to corporate R & D activities remain a key driver of investments, it is important to devise a public-private paradigm which incentivizes private companies to increase their investments in applied research. The author offers insights into these issues through several case studies that validate why African policymakers must ensure the level of private sector investments in R & D does not fall below the socially optimal level.

Africa is home to a dynamic and growing digital ecosystem. In the last decade, the financial technology sector on the continent has witnessed unprecedented growth, with the influx of international private capital and multiple large fundraises and exits. The rise of the digital economy on the continent provides a unique opportunity for policymakers to implement reforms that can help unlock further private investments. While the slow spread of ICT remains a bottleneck, if properly harnessed to kickstart a new growth cycle, the booming digital sector offers a glimmer of hope. The author offers a compelling argument vis-à-vis the role of Startup Acts as a policy innovation tool for the dynamic venture capital ecosystem on the continent. This is particularly appealing because digitization is a powerful growth enabler that can facilitate job creation and improve livelihoods on the continent.

The global energy transition is gathering momentum. However, given recent disruptive and unpredictable geopolitical shifts, the issue of energy security – in the context of the decarbonization of the global economy – has moved to the front burner of the policy debate. Like other regions in the world, this has implications for Africa's fight against the climate crisis and other measures necessary to expedite the energy transition. Africa's energy deficit poses a substantial challenge for development; the author recommends digital economic innovation and industrial diversification as a potent strategy that can help decrease emissions and drive the gradual decarbonization of the continent's fuel mix.

While the literature on the effect of policy change on development is vast, situating the critical role of public-private policy partnerships in policy innovation is an underexplored issue in the African context. Given the vastly heterogenous nature of Africa and its varying economic, political, cultural, and social realities, this work is quite timely and relevant.

Leadership matters and African leadership has evolved over the years. This has helped governance on the continent, especially in contemporary times. Gradually, economic modernization, social justice, and the provision of public goods are receiving the attention they deserve – but there is more work to be done.

Hope springs eternal. The recently approved and endorsed African Continental Free Trade Area (AfCFTA) aligns with the 2030 Agenda for Sustainable Development, as well as Agenda 2063 of the African Union. These policy paradigms and instruments hold the promise of launching Africa into the mainstream of global commerce – along with the competitive advantage that comes with that. However, stakeholders must be wary of cumbersome bureaucratic processes that may hinder implementation.

Fred Olayele understands policy, markets, and society – and he makes a compelling case for leveraging the private sector to spread socially beneficial innovations. This is an indispensable guide for anyone interested in understanding our continent's journey towards sustainable development, particularly the political economy of policy innovation.

Ameenah Gurib-Fakim
Former President of Mauritius

Preface

It is not from the benevolence of the butcher, the brewer, or the baker that we expect our dinner, but from their regard to their own interest.

— Adam Smith

THIS BOOK HAS BEEN IN THE WORKS for a while now, with the earlier drafts based on my research and practice around fostering synergistic interactions and outcomes in the academic and public policy domains. As an educator, researcher, and policy innovation enthusiast with a keen interest in the role of the science-policy-industry-society nexus in understanding the innovation system, I have always been fascinated by incremental innovations through public-private collaborations.

To make sense of the political economy of development in Africa in the context of the appropriateness of contemporary policy devices and paradigms, I explore the implications of contemporary theories of policy change for the African Union's Agenda 2063 and the African Renaissance. To build the Africa we want, I advance a multi-stakeholder development policy and programming framework which recognizes Africa's vastly heterogenous economies and societies.

Much of the discussion in the book is focused on the often complex and non-linear nature of policymaking – and the implications for harnessing the policy-market nexus to increase aggregate economic welfare. As such, the various themes traverse the highly interdisciplinary nature of policy innovation and political economy. From local communities and NGOs to African governments and international development agencies, public-private policy partnerships are a key enabler of policy innovation.

Being an academic operating simultaneously across several economic policy domains in multiple government agencies over the years meant that much of my work has been driven by a search for knowledge – at the intersection between economics, public policy, and society – that can help address many of the pressing challenges of our era. This explains, largely, my passion for a pragmatic approach to public policymaking vis-à-vis not only understanding what works in different contexts, but also resolving the inherent challenges associated with translating academic research and theory into practice and policy.

In the African context, the politico-juridical and neoliberal systems in the Western industrialized nations, based largely on individualism, are not fully aligned with traditional African communalism. While the fallacy of the rational utility maximizing agent in mainstream neoclassical economics has been laid bare by the failure of the Washington Consensus to grasp the economic and social realities of development through the micro implications of the price system, it often surprises me that much of the knowledge mobilization in the economic policy domain on the continent still depends on neoliberal models, paradigms, and policy devices.

The lightweight nature of the debate on why the paradigm of individualism in industrial capitalist societies is frequently at odds with mainstream social and economic ideologies like Ubuntu and traditional African values like familyhood, interpersonal relationships, and togetherness – which matter in the resource allocation decisions of Africans – is concerning. Perhaps even more disturbing is the fact that in the year 2022, we still do not have textbooks on African economic policy that not only unpack how these contradictions are suppressed, but also offer Africa-centric policy paradigms and theoretical representations of economic growth based on the implications of cultural and institutional arrangements for individual and household choices.

To the extent that Ubuntu creates a gap in the individualism-collectivism dichotomy, this misalignment is, to some degree, the antithesis of successful policy designs and macroeconomic stabilization programming efforts across Africa. I have written this book to sensitize the African development policy community on the need to fill this void.

Policy capacity, a derivative of good governance and institutional quality, remains a key driver of public policy innovation. Nowhere is this more compelling than in Africa – given historical and structural barriers which continue to perpetuate fragmentation, informality, extreme poverty, conflicts, and other colonial institutional vestiges. Based on this premise, I use the lens of political economy to examine the development trajectory of Africa and how the various detours and interruptions on the journey led to the emergence of the independent and heterogenous economies that are collectively referred to as Africa today. I extensively examine and discuss the literature, both Africa- and Western-centric, useful to this inquiry.

It is also worth mentioning that my approach is to first put forth the flaws in existing models and paradigms, before presenting alternative arguments that, in my view, can help in moving the needle based on incrementalism. Of course, along with the harsh critique of the current situation in some of the countries, many bright spots and policy innovations enabled by the burgeoning digital economy and improved governance on the continent are highlighted.

To achieve the Africa of our dreams, policy innovation is key. Policies, actions, and institutions matter. And given the potential of the African Continental Free Trade Area (AfCFTA) in changing the regional economic integration narrative in Africa, the need for policy innovation and institutional reforms across the continent to help spread beneficial social innovations by optimizing state-market relationships cannot be overemphasized. It goes without saying that there is no one-size-fits-all template to broaden the continent's productive base and deliver long-term economic growth through diversification. Policy innovation is required in devising the multiple pathways to fast-track Africa's development journey.

STRUCTURE

The book is divided into five sections. Section 1, "Unpacking African Development Dynamics: A Political Economy Perspective," explores the political economy nuances of African countries and the implications of various interrelationships on the overall economy and society.

Section 2, "Africa in the Context of Policy Innovation," focuses on policy innovation, the political economy of capitalism and Africa's development dynamics, and the theories of policy change vis-à-vis how the policy cycle helps in translating the vision and mission of governments into implementation. Among other issues, tools, models, paradigms, and techniques of policymaking and Africa's economic transformation in the context of the 2030 Sustainable Development Goals (SDGs) and Agenda 2063 are examined here. This part sets the pace with contemporary discussion on the philosophical foundations of political-economic interactions, the limits of conventional neoclassicism, pragmatism and policymaking, policy devices, policy capacity, and the various arguments on the call for a new approach to policymaking.

The increasingly complex nature of society poses policy questions that are also becoming more difficult to address. Schumpeterianism and policy innovation, the limits of physical laws in economic phenomena, the nexus between technology and policymaking, transaction costs, policy diffusion, and the applicability of the helix models of innovation are thoroughly analyzed, while the implications for policy innovation potential are articulated.

Section 3, "Political Economy of Policy Innovation," examines demographic shifts, global inequality and rentier capitalism, the political economy of industrial transformation and its theoretical ramifications, and lessons from economic rebasing in Africa. This segment of the book unpacks the implications of the interplay of policy, markets, and innovation for inclusive economic development, the dynamics of redistribution in the new economy, economic systems and state structures in the context of innovation capacity, the innovation-federalism nexus, the resource economy and competitiveness, and the theoretical underpinnings of fiscal decentralization in the context of redistributive fiscal flows.

In addition, themes on the diversification-specialization debate and the deleterious effects of governance failures – like authoritarianism, conflict, and social inequity – on political economy outcomes are discussed. This part covers the pros and cons of the arguments on institutional quality and resource extraction, innovations in the extractives sector, climate change and competitiveness, structural shifts and the pandemic, and comparative case studies on the political economy of decarbonization and the energy transition. Starting with the interplay between policy and markets, the ongoing shift in the energy landscape and what it means for policy incentives and pathways that may help strengthen Africa's adaptive capacity are considered. Policy innovation lessons from other regions of the world are examined.

Section 4, "Public-Private Policy Partnerships," focuses exclusively on the relevance of public-private partnerships (PPPs) as a policy innovation approach, with several case studies across Africa. By arguing that PPPs remain a vital tool for policymakers in harnessing important components of the innovation economy, the pros and cons of the leapfrog effect, development finance innovations, infrastructure, venture capital ecosystem, policy diffusion in the startup economy, tax policy and supply-side economics, ocean finance, the global minimum tax debate, and higher education under disruptive technologies are broadly dissected.

This segment of the book also adopts the innovation supercluster sectoral approach in the context of the AfCFTA to consider the pathways to economic resilience and sustainability in Africa. I shed light on the implications of the digital economy for the high representation of women and low-income earners working under poor conditions in Africa's informal economy. Productivity gaps and the distributional implications of the AfCTFA in the context of Africa's heterogeneous markets receive particular attention here. Additional case studies on harnessing sectoral policy innovation opportunities in Africa are presented across the agriculture, maritime, tourism, and mining sectors.

Section 5, "No Foot-Dragging: Let's Transform Africa," concludes with a clarion call for African policymakers, business leaders, civil society actors, development partners, and other key stakeholders to avoid foot-dragging. There has never been a more important time to reimagine Africa's economic system; the COVID-19 crisis presents a once-in-a-lifetime opportunity to address agelong structural barriers and vulnerabilities that stand in the way of sound public policy. From the Botswana miracle to policy learning in the context of the reinvention in Rwanda after the genocide, I underscore how lessons from adversity and crises can serve as a catalyst for reinvention.

The implementation of the AfCFTA must proceed simultaneously with other key political and institutional reforms across the continent to ensure public-private policy partnerships – through sound and well-crafted state-markets relationships – support industrial transformation capable of driving stable market expectations and a seamless business environment that can help build the Africa we all want.

Fred Olayele
Sprott School of Business,
Carleton University, Canada

Acknowledgment

For almost two decades now, I have had the privilege of collaborating with several brilliant and dedicated academics, public policy professionals, senior government and business leaders, bankers, researchers, development experts, and non-profit executives. Years of harnessing the policy-market nexus and pushing the boundaries of policy innovation through the quadruple helix approach contributed in no small measure to my decision to write this book. My affiliation, over the years, with the following institutions had a huge impact on this research and its framing: Sprott Centre for African Research and Business at Carleton University, Economic Innovation Institute for Africa, Economic Club for Africa in New York, and the Pan-African School of Policy Innovation. To all the wonderful colleagues who, knowingly or unknowingly, piqued my curiosity in one way or another, I am grateful.

A fairly significant chunk of the book content is a popularization of my research and teaching in economics, strategy, and public policy over the years at the University of Regina and Carleton University, both in Canada. The book is also deeply enriched with lectures and speeches I delivered as a visiting professor and guest speaker across universities and academic institutions abroad. Part of the research I conducted as a visiting scholar at the World Trade Institute in Switzerland informed some of the arguments in this work. The constant brainstorming and workshops jointly organized with academic colleagues – particularly my co-Principal Investigators on a number of trade policy and development projects – were very helpful in devising creative solutions to the many economic policy challenges we set out to tackle. It goes without saying that I received tremendous inspiration from my undergraduate and graduate students over the years. I owe these wonderful people a debt of gratitude for joining me in advancing the debate.

In 2017, I invented the "TFi4SD" (Trade, FDI, and Innovation for Sustainable Development) framework – based on my research around harnessing productivity gains from trade, FDI, and innovation linkages for sustainable and inclusive development. The premise is simple: leveraging trade and FDI for sustainable growth is rarely a linear process. Innovation remains an important element in maximizing the benefits of the digital economy for inclusive development. In the last five years, I have deployed the TFi4SD paradigm in a policy-market context to help several African economies optimize the benefits accruing from trade and FDI. Some of the case studies are presented in this book.

It takes a dedicated crew to accomplish the goal of writing a book. My sincere appreciation goes to the editors for overseeing the several iterations of the manuscript and the reviewers for the thoughtful comments. Needless to say, all errors and oversights in this book are my sole responsibility.

To my late mom, Comfort Adefisola, without whom none of my success would be possible, my heartfelt thanks for the many sacrifices.

Together, we can build the Africa of our dreams. The new Africa is possible. To the many policy change agents out there working day and night towards the African Renaissance, thank you for all you do.

Last but not least, I acknowledge with gratitude, the support and love of my family. Without them, this book would not exist. Writing a book is hard. Doing so without a strong support system is much harder. To my caring and loving wife, Titi, thank you for being a constant source of support and inspiration, and for reading through the drafts and offering useful suggestions. To my sons, Feran and Fisola, thank you for the unwavering affection and for enduring my frequent absences while working on the manuscript.

Fred Olayele
Sprott School of Business,
Carleton University, Canada

Section 1
Introduction

Chapter 1
Unpacking African Development Dynamics:
A Political Economy Perspective

ABSTRACT

At the heart of political economy is how politics affects the economy and vice versa. Society wants the supply of public services like healthcare, education, security, and infrastructure to be flexible, innovative, and efficient. However, the barriers created by bureaucracies often stifle innovation. The argument for harnessing the policy-market nexus to increase aggregate economic welfare remains compelling. While conventional arguments on the ability of the private sector to intrinsically generate efficiency gains remain valid, governments' traditional role of providing an enabling environment to foster private risk taking for capital accumulation is no less important. This chapter offers insights into the political economy of the public policy dynamics of the African economy and society, with emphasis on public-private collaborations for policy innovation. To break new ground and solve some of the most pressing challenges of our era, innovating the public policy cycle is key. Nowhere is the policy innovation imperative more compelling than in Africa.

DOI: 10.4018/978-1-7998-7383-9.ch001

Massive poverty and obscene inequality are such terrible scourges of our times — times in which the world boasts breathtaking advances in science, technology, industry, and wealth accumulation — that they have to rank alongside slavery and apartheid as social evils.

– Nelson Mandela

A core political economy issue in the growth literature is how to structure the relationship between the public and private sectors to ensure optimal outcomes. While conventional arguments on the ability of the private sector to intrinsically generate efficiency gains remain valid, governments' traditional role of providing an enabling environment to foster private risk taking for capital accumulation is no less important.

Borrowing from contemporary theories of policy change, in this book, I raise some fundamental questions about the political economy of development in Africa vis-à-vis the appropriateness of contemporary policy devices and paradigms, the compatibility of individualistic analytical frameworks with the African philosophy of Ubuntu, the debate on the rise of neoliberalism vs. Africa's traditions and values, and the implications of path dependence and the vestiges of colonization for the African Union's Agenda 2063 and the African Renaissance. From local communities and NGOs to African governments and international development agencies, to build the Africa we want, a multi-stakeholder development policy and programming framework which recognizes Africa's vastly heterogenous economies and societies is needed.

Society wants the supply of public services like healthcare, education, security, and infrastructure to be flexible, innovative, and efficient. However, the barriers created by bureaucracies often stifle innovation. Harnessing the policy-market nexus to increase aggregate economic welfare depends, to a large extent, not only on how business-government relations are designed and managed, but also on the specific dimensions of such relationships (Maxfield & Schneider, 1997). Amid the current wave of digital transformation, new innovations that can help governments fulfil their social contracts are increasingly emerging. And while the role of the state in creating incentives and reducing transaction costs is clear, a nuanced understanding of contemporary social policy requires a firm grasp of the role of business. At the same time, most public policy challenges are complex and non-linear in nature. To break new ground and solve some of the most pressing challenges of our era, innovating the public policy cycle is key. It goes without saying that nowhere is the policy innovation imperative more compelling than in Africa.

Africa continues to grow in importance. On March 7, 2019, the online edition of The Economist characterized the new scramble for Africa thus: "Governments and businesses from all around the world are rushing to strengthen diplomatic, strategic and commercial ties." Regional integration is progressing fast across the continent. And not just that. There is broad-based support from African governments and other important stakeholders both on the continent and within the broader international community. For instance, the AfCFTA, aimed at establishing a single market across the continent, represents an important milestone in achieving the bold objective of an economically integrated Africa.

Indeed, this is a pivotal moment for Africa in the context of policy development. Given the scope, size, and potential development impacts of the AfCFTA, it is arguably one of the most consequential contemporary policy developments on the continent. Not only is the AfCFTA expected to launch Africa into the mainstream of global commerce, but the pact is also poised to make the continent more competitive globally (World Bank, 2020). In the context of coherence and reinforcing policy actions across countries and sectors to achieve synergistic outcomes, it is also worth mentioning that the AfCFTA is aligned with the 2030 Agenda for Sustainable Development – with its 17 Sustainable Development Goals (SDGs) – as well as Agenda 2063, the African Union's continent-wide policy blueprint for inclusive growth and sustainable development.

My central argument in this book is direct: to the extent that policy innovation is a complex, non-linear process, "practice-based innovation" and public-private policy partnerships are fundamental to improving governance and public sector performance in Africa. At the core of this is an institutional arrangement that maximizes the benefits that accrue from the interactions between public and private sector actors. Based on this proposition, I offer a fresh perspective for examining richer dynamics by which the political economy nuances of African countries pave the way to distill the effects of other interrelationships on the overall economy and society. From a historical perspective, prior to 1870, European presence in Africa was limited to a few coastal ports and their surroundings, with only about 10 percent of the continent under formal European control. Over the next 40 years, the "Scramble for Africa" by seven Western European countries resulted in the occupation and colonization of the continent during the period of New Imperialism – which was marked by extensive overseas territorial acquisitions. While decolonization on the continent happened largely in the mid-to-late 1950s to 1975, several other countries became independent under varying circumstances.[1]

AFRICA'S DEVELOPMENT TRAJECTORY

Following Ghana's independence from colonial rule in 1957, 47 other countries on the continent gained independence between 1957 and 1990. As such, the public policy development process in immediate post-independence Africa was largely influenced by the struggles for Africa's national sovereignty and policy autonomy. This produced different strands and hybrids of African socialism based on varying economic systems, national struggles, and cultural and political debates. In much of the 1950s, leftist ideologies were prominent on the continent, partly as a backlash against colonialism – since most African leaders of the era recognized capitalism as being pivotal to the perpetuation of European dominance and imperialism.

To put this into perspective, between 1950 and the mid-1980s, important production and exchange decisions in 35 countries on the continent prioritized greater equality in the distribution of income based on the socialist mode of resource allocation. During this period, contrary to the classic individualism in much of the Western world, there was a rise in the paradigm of African socialism – a model that integrates traditional African values in resource allocation decisions. Through Africa-specific social and economic ideologies – from Tanzania's Julius Nyerere and Ghana's Kwame Nkrumah to Mali's Modibo Keita and Senegal's Léopold Senghor – prominent leaders of the era steered economic, social, and politico-legal affairs with the primary motive of shedding the vestiges of colonialism (Friedland & Rosberg, 1964).

From Ghana and Zambia to Mozambique and Angola, the political economy doctrine of socialism permeated Africa, and much of post-independence Africa was organized as centrally planned economies because, as Kumssa and Jones (2015) put it, "...nationalist African leaders embraced a state-controlled development strategy because it gave them the opportunity to control private and foreign enterprises, which they viewed as agents of exploitation and domination." (p.12). Nonetheless, it is important to clarify that despite the varying nature of socialist ideologies embraced across the continent over the aforementioned decades, most of these economies were largely market-oriented with varying degrees of controls, albeit their highly fragmented and informal nature might have obscured this reality.

Collier and Gunning (1999) question why Africa's political self-determination and economic fortunes recorded positive outcomes in the period immediately after independence, while both components witnessed declines in the 1970s. After three decades of dominant socialist doctrines on the continent, neoliberal capitalist tendencies staged a comeback, albeit in different forms and for varying reasons. While the socialist ideologies put in place by African nationalist leaders to enhance socioeconomic progress through public control of the health, education, and welfare systems achieved modest results in some areas, the inefficiencies and bureaucratic failures associated with centrally planned systems contributed to the decline of this political economy approach.

The three-sector model proposition that the development trajectory of countries needs to proceed from agrarian and extraction to manufacturing and ultimately service industries informed much of the debate on enhancing economic mobility and improving the lives of poor people in developing countries in the last century. The economic ascent of many Western industrialized nations through agricultural transformation was marked by rising shares of services in not only production, consumption, employment, and trade, but also in much of the intermediate inputs required to power production in other industries. However, due to the leapfrog effect[2] and the drastic changes in the post-industrial economy in the face of digitalization, the applicability of this reasoning has become somewhat limited, with important caveats. Africa is a classic example in this regard, and much of this monograph examines this in detail.

THE WASHINGTON CONSENSUS

Until recently, African leaders – especially in the immediate post-independence era – were typically from the military, academia, or the law profession. This meant that social justice and the provision of public goods were ranked highly in state affairs. However, in the face of proliferating underground economies, rising debt levels, inefficiently run state enterprises, coup d'états, bourgeoning dictatorships, and massive public sector corruption, free markets and democratization provided an alternative pathway to creating socioeconomic and political stability. This led to policy reversals and drastic cuts in social services and subsidies in public programs and state-run enterprises.

In the aftermath of the collapse of the Soviet Union in 1989, the end of the Cold War in 1991, and the rapid advances in digital technologies and multilateralism, the forces of globalization became entrenched. The more interconnected and interdependent global economy paved the way for neoliberalism to permeate African economic systems, with the Bretton Woods Institutions (BWIs) serving as conduit pipes.

The World Bank and the International Monetary Fund (IMF) created the Structural Adjustment Program (SAP) as a panacea for economic underperformance in the Global South. SAP was designed to fix structural imbalances in the economy through diversification, fiscal stability, positive balance of payments, non-inflationary growth, and reduced budget deficits (Mills, 1989).

Many African leaders embraced political and economic reforms, predominantly under the auspices of SAP, anchored on limited government and a market-oriented economy. However, while this economic prescription succeeded partly in its ability to put hyperinflation under control and maintain debt payment schedules – due to the uniquely different nature of African economies and societies – it caused huge economic dislocation and heralded unprecedented levels of poverty, unemployment, and inequality across the continent (Konadu-Agyemang, 2001).

Clearly, the BWIs missed a key point in the design of the SAP framework. Given that the key pillars in the economic management recipe was rooted in mainstream neoliberalism, the prioritization of macroeconomic stabilization over equity considerations and the vulnerability of the poor in economic systems largely characterized by informality, subsistence, and fragmentation contributed to its failure. This had grave consequences. In many ways, the inability of the Washington Consensus[3] to improve the socioeconomic fortunes of African countries has contributed to a backlash which has largely discredited it in many economic policy circles.

In their 2021 analysis in a Brookings article, Belinda Archibong, Brahima Sangafowa, and Ngozi Okonjo-Iweala examine countries in sub-Saharan Africa under the Washington Consensus framework. While the authors agree that there is mixed evidence on the socioeconomic effect of the policy reforms instituted by the BWIs, they nonetheless conclude that the policies failed to substantially achieve the intended objectives – because of the inability to strike a right balance between the implementation of pro-poor policies alongside market-oriented reforms. The authors put the key lesson from the Washington Consensus reforms straight:

The speed with which many of the reforms were carried out initially, especially domestic reforms like privatization of state-owned enterprises, without careful consideration of the environment of incomplete markets and the institutional challenges faced by African governments, affected the initial effectiveness of policy implementation and contributed to lower growth rates during the 1980 to 1999 reform period (Archibong, Sangafowa, & Okonjo-Iweala, 2021; para 8).

Perhaps more importantly though – especially in the context of the central thesis of this book – these findings corroborate the need for policy innovation and reform efforts to account for a stable government, conducive sociopolitical environment, and other important political economy nuances, particularly structural dynamics, institutional idiosyncrasies, and local ownership in domestic economic policy. To gain public support for policy reforms, the theories of policy change (discussed extensively in the subsequent chapters) offer insights on the pros and cons of incrementalism vs. radical policy innovation. Either way, safety nets and other inclusive approaches that can minimize the negative welfare impacts of policy reforms on vulnerable populations are key for success. Five key lessons for future policy reforms in the Brookings discussion corroborate this:

Even though there is no panacea when it comes to economic reforms, the following lessons provide a useful general guide going forward: First, while market-oriented reforms can be beneficial for growth, each reform policy needs to be carefully considered in the institutional contexts, initial conditions of development and sociopolitical environment, among others. Second, ownership of the reform agenda by local government with stakeholder buy-in is important to encourage support for the reforms and increase the likelihood of success. Third, the negative spillovers of reform policies need to be minimized. Investment in social safety nets is a crucial part of reforms to protect the most vulnerable populations within the countries. Fourth, where reforms aim to achieve macroeconomic stability, they should not trade away social investment in human capital like education and health. Finally, reforms should be a process of continuous reevaluation, adjustment, and recalibration over the reform period. There is not and will never be a one-size-fits-all approach when it comes to economic development, and the reform agenda should be approached carefully and with flexibility (Archibong, Sangafowa, & Okonjo-Iweala, 2021; para 10).

Two former Executive Secretaries of the United Nations Economic Commission for Africa – Adebayo Adedeji and Kingsley Amoako – underscored the need for policy pragmatism and the involvement of Africans in policy designs that have implications for their own affairs. After the release of the World Bank's publication: *Sub-Saharan Africa: From Crisis to Sustainable Growth* in 1989, Adedeji lamented the deleterious effects of policy experiments on the lives and livelihoods of the millions of Africans impacted and asked rhetorically: "Why should we turn Africa into a laboratory? Why don't we agree that the African problem is one of fundamental restructuring? It is not wholly economic. It is partly political, partly social." (as cited in Okolie, 1991).

Along the same lines, Amoako, in Mkandawire and Soludo (1998), reiterates the need for African perspectives in matters relating to the development of the continent. He decries the dominance of external theories and models in the development discourse of the continent and argues that:

A major irony of African development history is that the theories and models employed have largely come from outside the continent. No other region of the world has been so dominated by external ideas and models. A growing number of institutions and scholars have expressed serious concerns about this foreign domination, issuing a clarion call for Africans to lead in the reform process and to think for themselves (Mkandawire & Soludo, 1998; p. vii).

With 54 independent countries,[4] Africa is vastly heterogenous, resulting in varying economic, political, cultural, and social realities. While research abounds on the role of policy change in the socioeconomic development of the continent, the role of policy innovation through public-private policy partnerships is, however, grossly underexplored in contemporary political economy discourses. This work explores varying economic, social, and political contexts – under a pan-African framework – to offer real-world insights into the highly complex, dynamic, and regionally differentiated innovation economies on the continent.

THE BOTTOM LINE

The primary goal of this book is to offer insights into the political economy of the public policy dynamics of the African economy and society, with emphasis on the implications of policy capacity and public-private collaborations for policy innovation. As such, while academic disciplines and professional specializations such as economics, political science, sociology, anthropology, physical sciences, policy analysis, and policymaking provide the foundational basis for much of the argument, subject matter expertise in these domains is not required to make sense of the central argument in the monograph. As might be expected, the themes cut across several fields of study and support the highly interdisciplinary nature of the discourses. Therefore, like a deductive argument, readers do need to take cognizance of the logical relationships and how the various premises pave the way for the conclusion.

At the heart of political economy is how politics affects the economy and vice versa. As most questions in political economy discourses do not have binomial yes or no answers, philosophical foundations matter to the extent that differing research philosophies inform various strands of economic policy debates. While I have chosen somewhat differing topics to explore the various issues in the political economy of public-private policy partnerships, each topic is unique in its own sense. The topics have been chosen with a wide range of stakeholders in the policy cycle in mind – both in terms of their role and influence in the public policy development process. Academics, policy analysts, researchers, graduate students, policymakers, industry experts, development practitioners, and stakeholders across institutions that support public policy research and theory development will find this work useful.

The book builds on the works of a handful of economists, political scientists, sociologists, and other public policy experts who have navigated and studied economic and bureaucratic systems in the context of policy-market dynamics. To the extent that the public policy cycle is a dynamic endeavor in need of continuous reforms, the first major objective of this monograph is to extensively examine the theoretical and empirical underpinnings of the political economy dynamics of Africa in a bid to offer fresh insights based on institutional and jurisdictional exemplars from within the continent and elsewhere.

Far from the fallacy of the rational utility maximizing agent in the neoclassical economics domain, the reality that individual and household choices are indeed shaped by cultural and institutional arrangements is key to understanding the policy innovation discourse in Africa. This has implications for the holy trinity of rationality, selfishness, and equilibrium in neoclassicism (Colander et al., 2004). For different historical, social, and political economy reasons, economic systems across Africa are unique. Contrary to the dominant tenet of individualism in industrial capitalist societies, social and economic ideologies like Ujamaa, Ubuntu, and Harambee are important in the resource allocation decisions of Africans – since these philosophies reinforce traditional African values like familyhood, interpersonal relationships, and togetherness.

In sharp contrast, the politico-juridical dynamics and neoliberal economic systems in many Western industrial societies are based on individualism. Since Ubuntu is a normative ethical paradigm, the notion of an individual in the African context is largely community-based. This seeming gap in the individualism-collectivism dichotomy is a subtle source of failure in many policy designs and macroeconomic stabilization programming efforts. This is particularly important for understanding the ramifications of policy innovation on the continent, since transaction costs are fundamental to how economic systems work. This is another key objective of this work.

As the COVID-19 crisis unfolds, the feeling of déjà vu is palpable in many jurisdictions. Will African countries be able to ramp up capacity to manufacture vaccines? Is the pandemic going to replicate the wage stagnation and deep inequalities that accompanied the recovery from the 2008 global financial crisis (GFC)? And considering that the lines between technology and traditional industries are increasingly blurring, how will the challenges associated with vaccines and treatments for COVID-19 manifest in both traditional and emerging sectors of the economy? How might the swift upward trajectory in global healthcare and life sciences spending in the aftermath of the pandemic unlock further investments? Certainly, these questions have major implications for the transformation of economic systems across Africa and the rest of the world. And policy innovation is a key differentiator. This captures the third fundamental objective of this book. I offer a comprehensive, cutting-edge analysis of the paradigms, tools, and political economy analytical frameworks for making sense of policy innovation, in the context of policy capacity, ideas, and experiences of national and regional ecosystems, with a focus on Africa.

Last but not least, I offer insights on specific policy domains in relation to Africa's journey on PPPs. From bridges and airports to highways and sewer plants, extensive literature abounds on conventional PPPs for infrastructure projects on the continent. However, there is a dearth of comprehensive, rigorous analytical research on the collaboration between government and the private sector across specific policy spheres. It is important to emphasize that my focus in this regard is not on conventional PPPs, but public-private policy partnerships. The core argument on the role of PPPs as a policy innovation tool has underlying questions that are either matters of political economy or public policy. In part, the lack of broad-based support for the neoliberal policies of privatization, liberalization, and marketization in the 1990s underpins the popularity of the Keynesian welfare-state institutional arrangements that re-emerged, long after its initial dominance after World War II.

Economic theory asserts that market failures due to the externalities created by public goods provide the basis for the provision of such goods. Based on this premise, public goods are defined as goods that are both non-rivalrous and non-excludable. Such non-excludability and non-rivalry properties make collective action important in ensuring adequate and sustained provision of public goods. To the extent that some goods and services can be public and private at the same time in varying degrees, this has key implications for public-private policy partnerships as a policy innovation approach. I explore the various intersectoral collaboration possibilities between the public and private sectors around key policy themes in the trade, energy, technology, climate, blue economy, taxation, and tourism domains, among others. This book fills a critical void by shedding light on success stories around public-private policy partnerships in various sectors and jurisdictions in Africa, while also highlighting critical gaps and appropriate policy and programmatic interventions.

ANALYTICAL FRAMEWORK

My methodological approach relies heavily on epistemology and the institutional economics research tradition. From risk allocation and incentive to property rights and governance, the institutional economics literature is largely about the dynamics of institutions and how they influence economic behavior. And in both the old and new traditions, the central thesis is the role of social institutions in the exchange economy and the concomitant social relations. In terms of differences, the major distinction lies in the theoretical underpinning of the analysis of individual decision-making.

While the new institutional economists treat the preferences of the individual as given in their institutional analysis, the old institutional school of thought explores patterns and regularities of human behavior vis-à-vis how they are shaped by social circumstances. And based on efficiency gains argument, transaction costs lie at the heart of this model. Simply put, compared to existing models, institutions thrive in a sustainable fashion when the benefits of their value proposition far outweigh the transaction costs incurred. To a large extent, group preferences in societies determine institutional outcomes since lower aggregate transaction costs signal efficiency in the resource allocation process.

In much of the monograph, I rely on case studies, grounded theoretical constructs, and several inductive comparative methodologies that systematically synthesize, analyze, and present the relevant facts. Where there are options, I select multiple case studies over single ones. Apart from allowing a high degree of detail, multiple case studies ensure the four key criteria of construct validity, internal validity, external validity, and reliability are met in the research design process (Yin, 2003). As well, secondary literature and decent doses of empirical findings from primary research form a large part of the methods and strategies adopted in the investigation.

Following Hodgson (2015b), much of the generalizations in the book relies on theory only to the extent that it clearly helps in making sense of, and influencing, real-world complexities in the policy cycle. By focusing more on patterns, while relying on theory only when it helps in resolving counterintuitive cases, I adopt an approach that attempts, on a case-by-case basis, to strike a right balance in the context of social institutional dynamics and their implications for the workings of the economy. In effectively linking science to practice, the research design process ensures sound epistemological grounding and pragmatism inform the major takeaways and policy recommendations. My views and suggestions on incremental policy improvements are based largely on context and circumstance rather than some rigid principles.

As mentioned above, a major delimitation in this work is in the context of the definition of PPP. While PPP has traditionally been leveraged to address challenges in physical and digital infrastructure, its application to core public policy problems in the African context is somewhat limited. Therefore, the appropriateness, legitimacy, effectiveness, or efficiency of PPPs as a service delivery framework is not relevant for the purposes of the discussion in this book. Rather, my intention is to examine public-private policy partnerships based on the involvement of private actors in traditional public sector operations in specific policy domains.

The poverty of what now came to be known as "underdeveloped countries", a dynamic term, became recognized to be a problem. This represented a momentous redirection of public interest. Within this movement there went also an equally radical redirection of economic research, for the first time giving importance to these countries' abject poverty and also to the policy methods, which could initiate progress there by planning for development.

— *Gunnar Myrdal*

REFERENCES

Archibong, B., Coulibaly, B. S., & Okonjo-Iweala, N. (2021). How have the Washington Consensus reforms affected economic performance in sub-Saharan Africa? In *Africa in focus*. Brookings Institute. https://www.brookings.edu/blog/africa-in-focus/2021/02/19/how-have-the-washington-consensus-reforms-affected-economic-performance-in-sub-saharan-africa/

Colander, D., Holt, R., & Rosser, B. Jr. (2004). The changing face of mainstream economics. *Review of Political Economy*, *16*(4), 485–499. doi:10.1080/0953825042000256702

Collier, P., & Gunning, J. W. (1999). WhyHHas Africa Grown Slowly? *The Journal of Economic Perspectives*, *13*(3), 3–22. doi:10.1257/jep.13.3.3

Friedland, W. H., & Rosberg, C. G. (1964). *African Socialism*. Stanford University Press.

Hodgson. (2015). What Humpty Dumpty might have said about property rights – and the need to put them back together again: a response to critics. *Journal of Institutional Economics, 11*(4), 731–747. doi:10.1017/S1744137415000260

Konadu-Agyemang, K. (Ed.). (2001). *IMF and World Bank Sponsored Structural Adjustment Programs in Africa: Ghana's experience, 1983-1999* (1st ed.). Routledge. doi:10.4324/9781315210414

Kumssa, A., & Jones, J. (2015). Post-independence African policy: African socialism and the organization of African unity. *Public Administration Review*, *4*(1), 12–23. doi:10.5539/par.v4n1p12

Maxfield, & Schneider, B. R. (1997). *Business and the state in developing countries*. Cornell University Press.

Mills, C. A. (1989). *Structural adjustment in sub-Saharan Africa*. Economic Development Institute policy seminar report: no. EDI 18 - World Bank Institute. https://documents.worldbank.org/en/publication/documents-reports/documentdetail/570911468768036645/structural-adjustment-in-sub-saharan-africa

Okolie, A. C. (1991). Economic Crisis, Structural Adjustment, and Prospects for Political Stability in Nigeria's Third Republic. *Ufahamu. Journal of African Studies*, *19*(1). Advance online publication. doi:10.5070/F7191016804

Soludo, C. C., & Mkandawire, P. T. (1998). *Our Continent, Our Future: African Perspectives on Structural Adjustment*. Africa World Press.

The Economist. (2019). *The new scramble for Africa: This time, the winners could be Africans themselves*. https://www.economist.com/leaders/2019/03/07/the-new-scramble-for-africa

Williamson, J. (1989). What Washington means by policy reform. In J. Williamson (Ed.), *Latin American readjustment: How much has happened* (pp. 7–20). Institute for International Economics.

World Bank. (1989). *Sub-Saharan Africa: From Crisis to Sustainable Growth*. Errata Sheet. Retrieved from https://documents1.worldbank.org/curated/en/498241468742846138/pdf/multi0page.pdf

World Bank. (2020). *The African Continental Free Trade Area*. Retrieved from https://www.worldbank.org/en/topic/trade/publication/the-african-continental-free-trade-area

Yin. (2003). *Case study research: design and methods* (3rd ed..). Sage Publications.

ENDNOTES

1 Liberia (1847), South Africa (1910), Egypt (1922), Ethiopia (1942), Eritrea (1947), Libya (1951), Sudan (1956), South Sudan (1956), Tunisia (1956), and Morocco (1956).

2 Leapfrogging refers to the notion that contrary to the dictates of development orthodoxy, a low-income country can skip some stages in its development journey by leveraging the digital revolution to move directly from traditional industry into modern industry.

3 The Washington Consensus, a term coined by economist John Williamson in 1989, refers to a list of 10 policies targeted at addressing the macroeconomic imbalances and debt crisis of developing countries in Latin America from the early to mid-1980s. These policies, as prescribed, were focused on tax overhaul, fiscal discipline, openness to trade and investment, market-oriented reforms, and property rights.

4 The United Nations recognizes 54 countries, while the African Union recognizes 55.

Section 2

Africa in the Context of Policy Innovation

Chapter 2
Policy Innovation in Africa:
Problems and Promises

ABSTRACT

Mainstream discourses often construe policy innovation in the context of public policy targeted at achieving innovation in a particular domain. However, this chapter argues this is not the same as fostering innovation within the public policy life cycle. The innovation discourse has transitioned from its purely scientific and technical focus to include digital opportunities and the evolution of new business models. Africa has underlying political economy issues manifesting as social, economic, and policy challenges. To understand what has happened to the African economy and society, it is important to situate the varying degrees of state and market involvement in resource allocation dating back at least to the immediate post-independence period. Policy learning provides a more feasible pathway for policy entrepreneurs and innovators to bridge existing practical knowledge gaps by learning and creating opportunities through innovative and creative approaches. The parameters of a policy implementation path are key drivers of the eventual policy outcome.

DOI: 10.4018/978-1-7998-7383-9.ch002

Never before in history has such a sweeping fervor for freedom expressed itself in great mass movements which are driving down the bastions of an empire. This wind of change blowing through Africa, as I have said before, is no ordinary wind. It is a raging hurricane against which the old order cannot stand.

— *Kwame Nkrumah*

The increasingly complex nature of society poses policy questions that are also difficult to address. The interplay of policy and markets, through its various manifestations in the form of state-business relations and public-private collaborations, is a major political economy paradigm shaping economic outcomes – particularly in emerging markets and developing economies (EMDEs). Whether in the macroeconomy, or in specific sectors, the policy-market forces have implications for short- and long-term structural, institutional, and political economy dynamics. The barriers created by bureaucracies often stifle innovation, and amid the current wave of digital transformation, new innovations that can help governments fulfil their social contracts are increasingly emerging.

The innovation discourse has transitioned from its purely scientific and technical focus to include digital opportunities and the evolution of new business models. The notion of the knowledge economy lies at the heart of contemporary economic growth narratives. Not only has it shifted attention from the industry-government dyad to the "triple helix" of university-industry-government interactions – and more recently the "quadruple helix" – but it has also increased the attention given to these latter frameworks as reliable analytical paradigms for innovation policy and practice. While globalization has intensified technology diffusion globally, leading to increased productivity in EMDEs, the extent of income convergence predicted by theory has not been realized – due, partly, to changes in the patterns and processes of capital accumulation during the post-World War II economic boom, and the concomitant highly dynamic nature of the capitalist mode of production.

Economic diversification is often associated with higher levels of productivity because structural transformation leads to factor reallocation within and between sectors. In a global context, Autor et al. (2020) use the "superstar firm" framework to explain how economic activity reallocation among firms with differing heterogeneous productivity and labor shares is key to understanding the fall in the aggregate share of labor in total output in a dynamic product market environment. The authors contend that the "winner take most" syndrome, where a few capital-intensive firms gain a large share in key sectors of the economy, is increasingly becoming widespread.

Africa's structural economic transformation challenges are well-documented. From fragmentation and low productivity to poor infrastructure and the presence of large informal sectors, industrial diversification remains a mirage –despite its prominence on the front burner of the economic policy debate in the last six decades. Of the world's 15 least diversified economies, the continent is home to eight (International Monetary Fund, Export Diversification Index, 2020). Due to institutional and structural constraints, diversification has been largely elusive, particularly in the poorest countries in sub-Saharan Africa. Nonetheless, the digital knowledge economy beckons.

Given Africa's inability to harness the benefits of both the agricultural and industrial revolutions – as envisaged for a long time in contemporary development orthodoxy – the rise of the digital knowledge economy is generating a lot of hope for the socioeconomic transformation of the continent, albeit with cautious optimism. While a handful of players are reaping bountifully from the acceleration of technological uptake across key sectors and digital innovation ecosystems on the continent, the reality remains that many Africans still do not have access to digital resources at a scale large enough to spark a continent-wide industrial revolution that can move a significant number of Africans above the poverty line. This has implications for the innovation discourse. We discuss this in detail below.

INNOVATION AND DIVERSIFICATION IN A GLOBAL CONTEXT

The knowledge economy is here to stay. Know-how and technological innovations have become the key drivers of economic competitiveness; the outputs of the research and development (R & D) activities in the ivory towers are key ingredients for creating prosperity and inclusive development. Increasingly, innovation is becoming a subject of much interest to players in the academic, corporate, and policy spheres. While the academic-government interaction phase in the innovation discourse signifies the knowledge production component when the competitive edge is identified, the academic-industry phase enhances the process through which innovation and knowledge reduce transaction costs through the spillover effects. This explains the popularity of the endogenous growth model (Romer, 1994) in the policy circle because it recognizes the importance of the spillover effects of innovation on economic development, partly because subsidies or industrial policy in some areas can produce a net positive effect.

Understanding the different innovation types and capabilities remains important in crafting and improving on existing ones. Meijaard (2001) argues that the innovative advantage has moved from big and established corporations to new small and medium-sized enterprises (SMEs) because the recent advances in technology have reduced the constraints imposed by scale economies in key sectors. While this contradicts, in a way, the notion that the disproportionate displacement of labor by capital explains the rise of the superstar firm, it does resonate when viewed in the context of the argument that most of the new jobs in an economy are created by SMEs (Birch, 1987).

Looking at this from the lens of economic theory, while the literature is united on the notion of a falling labor share, evidence on the reasons for the recent decline is still mixed. Karabarbounis and Neiman (2013) argue that the fall in the cost of capital relative to labor, under a quality-adjusted price of ICT, would further erode the share of labor if the elasticity of capital-labor substitution is greater than one. While a large chunk of the empirical literature agrees that the elasticity is less than one (Oberfield & Raval, 2014; Antras, 2004), a few support an elasticity above one, including Karabarbounis and Neiman. Acemoglu and Restrepo (2019) corroborate how tasks automation can exacerbate the reduction in the labor share, through digitization, if the resultant worker displacement effects more than compensate for the increased demand seen in the new non-automated tasks that emerge.

As might be expected, productivity improvements happen fast in firms and industries with significant digital processes, while traditional social sectors like education, healthcare, public administration – and parts of the real economy in agriculture and manufacturing – remain stagnant, with little or no productivity gains. This trend is not limited to industry sectors; it can be extrapolated to cities, regions, and individuals (Bogers et al., 2018). Melhem (2016) highlights the importance of leveraging the complementarities in digital and analog processes to advance policy innovation. For context, the urban innovation literature supports the view that the positive agglomeration effects of firms in urban centers often generate or induce new knowledge. Given the rapid rate of urbanization on the African continent, the right dose of policy can trigger an increase in new SMEs and the rate of job creation. This has implications for the policy development discourse.

CORPORATE INNOVATION AND PUBLIC POLICY

Strategic innovation reduces transaction costs by reducing risks and creating positive externalities among key actors in government, academia, industry, and civil society. The digital revolution is fostering more global, open, and collaborative science and innovation ecosystems and the knowledge for innovation in the global economy has become widely distributed (Bogers et al., 2018). For instance, the Open Government policies of the Obama Administration in 2009 heralded the rapidly evolving concept of open government and open data, with the concomitant effect being the entry of new players into the government open digital ecosystem. In addition to fostering collaborations across industries with private sector stakeholders over the years, public agencies have become more efficient in their service delivery (Chenok, 2019). This is a major advance.

Grant (2016) proposes long-term, and often irreversible, value creation which involves huge resource commitment as a viable model since strategic innovation implies value creation from varying experiences or models of product delivery. Grant's logic is premised on the notion that to constitute a competitive advantage, governments and corporations must be willing to support economic redesign through long-term commitments and investments capable of establishing a threshold to incentivize behavioral changes. In a way, this underscores the reality that government resources alone cannot address the needs of society; major innovations can occur when markets are leveraged to create positive social impacts.

In relative terms, while the literature on corporate innovation – particularly in the management and technology domains – is extensive, not a lot is available on the policy dimension. Due to the absence of a unified framework, defining innovation is not quite straightforward. This is somewhat counterintuitive given the burgeoning interest in this field. Depending on the context, discipline, industry, and circumstance, innovation has different meanings in diverse academic, business, and policy settings. For instance, while economic innovation is often explained in the context of increased industry-level productivity, technology innovation focuses more on the process by which new technologies become the drivers of other innovations (Gopalakrishnan & Damanpour, 1997).

In the strategic management domain, innovation is analyzed largely through the resource-based model of competitive advantage, where long-term corporate success depends on the so-called "strategic resource"[1] of a firm.

To the extent that a firm's strategic resources constitute the major sources of competitive advantages over its rivals, maintaining such edge in a sustainable manner means the firm must accumulate and deploy its resources in ways that make them difficult to imitate and nonsubstitutable. This has implications for innovation decision-making vis-à-vis the creation or destruction of a firm's competitive advantage.

The literature on innovation and competitive advantage is extensive. Giménez et al. (2019) provide empirical insights into specific policy innovations capable of sustaining the competitive advantages of companies in the construction sector. Based on a sample of 94 Spanish construction companies over the 2009–2011 period – an era associated with economic downturn in the aftermath of the Great Recession – the authors shed light on the specific capabilities that can increase innovation and performance for companies operating in the sector, in an era characterized by a dire need for economic rebound. Their results identify gains in financial and human capital innovation capabilities as critical ingredients for driving competitive capabilities for better performance.

In the resource-based tradition, Schroeder et al. (1989) distinguish further between management innovation and manufacturing innovation. They opine that innovation, in a management sense, is "the generation, evaluation, and implementation of new ideas to meet organizational objectives" (Schroeder et al., 1989; p. 6), while in the manufacturing sphere, "the application of new or different approaches or methods or technologies resulting in improved quality or reduced cost relative to competition" (Schroeder et al., 1989; p. 6) constitutes innovation. Digital platforms are increasingly helping to drive innovation and help government fulfil their social contracts. And open innovation is at the heart of this trend, as it is becoming commonplace in academic, business, and public policy circles to rely on both internal and external sources of information – contrary to the secrecy-driven models of closed innovation in traditional corporate research supply chains, where intellectual property control and ownership remain key.

Henry Chesbrough in his 2003 book, *Open Innovation: The New Imperative for Creating and Profiting from Technology*, explains the concept of open innovation in terms of how useful knowledge and technology can no longer be restricted to supply chains denominated by individual inventors or academia. Chesbrough details the corporate research management process and strategies for bringing the commercialization of new technologies, corporate venturing, licensing, and intellectual property under one umbrella. Along the same lines, open innovation can be viewed as "a distributed innovation process based on purposively managed knowledge flows across organizational boundaries." (Chesbrough & Bogers, 2014; p. 1).

THE POLICY INNOVATION IMPERATIVE

What's the fuss about policy innovation? Well, innovation has become the success factor in the current highly competitive and digital global economy. Not only because of the positive spillovers, but also because a strategic innovation policy enables decision-makers to take advantage of future opportunities. At the heart of policy innovation is pragmatism. It is hard to find a scenario in which the linear policy cycle resolves a policy challenge in its entirety. As the ongoing wave of digital transformation intensifies, new methods and innovative paradigms in the public policy design and development domains are emerging. For instance, in the last decade, innovation in public service delivery has focused largely on Policy Innovation Labs (PILs).

PILs are frameworks, both within and outside government establishments, that leverage the conventional methods adopted in scientific laboratories – testing, piloting, prototyping, and experimentation – to address a wide range of social, urban, and climate concerns. Using a multi-stakeholder approach, such collaboration often involves key actors in the public, private, academic, and civic sectors. While the notion of strict evidence-based policymaking exercises considerable influence, it often comes into conflict with a normative and more pragmatic approach that recognizes the limits of the policy cycle construct in real-world policymaking, as opined below:

In fact, it is more common to describe counterintuitive processes in which, for example, by the time policymaker attention rises to a policy problem at the 'agenda setting' stage, it is too late to formulate a solution. Instead, 'policy entrepreneurs' develop technically and politically feasible solutions then wait for attention to rise and for policymakers to have the motive and opportunity to act. (*Cairney, 2018; para 4)*

To the extent that the theoretical underpinnings of evidence-based policymaking provide a good intellectual base for distilling the key issues, policy learning provides a more feasible pathway for policy entrepreneurs and innovators to bridge existing practical knowledge gaps by learning about, and creating opportunities, through innovative and creative approaches.

Mainstream discourses often construe policy innovation in the context of public policy targeted at achieving innovation in a particular domain. This is not the same as fostering innovation within the public policy life cycle, which is the focus of this book. Among others, this involves leveraging new paradigms, tools, frameworks, and techniques to generate incremental improvements in all five components of the policy life cycle: agenda-setting, policy formulation, adoption, implementation, and evaluation (Howlett & Ramesh, 2003). In addition to harnessing complementarities that can lead to an increase in aggregate economic welfare, this could mean including a diverse range of voices in the policy process. A classic example is leveraging the quadruple helix model of innovation, which involves stakeholders from the public, private, academic, and community sectors (this is discussed later in the book).

Joseph Schumpeter advanced the theory of innovation to account for industry growth through three channels: creative accumulation, creative destruction, and rejection of competitive market equilibria (Sweezy, 1943). In all three channels, the entrepreneur – who is willing to leverage market dynamics, profit expectations, and long-run growth expectations to drive evolutionary growth and endogenous innovation – remains the driving force behind capitalism. Much of the recent neo-Schumpeterian literature provides insights into how innovation has contributed to a better understanding of the technology-economy-society nexus, with technology remaining a force capable of generating economic growth, while also improving social welfare – the so-called inclusive growth.

As discussed in the subsequent chapters, the parameters of a policy implementation path are key drivers of the eventual policy outcome. This implies that the combined effects of power relationships among various stakeholders and social groups have a major influence on the impacts of a policy, as well as how well the policy achieves its intended objectives. Economic growth and social inclusion are not mutually exclusive; policy interventions targeted at promoting inclusion can ensure mobility for those on the lower end of the socioeconomic ladder. This is achievable through a broad range of reforms targeted at competitiveness and economic growth, while creating social impact by advancing inclusive and equitable economic development. Policy innovation through market channels can achieve this.

INNOVATION CAPACITY IN THE AFRICAN CONTEXT

The World Intellectual Property Organization (WIPO), INSEAD, and Cornell University (2020) define innovation leaders in terms of complementarity and balance across the different areas of their innovation system. "A successful innovation system balances the forces that push knowledge creation, exploration, and investments—the innovation inputs— with the forces that pull ideas and technologies towards application, exploitation, and impact—the innovation outputs" (WIPO, 2020; p. 15). Through the annual Global Innovation Index (GII) – a model that captures innovation metrics for 131 economies with varying weights on factors that help create an environment that fosters innovation – Africa's performance is reported relative to other regions.

In terms of performance, regional differences appear across Africa in the 2020 GII, with Mauritius (52nd), South Africa (60th), Kenya (86th), Tanzania (88th), and Botswana (89th) occupying the first to fifth positions in sub-Saharan Africa in the order indicated.[2] Compared to 2019, all five economies improve their 2020 GII ranking, except for Kenya. Rwanda (91st) and Cabo Verde (100th) are among the top 100, while Malawi (111th), Madagascar (115th), Zimbabwe (120th), Zambia (122nd), and Togo (125th) witness increases in their rankings. Five out of the 12 lower middle-income economies that perform below expectations (in terms of innovation outputs relative to the levels of innovation investments) are from sub-Saharan Africa (Cameroon, Côte d'Ivoire, Ghana, Nigeria, and Zambia), while Tunisia, Morocco, Tanzania, Madagascar, and Niger are termed innovation achievers – having performed at expectations for their level of development.

Based on their relatively deterministic model of the innovation-development relationship, the GII notes some outliers that perform above or below expectations, relative to their predicted performance. A joint GII, IMF, and Boston Consulting Group's analysis shows that while developing countries tend to rank low on the GII – compared to the average score of 29 for all emerging markets – the average innovation index score for Africa is 22.4 – below the average for all emerging markets (Figure 1).

Figure 1. Innovation performance: Africa vs. emerging markets
Source: Maher et al. (2021): Boston Consulting Group

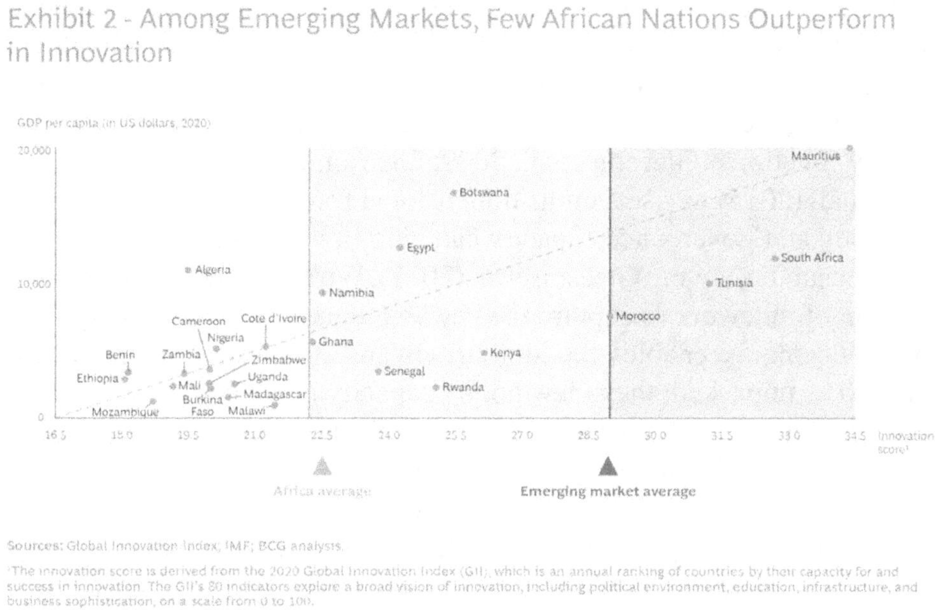

Sengupta (2014) explains the innovation-development nexus using productivity gains as a theoretical underpinning. He argues that recent advances in ICT and the rise of the knowledge economy have led to a dynamic shift from material manufacturing to a digital economy driven by research and development (R&D) and human capital. The GII notes that historically, sub-Saharan Africa is home to the largest number of economies with above-expectations innovation performance, compared to their level of development. Again, this offers a glimmer of hope for Africa's development journey in the context of the leapfrog effect.

POLICY CAPACITY AND INNOVATION

Depending on the context, policy capacity has multiple and varying definitions. While the divergence in opinions on how this concept can be scientifically measured and operationalized is widely acknowledged in the literature, the policy innovation discourse continues to present a clear consensus that policy capacity is essentially about governments' ability to improve the instrumental rationality of policymaking. This could be a cost-benefit analysis of alternative policy scenarios (Bakvis, 2000); systematic and strategic use of knowledge to improve policymaking (Parsons, 2004; Peters, 2005); environmental scanning to aid strategic planning (Howlett & Lindquist, 2004); deploying necessary resources to inform intelligent choices (Painter & Pierre, 2005); and acquiring the necessary skills and resources necessary for the discharge of policy functions (Gleeson et al., 2009; Gleeson et al., 2011).

Wu et al. (2015) devise a multi-dimensional framework in the analysis of how policy and governance capacity can help in understanding why policy failures occur. Following Gleeson et al. (2011), Wu et al. devise a rather broad conceptual framework to capture the key elements of policy capacity. Their adopted taxonomy enables the similarities and differences of the various strands to be unpacked; they view policy capacity in the context of the skills and resources (i.e., competences and capabilities) needed to accomplish the objectives of the key stages of the policy cycle. They categorize such skills or competences into three types: analytical, operational, and political. Furthermore, they contextualize how each type is driven by resources or capabilities at three different levels: individual, organizational, and systemic.

A major advance in the use of this approach is its ability to adopt a multi-stakeholder approach in public policy innovation, by tapping into the capacity and resources of other key stakeholders beyond the public sector. The recognition that addressing societal challenges through policy requires governments to be more open and receptive to ideas from the private sector and civil society – by harnessing opportunities in the policy-market nexus – fosters an entrepreneurial environment in the public policy development process. This framework is particularly relevant in the African context not only because it serves as a tool for diagnosing and addressing policy capacity deficits across governments, but also because it helps to pioneer novel policy solutions by taking full advantage of the burgeoning digital economy to reimagine and redefine policy innovation on the continent.

To put the analysis above into perspective, let's consider the argument on how best to fix global inequality and poverty. While there are various opinions on the way forward, the core of the argument is fundamental: policy focus on overall economic growth versus the distribution of the growth itself. While much of the debate in the advanced industrial nations has always focused on the pros and cons of progressivism, the limits of the fiscal tax-and-transfer system as the only panacea to inequality and poverty must be recognized. In the new global digital economy, technological innovations will only cause further disruptions; this has implications for the limits of fiscal policy omnipotence.

An innovative policy regime that recognizes the role of the state in creating incentives and reducing transaction costs is important.

A nuanced understanding of contemporary social policy requires a firm grasp of the role of markets. Bivens (2016) further unpacks this by dividing contemporary progressive economic policy into three pillars: the use of macroeconomic stabilization tools to achieve genuine full employment, boosting investment in public goods underserved by the markets in the hope for potential (evidence-based) large returns, and market failures correction through legislation or regulatory channels. He then cautions that the three planks above require effective public structures and well-run governments – and not just taxing and spending – that recognize the efficiency implications of a smarter and fairer taxing and spending regime under a progressive system. To the extent that policy recommendations and budgetary considerations drive real-world outcomes, the disconnect between policy planning and policy implementation has major implications. This explains why, to a large extent, innovation hubs and policy laboratories aimed at experimenting and applying new approaches to policy development are increasingly commonplace in much of the developed world (Brookfield Institute, 2018).

TAKEAWAYS AND IMPLICATIONS FOR AFRICA

Of course, these issues are more nuanced in the African context. While the continent continues to make giant strides in the adoption of digital technologies across industries – leading to wealth creation and social mobility in many communities and households – existing structural and institutional barriers preclude many national governments from deploying flexible, innovative, and efficient policy innovation templates that have become a new normal in the developed world. To ensure that Africa's heterogenous dimensions are accounted for, the subsequent chapters examine diverse issues such as state structures, institutions, redistributive fiscal policy, regional innovation ecosystem, economic structure, and other political economy considerations.

To date, policy innovation has not received the level of attention it deserves in Africa. Forging a more dynamic economy across the continent requires solutions based not only on research, but also on testing, piloting, prototyping, and experimentation with innovative approaches in the policy development process. Whether through competitive markets or public sector operations, society wants the supply of public services like healthcare, education, security, and infrastructure to be flexible, innovative, and efficient. Many of these policy challenges cannot be solved through traditional, linear channels. The discourse on innovation has transitioned from its purely scientific and technical focus to include digital opportunities and collaborations across the state-business nexus.

Traditionally, policymakers have crafted innovation strategies and policy instruments to attract investments in science and technology for long-term economic growth – through incentives for academic research, preferential tax treatment and subsidies on R&D expenditures, etc. However, given recent advances in the digital economy, multipronged approaches and policy framings are becoming popular in the public policy development value chain. This underscores the importance of a well-designed policy framework as an important foundational element for a thriving innovation economy. Indeed, the digital revolution provides a unique opportunity for Africa to transition to the mainstream of global commerce, increase productivity, and break the shackles of poverty. Much has been written about the implications of the leapfrog effect for socioeconomic transformation in Africa; many in the policy and development circles see leapfrogging as a potent strategy to address decades of elusive development objectives.

The First Industrial Revolution relied on water and steam power for mechanized production; the Second leveraged electric power for mass production; and the Third automated production processes through ICT. Unlike these previous waves of revolutions, however, the Fourth Industrial Revolution is about efficiency in the utilization of capabilities made possible by digitization. A statement submitted by Uganda's Minister of Science, Technology, and Innovation, Elioda Tumwesigye, to the United Nations Commission on Science and Technology for Development in 2019 reads, "We must support and invest in R&D so that we can leapfrog the technological trends and developments, as we modernize our industrial base and become a player on the global technological platform." (United Nations Conference on Trade and Development, 2019; p.4).

While scientific research, capital investments, and the knowledge economy are important in the value creation process, they are not an absolute precondition for success in the current digital economy. Instead, talent, business model, digital savviness, execution, and allied variables have more explanatory power. While this offers a slight but meaningful glimmer of hope for Africa, other important underlying structural and institutional issues must be considered, as espoused in terms of the pros and cons below:

Granted, Africa still has a long way to go before it can take full advantage of the digital industrial revolution. Despite impressive progress over the past decade, in virtually every metric—from internet penetration to venture capital investment to skilled workforces to "ease of doing business" rankings—the continent as a whole lags behind the rest of the world in its capacity to widely deploy cutting-edge knowledge in fields such as artificial intelligence, big data analytics, and advanced robotics........From the ground level, however, the view in parts of Africa is encouraging. Several global growth hot spots are emerging. Morocco's 200-company automotive cluster, for example, is launching R&D initiatives linking manufacturers to universities. Nigerian startups have attracted hundreds of millions of dollars in equity funding, and Kenya has emerged as a hotbed for fintech. South Africa's dynamic health technology ecosystem includes more than 120 companies. Incubators, entrepreneurship training, and investment funds are making Egypt the region's fastest-growing startup ecosystem (Maher et al., 2021; para 3-4).

From land and exchange rate reforms to tax overhaul and improved access to markets, policy innovation can create efficiency gains for increased economic prosperity on the continent. Targeted policy innovations through a multi-stakeholder approach which bring startups, investors, governments, and other key actors in the innovation ecosystem together will be important in ensuring sustainability. Among other things, this could be as simple as creating legislation to ensure the business environment is conducive for the fledgling tech ecosystem, while also supporting upcoming African entrepreneurs. African governments must collaborate with industry, academia, and the civic sector to unleash the immense potential of the innovation economy through sector- and jurisdiction-specific policy innovations that can help young and dynamic African founders scale, unleash growth, and create prosperity.

To conclude, Africa has underlying political economy issues manifesting as social, economic, and policy challenges. Simply put, underperformance on critical economic and social indicators on the continent is grounded in a political economy ramification that has persisted for decades. To understand what has happened to the African economy and society, we need to look back at least to the immediate post-independence period. The varying degrees of state and market involvement in resource allocation often present Africa as a mixed economy under policy design scenarios. This leaves a wiggle room for experiments that may not fully capture the continent's core underlying social and political context. Based on history and experience, we know that development is a complex, non-linear process. As well, policy innovation is inextricably dependent on political economy dynamics. And to the extent that no one has all the answers, iterations and designs through policy tools that effectively and efficiently capture the economic, political, social, cultural, and demographic realities of complex systems are a sine qua non.

These conundrums, while entrenched, can be addressed. The foundational issues on policy innovation have been discussed in this chapter, but making incremental gains in the policy life cycle requires building a shared understanding of the continent's journey. This is the only way strategies targeted at fixing almost a century of policy incongruence can be effective. Needless to say, much progress has been made in the context of Africa's contemporary policy environment –à la Agenda 2063 and the AfCFTA – but strengthening the link between policy learning and policy change can move the needle in a critical way. This is discussed in detail in the next chapter.

Whether you're a farmer, builder or engineer, the opportunities are equal: Just add a little innovation.

— *Strive Masiyiwa*

REFERENCES

Acemoglu, D., & Restrepo, P. (2019). Automation and new tasks: How technology displaces and reinstates labor. *The Journal of Economic Perspectives*, *33*(2), 3–30. doi:10.1257/jep.33.2.3

Antràs, P. (2004). Is the U.S. aggregate production function Cobb-Douglas? New estimates of the elasticity of substitution. *The B.E. Journal of Macroeconomics*, *4*(1), 1–36. doi:10.2202/1534-6005.1161

Autor, D., Dorn, D., Katz, L. F., Patterson, C., & Van Reenen, J. (2020). The fall of the labor share and the rise of superstar firms. *The Quarterly Journal of Economics*, *135*(2), 645–709. doi:10.1093/qje/qjaa004

Bakvis, H. (2000). Rebuilding policy capacity in the era of the fiscal dividend: A report from Canada. *Governance: An International Journal of Policy, Administration and Institutions*, *13*(1), 71–103. doi:10.1111/0952-1895.00124

Barney, J. B. (1991). Firm resources and sustained competitive advantage. *Journal of Management*, *17*(1), 99–121. doi:10.1177/014920639101700108

Birch, D. G. (1987). *Job creation in America: How our smallest companies put the most people to work.* The Free Press.

Bivens, J. (2016). *Progressive redistribution without guilt: using policy to shift economic power and make U.S. incomes grow fairer and faster.* Economic Policy Institute. https://www.epi.org/publication/progressive-redistribution-without-guilt-using-policy-to-shift-economic-power-and-make-u-s-incomes-grow-fairer-and-faster/

Bogers, M., Chesbrough, H., & Moedas, C. (2018). Open Innovation: Research, Practices, and Policies. *California Management Review, 60*(2), 5-16. doi:10.1177/0008125617745086

Brookfield Institute for Innovation + Entrepreneurship. (2018). *Exploring policy innovation: Tools, techniques + approaches.* https://brookfieldinstitute.ca/wp-content/uploads/BrookfieldInstitute-PIP-Landscape-1.pdf

Cairney, P. (2018). *Evidence-based policymaking: political strategies for scientists living in the real world.* Retrieved from https://paulcairney.wordpress.com/2018/04/26/evidence-based-policymaking-political-strategies-for-scientists-living-in-the-real-world/

Chenok, D. (2019). How open innovation can transform the government technology playing field. *FCW: The Business of Federal Technology.* https://fcw.com/articles/2019/12/17/comment-chenok-open-innovation.aspx

Chesbrough, H., & Bogers, B. (2014). Explicating open innovation: Clarifying an emerging paradigm for understanding innovation. In H. Chesbrough, W. Vanhaverbeke, & J. West (Eds.), New Frontiers in Open Innovation (pp. 3-28). Oxford University Press.

Chesbrough, H. W. (2003). *Open innovation: The new imperative for creating and profiting from technology.* Harvard Business Press.

Chi, T. (1994). Trading in strategic resources: Necessary conditions, transaction cost problems, and choice of exchange structure. *Strategic Management Journal, 15*(4), 271–290. doi:10.1002mj.4250150403

Cornell University, INSEAD, & WIPO. (2020). *The Global Innovation Index 2020: Who Will Finance Innovation?*

Giménez, J., Madrid-Guijarro, A., & Duréndez, A. (2019). Competitive Capabilities for the Innovation and Performance of Spanish Construction Companies. *Sustainability (Basel, Switzerland), 11*(19), 5475. doi:10.3390u11195475

Gleeson, D., Legge, D., O'Neill, D., & Pfeffer, M. (2011). Negotiating tensions in developing organizational policy capacity: Comparative lessons to be drawn. *Journal of Comparative Policy Analysis, 13*(3), 237–263. doi: 10.1080/13876988.2011.565912

Gleeson, D. H., O'Neill, D., & Legge, D. G. (2009). Evaluating health policy capacity: Learning from international and Australian experience. *Australia and New Zealand Health Policy, 6*(1), 3. Advance online publication. doi:10.1186/1743-8462-6-3 PMID:19245704

Gopalakrishnan, S., & Damanpour, F. (1997). A Review of Innovation Research in Economics, Sociology and Technology Management. *Omega, 25*(1), 15–28. doi:10.1016/S0305-0483(96)00043-6

Grant, R. M. (2016). *Contemporary strategy analysis: Text and cases* (9th ed.). Wiley.

Howlett, M., & Lindquist, E. (2004). Policy analysis and governance: Analytical and policy styles in Canada. *Journal of Comparative Policy Analysis, 6*(3), 225–249. doi:10.1080/1387698042000305194

Howlett, M., & Ramesh, M. (2003). *Studying Public Policy: Policy Cycles and Policy Subsystems* (2nd ed.). Oxford University Press.

International Monetary Fund. (2017). *Export Diversification Index, 2020.* https://data.imf.org/?sk=A093DF7D-E0B8-4913-80E0-A07CF90B44DB

Karabarbounis, L., & Neiman, B. (2013). *The global decline of the labor share.* National Bureau of Economic Research. doi:10.3386/w19136

Maher, H., Chraïti, A., Laabi, A., Oikawa, T., Oyekan, T., & Bosson, A. (2021). *Igniting Innovation-Based Growth in Africa.* Boston Consulting Group. https://www.bcg.com/publications/2021/innovation-in-africa

Meijaard, J. (2001). *Making sense of the new economy.* Research Report 0009/E. https://www.researchgate.net/publication/5012541_Making_sense_of_the_New_Economy

Melhem, S. (2016). *Harnessing the Internet for Development.* World Bank. https://www.worldbank.org/en/news/feature/2016/01/13/connections-note-31

Oberfield, E., & Raval, D. (2014). *Micro data and macro technology*. National Bureau of Economic Research. doi:10.3386/w20452

Painter, M., & Pierre, J. (2005). *Challenges to state policy capacity: Global trends and comparative perspectives*. Palgrave Macmillan. doi:10.1057/9780230524194

Parsons, W. (2004). Not just steering but weaving: Relevant knowledge and the craft of building policy capacity and coherence. *Australian Journal of Public Administration, 63*(1), 43–57. doi:10.1111/j.1467-8500.2004.00358.x

Peters, B. G. (2005). Policy instruments and policy capacity. In M. Painter & J. Pierre (Eds.), Challenges to state policy capacity: Global trends and comparative perspectives (pp. 73-91). Palgrave Macmillan. doi:10.1057/9780230524194_5

Romer, P. (1994). The Origins of Endogenous Growth. *The Journal of Economic Perspectives, 8*(1), 3–22. doi:10.1257/jep.8.1.3

Schroeder, R. G., Scudder, G. D., & Elm, D. R. (1989). Innovation in manufacturing. *Journal of Operations Management, 8*(1), 1–15. doi:10.1016/S0272-6963(89)80002-6

Sengupta, J. (2014). *Theory of innovation: A new paradigm of growth* (1st ed.). Springer International Publishing. doi:10.1007/978-3-319-02183-6

Sweezy, P. M. (1943). Professor Schumpeter's Theory of Innovation. *The Review of Economics and Statistics, 25*(1), 93–96. doi:10.2307/1924551

Tumwesigye, E. (2019). The impact of rapid technological change on sustainable development. *United Nations Conference on Trade and Development.* https://unctad.org/system/files/non-official-document/ecn162019s17_Uganda_en.pdf

Wu, X., Ramesh, M., & Howlett, M. (2015). Policy capacity: A conceptual framework for understanding policy competences and capabilities. *Policy and Society, 34*(3-4), 165–171. doi:10.1016/j.polsoc.2015.09.001

ENDNOTES

1. A strategic resource is defined in the context of being an asset that is valuable, rare, difficult to imitate, and nonsubstitutable (Barney, 1991; Chi, 1994).
2. The positions in brackets indicate global rankings.

Chapter 3
Policy Change:
Theories, Evidence, and Implications

ABSTRACT

Institutional quality lies at the heart of much of the work in comparative political economy, through paradigms such as agenda-setting, policy image, and the influence of the media. And while the growth and development trajectories of economies may encounter positive and negative political shocks, the broad effects have implications in both developing and advanced economies. This chapter presents political economy as a framework for understanding how policy choices emanate from the interactions between politicians and economic elites. With the aid of eight contemporary theories of policy change, the core arguments and worldviews about new paradigms, beliefs, and assumptions that can generate the necessary and sufficient conditions to improve policymaking are presented – while paying special attention to the differing implications for policy innovation. The theories are situated within the broader discussion on the political economy of public-private policy partnerships and, more specifically, within the discourse on policy entrepreneurship.

DOI: 10.4018/978-1-7998-7383-9.ch003

If your dreams do not scare you, they are not big enough

— Ellen Johnson Sirleaf

THEORIZATIONS IN POLICY CHANGE are essentially about translating the vision and mission of governments into implementation through policy tools, models, paradigms, and techniques. Addressing societal challenges through policy requires governments to be more open and receptive to ideas from the private sector and civil society, but it is often hard to innovate in large bureaucracies. The policy diffusion process is slow; this explains why innovation concentration at the upper rung of the spectrum is a major driver of uneven growth in productivity and prosperity across industry sectors and regions. This has implications for the high levels of inequality in society. Varying social, political, economic, and cultural settings inform how policies are developed and implemented.

For complex policy problems that require unconventional nonlinear solutions, ill-defined problems can generate large inefficiencies along the policy value chain. Patton et al. (2012) in *Basic Methods of Policy Analysis and Planning*, describe a set of systematic procedures that can help address a wide range of policy problems. The authors' six-step model of policy analysis summarizes the problems of modern society below:

1. They are not well defined.
2. Their solutions cannot usually be proven to be correct before application.
3. No problem solution is ever guaranteed to achieve the intended result.
4. Problem solutions are seldom both best and cheapest.
5. The adequacy of the solution is often difficult to measure against notions of the public good.
6. The fairness of solutions is impossible to measure objectively.

Following the rationalist model, they argue that policymaking is based on a rigid framework that follows some sequences like problem definition, possible outcomes, feasible alternatives, selection, and policy implementation. The policy process is essentially about policy actors interacting with public, private, academic, and civic stakeholders within existing institutional arrangements to influence policy outcomes. To the extent that citizens interpret the world around them through the lens of their beliefs, while also learning by combining systematic and scientific evidence with heuristics, policymakers must strike a right balance between evidence-informed policymaking and policy diffusion. Policy designs and implementations based partly on the experiences of the past, or other policies, can benefit from a wider range of examples.

Political economy scholarship is largely about devising a framework for understanding how policy choices emanate from the interactions between politicians and economic elites. In their 2006 book, *Economic Origins of Dictatorship and Democracy*, Daron Acemoglu and James Robinson argue that political power and resource allocation pattern influences how various social groups prefer different political institutions. Democracy, in their view, is preferred by most citizens and opposed by elites, but due to forces beyond their control, elites maintain social stability by credibly transferring political power to the citizens. They identify six channels: the strength of civil society, the structure of political institutions, the nature of political and economic crises, the level of economic inequality, the structure of the economy, and the form and extent of globalization.

Change is a constant feature of the capitalist mode of production, evidenced by the continuous churning that enables old firms, processes, paradigms, and products to pave the way for new ones, in alignment with Joseph Schumpeter's submission that innovation happens through a "perennial gale of creative destruction" that reorganizes the economic structure from within by "incessantly destroying the old one, incessantly creating a new one" (Schumpeter, 1942; p. 83).

THEORIES OF POLICY CHANGE

Quite simplistically, theories of policy change are worldviews about new paradigms, beliefs, and assumptions that can generate the necessary and sufficient conditions to improve policymaking. Moyson et al. (2017) identify three approaches in the understanding of the connection between policy learning and policy change: micro-, meso-, and macro-level approaches. The authors explain micro-level approaches "as a process of 'puzzling' among individual policy actors dealing with ideas and uncertainty," meso-level in the context of "the increase of knowledge and intelligence in organizations and changes in their effectiveness in resolving problems or in the policy positions that they advocate," and macro-level as "sequences in which policy decisions are made in one or several institutional systems, often times after similar decisions have been made in one or several other institutional systems." (Moyson et al., 2017; p. 162)

Peter John, in his 2018 work, contends that:

One of the most significant intellectual developments of recent years has been the revival of interest in political economy, especially with a comparative range. This approach to study operates on two related dimensions: one is the role of the economy in structuring political choices (and also the influence of politics on economic outcomes); the other is about the method, which comes from economics, in theorizing about how political and economic variables relate together, often through formal models and/or advanced statistical methods. Political economy involves a closer relationship between the discipline of economics with its modelling and theory testing approach, and political science, which is more interested in contexts, the role of institutions, comparative systems design, and the influence of actors, such as voters and interest groups. (John, 2018; p. 5)

Institutional quality lies at the heart of much of the work in comparative political economy, through paradigms such as agenda-setting, policy image, and the influence of the media. And while the growth and development trajectories of economies may encounter positive and negative political shocks, the broad effects have implications in both developing and advanced economies. John categorizes the discourse on decision-making in public policy into three distinct ages of theory building and testing:

The first was the classic period of studies of decision-making and rationality; the second was the age of synthesis when theories of decision-making were blended into accounts of agenda setting. The third—which is starting to take shape—is the age of the political economy of public policy, drawing on models and methods that have been applied to the study of international relations and comparative politics, which are increasingly addressing issues in public policy. (John 2018; p. 1)

In his 2012 book, *Analyzing Public Policy*, John explains that in the study of policy analysis, the core theories of public policy and the policy process comprise of five widely used paradigms and frameworks: institutions, groups and networks, society and the economy, individual interests, and ideas. This approach makes it obvious that no one framework unpacks the various developments in the public policy process in totality. Instead, a blended approach which recognizes the strengths and weaknesses of the various models offers a more pragmatic path to the understanding of public policy.

In this chapter, I summarize the core arguments of eight contemporary theories of policy change, while paying special attention to the differing implications for policy innovation. The theories are situated within the broader discussion on the political economy of public-private policy partnerships, and more specifically, within the discourse on policy entrepreneurship. The implications for incremental innovations and applicability in the policy cycle, more broadly, are discussed. These theories are grounded in diverse worldviews and disciplines aimed at helping policy actors unpack various entrenched beliefs and assumptions about the inner workings of the policymaking process. As with most scientific theories, eventual policy outcomes are under no obligation to conform to these ideas and theory-grounded expectations. But, at least, they provide reasoned justifications for why, and how, certain policy changes may or may not occur.

Punctuated Equilibrium Theory

Why do most public policies stay the same for extended periods while some change very rapidly and dramatically? Why are incremental policy changes seen in some socioeconomic systems for decades, only to be heralded by an agenda setting regime which charts a new policy trajectory? The Punctuated Equilibrium Theory (PET), pioneered in 1993 by Frank Baumgartner and Bryan Jones in *Agendas and Instability in American Politics,* explains long periods of policy stability punctuated by short periods of radical change. Baumgartner and Jones' thesis was later refined (see Jones et al., 2003; Jones & Baumgartner, 2005; & Baumgartner et al., 2006).

Baumgartner and Jones (1993) demonstrate how a wide variety of public policies – including energy policy, transportation policy, and urban policy – navigated long periods of stability punctuated by short periods of radical change. As a framework for unpacking the complex dynamics of social systems, the central tenet of the PET is that until social systems are punctuated by sudden events leading to a radical change, they tend to exist in stasis for an extended period.

The PET is essentially about making sense of the long periods of equilibrium before the abrupt punctuations that happen in political systems. At the core of it, the PET sheds light on why under certain conditions, policymakers may welcome evidence-informed recommendations that can trigger a major policy change, while in other instances, only marginal changes are considered. The model is rooted in pluralism, a paradigm in which power is distributed among specialized subsystems across all levels of government, due to the relatively limited attention and expertise of decision-makers – since public policy development is an inherently technical, and ongoing, process.

Paul Cairney, in *Understanding Public Policy: Theories and Issues*, explains how a combination of approaches provides insights on the dynamics of policy continuity and policy change. Cairney (2012) sees the PET as the combination of policy communities and agenda-setting – two approaches to the study of public policy. Policy communities are explained largely as identifying stable relationships between interest groups and public officials since these actors perpetuate a policy monopoly through a shared understanding of the nature of a policy problem. As such, incrementalism becomes the basis of policymaking since previous agreements between a small number of actors are all that is required, as espoused further below:

Policies stay the same within policy communities because there is minimal external interest or a limited ability of outsiders to engage. Policies change when there is sufficient external interest to cause the collapse of previously insulated communities. External attention rises and the issues are considered in a broader political environment where power is more evenly spread and new actors can set the agenda (Cairney, 2012; p. 2)

A major implication of unsuccessfully protecting a policy monopoly is opening up the policymaking process to a more competitive arrangement where stakeholders from a wider political spectrum have a chance to frame the policy issue. Under such breakdown of a policy monopoly, divergent outcomes from policy communities could trigger a demand for greater access to government and political instability, as corroborated, here:

While the successful definition of policy as a technical or humdrum issue ensures that issues may be monopolized and considered quietly in one venue, the reframing of that issue as crucial to other institutions, or the big political issues of the day, ensures that it will be considered by many audiences and processed in more than one decision-making venue (Cairney, 2012; p. 2)

The PET is a useful analytical framework for guiding the actions and strategies of government leaders as they seek to influence the policymaking process. Based on the theoretical underpinnings of the PET, Lundgren et al. (2018) take a critical look at the policy agendas – defined as “the allocation of policy output across policy topics” – of five international organizations with multi-issue orientations, comparable policy outputs, and geographic scopes: African Union, European Union, Organization of American States, Organization of Islamic Cooperation, and United Nations.

Based on data on about 20,000 individual policy decisions, between 1980 and 2015, their analysis assesses the presence of policy punctuations, in addition to explaining the variation in punctuation. In essence, until barriers and institutional constraints around vested interests, cultures, and defence mechanisms put in place around subsystems are disrupted, policy changes will only happen incrementally. Except the status quo is punctuated exogenously through changes in public opinions or intra-party dynamics within a ruling political party, political institutions may remain insular to the changing sociopolitical system. In an ideal world with no information asymmetry, policymakers know the implications of their choices, ex ante.

Incrementalism: The Baby-Steps Approach

Incrementalism, in the context of modeling policy change, is useful for tracking and analyzing viable options in the face of uncertain outcomes. Rational policymaking is the ideal scenario in which a democracy should work because it is "a process in which elected policymakers identify problems, clarify their aims and carefully weigh up solutions before making a choice (based on perfect information and no resistance from unelected implementing officials)" (Cairney, 2012; p. 95). However, the reality is that bounded rationality in policymaking is more about satisficing than optimizing, thereby limiting the efficacy of interventions (Deegan, 2021).

Charles Lindblom, in two articles in 1959 and 1979, underscores the limitations of rationality in the policymaking process in terms of the opportunity cost of relying on bounded rationality to close the gaps associated with the assumption of perfect information. Instead, Lindblom proposes incrementalism, or the so-called "muddling through" or "baby-steps" approach, as a more efficient and democratic approach to policymaking than comprehensive rationality. This is based on the view that when policy innovation occurs in gradual phases by improving on previous policies, the outcomes tend to be more efficient than when policy changes occur in a revolutionary manner.

Overall, incrementalism is viewed favourably as a relatively straightforward and empirically sound public policy formulation paradigm. For instance, incrementalism has become the holy grail of policymaking in the government budgeting sphere given its easy, step-by-step approach. In many ways, this model moves the needle in critical ways, on a marginal basis, while avoiding statis when radical policy reforms are not greenlit by society and policy actors. In Lindblom's view, incrementalism is a framework for reducing policy risk by engaging in trial and error to fix the deficiencies in the status quo. Incrementalism recognizes the tensions inherent in pluralistic situations where multiple actors and varying political consideration and interactions need a consensus in the public policy development process.

Multiple Streams Framework and Policy Entrepreneurship

The Multiple Streams Framework (MSF), pioneered by John Kingdon in his 1984 seminal book, *Agendas, Alternatives, and Public Policies,* with extensive applications by Zahariadis (1995), remains a powerful framework in understanding policy processes. Kingdon *(1984)* deploys the MSF as a tool for unpacking the policy process, and in particular, agenda-setting. The MSF identifies three streams of actors and processes in the policy cycle: a problem stream, a policy stream, and a politics stream. The problem stream is characterized by a data-driven approach to a policy problem; the policy stream is where solutions are proffered; and the politics stream constitutes the domain where leaders decide on specific interests and actions (Lasswell, 1936).

The policy stream, through the notion of the "policy entrepreneur", has attracted considerable attention in the policy change discourse. The term policy entrepreneur entered the public policy lexicon when Kingdon opined that policy entrepreneurs:

...could be in or out of government, in elected or appointed positions, in interest groups or research organizations. But their defining characteristic, much as in the case of a business entrepreneur, is their willingness to invest their resources – time, energy, reputation, and sometimes money – in the hope of a future return (Kingdon, 1984/2011; p. 122)

Through the active role they play in the policy stream through agenda-setting in the MSF, policy entrepreneurs devise policy alternatives and link them to policy problems. The significance of the policy entrepreneur in the MSF lies in the fact that even when they fail in moving a policy problem to the front burner of the political agenda, they still find a way to present the same issue to policymakers later or in another context. Policy entrepreneurs are energetic actors who, through problem definitions, determine what policies should be advanced, which actors will be interested in the problem, and the institutional dimension. This class of political actors engages in collaborative efforts in and around government to advance policy innovations (Figure 1). The diagram depicts a theoretical model of the policy process where policymaking and policy implementation are separate, but interdependent processes. This nested process, with several pillars in the policymaking process under the Kingdon MSF policy innovation paradigm, shows how the problems, policies, and politics streams are interconnected with policy implementation, with the policy entrepreneur playing a key role.

Figure 1. Policy innovation under the MSF
(Credit: Using the MSF to Connect Policy Adoption to Implementation, Fowler, 2020)

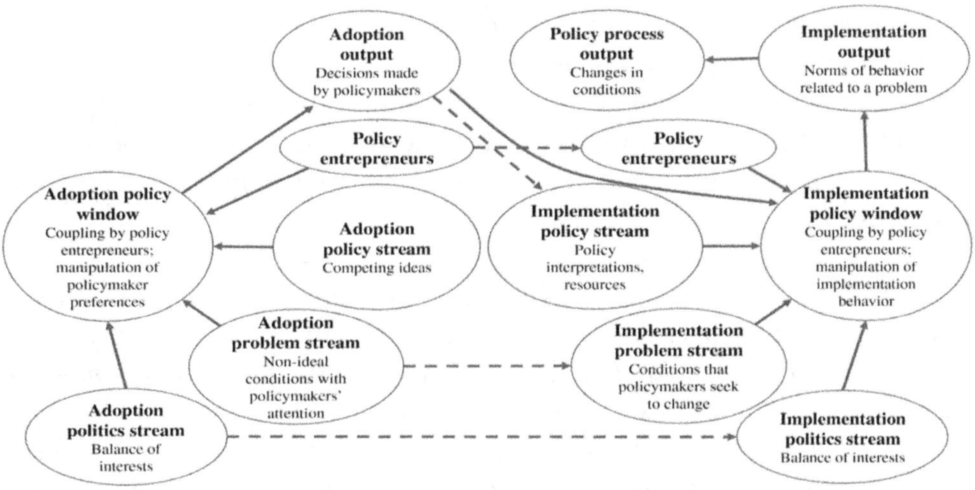

Just like Schumpeter, innovation is a trigger of economic change since new ideas, experimentations, and technological innovations are needed to create "a perennial gale of creative destruction," which typically happen through entrepreneurs and the startups in the innovation economy. Policy entrepreneurs are different from elected and appointed public officials and traditional political actors who belong to or represent certain interest groups.

Policy entrepreneurs, by and large, are the equivalent of corporate institutional entrepreneurs in the pubic policymaking process. Per Kingdon, in return for expected future rewards in the form of their ability to influence policy developments, these actors devise a way to influence the agenda-setting process. Not only that; they devote their energy and resources to ensure their efforts pay off by seeing the agenda-setting process through to policy actions. Herweg et al. (2018) take the MSF framework a step further by presenting it in a wide variety of ways, and how it is applicable to other stages of the policy process since the initial theoretical foundation of the MSF by Kingdon was limited to agenda-setting. For Mintrom (2019), the attributes of policy entrepreneurs can be encapsulated as: ambition, social acuity, credibility, sociability, and tenacity. This implies that policy entrepreneurship is a sine qua non for policy innovation; it is very disruptive since the pursuit of change is an arduous task that requires a lot of courage.

In the Schumpeterian tradition, the replacement of existing enterprises through new innovations is the core of capitalism in the context of the "the perennial gale of creative destruction." The Schumpeterian innovation model explains industry growth through three channels: creative accumulation, creative destruction, and rejection of competitive market equilibria. These channels underscore evolutionary growth and endogenous innovation, with the vital force behind capitalism being the innovation and the entrepreneur willing to make things happen through market dynamics, profit expectations, and long-run growth expectations. *Capitalism, Socialism, and Democracy* espouses this:

The opening up of new markets, foreign or domestic, and the organizational development from the craft shop to such concerns as U.S. Steel illustrate the same process of industrial mutation—if I may use that biological term—that incessantly revolutionizes the economic structure from within, incessantly destroying the old one, incessantly creating a new one. This process of Creative Destruction is the essential fact about capitalism. (Schumpeter, 1942; p. 83)

No doubt, this is even more true today, given the pace of disruptions due to the ongoing digital transformation of the global economy. While the context here is far from capitalism, this analogy resonates in many ways. Creative destruction is not a new concept, but it perfectly explains the role of policy innovation in creating a fairer and more equitable economy and society. This is essentially where policy entrepreneurs come in. They drive the policy process and transform ideas into innovations by disrupting the status quo.

The Helix Models of Innovation

Leveraging the helix models produces synergistic outcomes that drive innovation because of lower transaction costs. There are various strands, but I discuss two here: the triple and quadruple models. The triple helix of university-industry-government interactions model was developed by Etzkowitz (1993) and Etzkowitz and Leydesdorff (1995), based on the preceding works of Lowe (1982) and Sábato and Mackenzi (1982). The central thesis of the triple helix model is essentially about a thought process that led to a dramatic shift in the notion of the industry-government dyad that prevailed in the industrial society to take cognizance of the triadic relationship in the university-industry-government nexus considering the importance of the knowledge-based modern economy.

The theory unpacks how the linkages in the government-business-university nexus constitute the catalyst for advancing the innovation economies of nations. Even in the early era of economic thought, much of the debate on wealth creation was based on the notion of the most advanced practice of production (Unger, 2019). From mechanized manufacturing in the early phase of the First Industrial Revolution to late 19th century industrial mass production that defined the Second Industrial Revolution and the Third Industrial Revolution of the 20th century marked by partial automation and computers to the ongoing Fourth Industrial Revolution in which ICT is now integrated into production systems, recognizing the peculiar nature of the most advanced practice of production has major implications for the current knowledge economy.

The triple helix systems are a framework that systematizes university-industry-government interactions in an analytical manner into an 'innovation system' format (Ranga & Etzkowitz, 2013). Based on their systems theory's categorization as a set of components, relationships, and functions, Ranga and Etzkowitz establish three key distinctions of the triple helix systems (between R&D and non-R&D innovators; between "single-sphere" and "multi-sphere" (hybrid) institutions; and between individuals and institutions), while four types of relationships are identified between components (collaboration and conflict moderation, collaborative leadership, substitution, and networking).

The quadruple helix model has also become important in the innovation discourse. In addition to science, policy, and industry, society has become critical in understanding the innovation system. Recent advances in technological innovations continue to foster entrepreneurship and innovation, and this is increasingly integrating civil society into innovation systems. In the context of Leydesdorff's (2012) argument that the quadruple helix model elevates the important role of civil society in the innovation debate, political leaders are prioritizing greater public involvement in the innovation discourse. In essence, the fourth helix is essentially the human-centered aspect of the innovation system and encompasses things like democratic knowledge, values, media, culture, arts, artistic research, arts-based innovation, and the cultural fabric of a community.[1]

The significance of the various strands of the helix model of innovation is underscored by Lindberg et al.'s (2014) argument that civil society actors can transcend the commercial-political-scientific community because of their non-profit structure, in addition to being able to step in when certain projects do not fit the traditional organizational logic of the university or government financiers.

Advocacy Coalition Framework

The Advocacy Coalition Framework (ACF), pioneered by Paul Sabatier and Hank Jenkins-Smith in the early 1980s before being published as an edited collection in 1993, is a comprehensive theoretical approach to the policymaking process. The ACF explains the policy process as a policy cycle based on the notion that the policy world is comprised of several policy subsystems where political actors advance their policy priorities through advocacy coalitions.

The theory works on the premise that certain core ideas guide causation and value in public policy, and that "Policy change occurs through interactions between wide external changes or shocks to the political system and the success of the ideas in the coalitions, which may cause actors in the advocacy coalition to shift coalitions." (Cerna, 2013; p.5)

The ACF rests on seven foundational assumptions:

1. Policy Subsystems are the primary unit of analysis to understand policy processes. These subsystems are characterized by a geographical area, an issue, and policy actors.
2. The subsystem actors include participants that attempt to influence policy. These may include government officials, private or non-private organizations, experts, scholars, consulting firms, think tanks, and media among others.
3. The ACF assumes that policy actors are boundedly rational, and have limited cognitive abilities to process the information.
4. Subsystems aggregate actors into one or more coalitions. The ACF provides a lens to see the policy actors as members of coalitions. These coalitions are formed based on similarities and differences in policy core beliefs.
5. Policies often reflect and translate the beliefs of one or more coalitions.

6. Scientific and technical information is important for understanding subsystem affairs. Scientific and technical information, beside the day-to-day experience of the policy actors, inform the causal patterns adopted by the Belief systems.
7. To understand the policy process or policy change, the researcher must adopt a long-term perspective (e.g., 10 years or more). It takes a long time to understand the policy process because the winners of today could be the losers of tomorrow. Often, the debates among the coalitions last more than decades, and in order to understand the Coalitions, learning, and policy change, one must understand all the past events. (International Public Policy Association, 2017; para. 3)

The ACF is comprised of different public and private actors across various levels of government who harness their similar beliefs and aspirations with the overall goal of driving policy change by influencing policies and the resource allocation process. More profoundly, these agents are called advocates because of the altruistic way the beneficial impacts of the policy change they champion create positive spillovers in society. Like the role of policy entrepreneurs in the MSF, advocacy coalitions within policy subsystems comprise of concerned stakeholders – from the public sector, industry, academia, and civil society – who drive the policy change process.

Much like the policy entrepreneurs who "could be in or out of government, in elected or appointed positions, in interest groups or research organizations" are the catalysts that drive the policy process under the MSF construct, the advocates in the various policy subsystems exhibit common entrepreneurial dispositions regardless of whether they are functioning in political and governmental domains, market settings, academia, or social and community spheres.

Sabatier (1988) explains the use of policy analysis in public policymaking through the "belief systems of advocacy coalitions within policy subsystems (p. 129)." He argues these are the "critical vehicle for understanding the role of policy analysis in policy-oriented learning and the effect, in turn, of such learning on changes in governmental programs (p. 129)." When triggers or external shocks – due to broad changes in socioeconomic systems, public opinion, coalitions, and dynamics in the other subsystems –lead to a policy change, the outcomes on policy subsystems often depend on the existing structures of pluralistic and nonpluralistic political systems. For instance, Nohrstedt (2009) argues that the intensity and breadth of political conflict and strategic action are two fundamental determinants of the differing impact of policy change in contested policy areas.

Cairney (2013) espouses how responses from coalitions determine the net effect of a shock. While exogenous shocks like a global recession may trigger a policy change, coalitions may exploit the opportunity by shaping how such events are understood, interpreted, and handled. Internal shocks often manifest in the form of a policy failure leading to a confidence crisis in one coalition, thereby prompting another coalition to assert the superiority of its subsystem in terms of being able to offer a better policy outcome. In both cases, until an internal or external event is exploited by a coalition, the likelihood of it causing a disruption of the status quo is low, as elucidated below:

An external event is not enough to cause an external shock, and the perception of policy failure does not produce an internal shock inevitably. Events have to be exploited successfully by a coalition which is well led, and equipped to learn and adapt, using its resources to frame information, exploit public opinion, rally support, and (in some cases) secure funding. (Cairney, 2013; para. 14)

The ACF helps to make sense of a complicated policymaking environment where decisions are made amid ambiguity and high uncertainty with multiple stakeholders and tiers of government.

Path Dependence Theory

In simplistic terms, path dependence is about the role of history, rather than current conditions, in the interpretation of outcomes. Rooted in historical institutionalism, path-dependent policy paradigms have causal implications for institutional change. History matters. Institutions and policies have a constraining effect into the future because due to inertia, once particular paths are forged, enormous efforts are required to change course (Greener, 2005).

The basic tenet of this model is that policy changes are difficult because socioeconomic systems are complex, institutions are sticky, and initial conditions and strong inertia often perpetuate the status quo, even when it is suboptimal, because of the tendency of socioeconomic systems to "become "locked-in" to behavior patterns" (Greener, 2002; Aghion, et al., 2014).

In mainstream economics, a process is said to be path-dependent when a sequential resource allocation regime depends not only on typical a priori determinants – like technology, factor endowments, preferences, and institutions—but on some contingent events (Puffert, 2000). In the presence of multiple equilibria, explaining path-dependent economic outcomes entails looking at history – and not just deterministic, unique equilibria dictated by current conditions of technology, preferences, and institutions.

David (2007) argues that to correctly attribute path dependence to a deterministic process, a more precise definition must necessarily consider the "relationship between a system's process dynamics and the limiting configuration(s) that it ultimately takes on" (p. 6). If indeed economies of scale are a major source of market failure, he espouses the implications of economic processes in the context of path dependence for stochastic and deterministic processes.

Given the ambiguity in the reallocation process and how this complicates the final equilibria of winners and losers, he underscores why, due to increasing returns, competitive outcomes may be unattainable since the "micro-level irreversibilities in the behavior of agents" will preclude such. In his words:

While the logical relationship between path dependence and market failure is neither one of necessity nor sufficiency, there are indeed some potentially important underlying connections between the existence of path dependence and the welfare optimality of decentralized resource allocation in market economies. (David, 2007; p. 13)

David (1985) and Arthur (1994) use technology as an exemplar in the analysis of path dependence based on increasing returns. They argue that because of the knowledge-intensive nature of the innovation economy, a new technology subject to increasing returns will enjoy an initial advantage that may lock out potential competitors due to positive feedback effects. Extending the analysis to the distributional implications of welfare gains from the recent advances in technological innovations and globalization, David (1985, 1987) contends that private and public policy decisions must consider three critical conditions for path dependence: technical interrelatedness of system components, quasi-irreversibility of investment, and increasing returns to scale in the use of a common technique.

For instance, while technology has huge welfare implications, it rarely does provide a solution on its own. Certainly, technological innovations can help mitigate the deleterious effects of various social, political, demographic, and environmental shocks – e.g., inequality, poverty, and climate change – but policy must anticipate and guide against unintended consequences. The equity and social justice dimensions of income and wealth distributions in socioeconomic systems are fundamental to the analysis of policy change.

Geography and density have a role in the determination of path dependence. But how much of the distribution of economic activity is explained by history rather than by geography? In addition to technology, agglomeration economies from the spatial location of production offer insights into the path dependence paradigm. Urban agglomeration remains a major driver of innovation. The endogenous growth model explains how innovation and knowledge create positive externalities and spillover effects that drive the economic development process. In the presence of the right policy, R&D investments can generate secondary order impacts resulting in greater levels of innovation in dense urban centers. In a way, this explains how knowledge spillovers created by the R&D activities of a university support the commercial innovation activities of nearby firms. Increasing returns, through agglomeration economies, explain industry localization. Paul Krugman, in *History versus Expectations*, explores path dependence with the aid of a simple trade model which incorporates both external economies and adjustment costs. He underscores the importance of spatial economics in the path dependence discourse thus:

If there is one single area of economics in which path dependence is unmistakable, it is in economic geography-the location of production in space. The long shadow cast by history over location is apparent at all scales, from the smallest to the largest-from the cluster of costume jewelry firms in Providence to the concentration of 60 million people in the Northeast Corridor. (Krugman, 1991; p.80)

Pierson (2000) advances increasing returns arguments in the understanding of political dynamics. To the extent that economics lays the foundation for understanding the distinctive characteristics of politics, he contends that "Rather than simply apply extant arguments in economics to political phenomena, we need to consider the features of the political world that require modifications in the use of path dependence claims" (Pierson, 2000; p.252). Since the neoclassical axiom of diminishing marginal returns underpins rational expectations, Pierson worries that economic choices will trigger negative feedback which will generate a predictable outcome. In the context of extending increasing returns arguments to political analysis, he posits that:

Factors such as the prominence of collective activity in politics, the central role of formal, change-resistant institutions, the possibilities for employing political authority to magnify power asymmetries, and the great ambiguity of many political processes and outcomes make this a domain of social life that is especially prone to increasing returns processes. (Pierson, 2000; p.252)

Schienstock (2011) provides a good summary of the discussion in this section based on the premise that since path dependence approaches the explanation of organizational, institutional, and political change from a techno-economic view, the central arguments that historic events determine future paths are inefficient. As such, the creation of new and preferred paths through agency remains key:

Still, as the process of path creation entails high technical and market uncertainties, it does not generally get started without external socio-economic pressures coming particularly from the ongoing globalization process. This process triggers growing innovation competition. Radical, growth-enhancing innovations, however, become increasingly difficult to make along a traditional growth path. Additional pressures often come from key change events, such as an economic crisis or a political turmoil. (Schienstock, 2011; p. 69)

In the African context, Pylak's (2015) paper on developing economies offers some useful insights on the relevance of the path dependence model in the policy innovation discourse. Pylak argues that while varying development factors yield varying outcomes, exceptions apply in the context of the ability of economies to follow a development path. By implication, both the spatial and dynamic dimensions are key in identifying the breakthroughs of path dependence. To put this into perspective and distill the implications, the work of economist and political theorist, Walt Whitman Rostow, helps in further analyzing this proposition. In his 1960 book, *The Stages of Economic Growth,* Rostow opines that economic modernization happens in five stages: traditional society, preconditions for take-off, take-off, drive to maturity, and high mass consumption. Based largely on evidence from Britain's Industrial Revolution, the book had a major influence on much of the development literature of the era:

We must demonstrate that the underdeveloped nations—now the main focus of Communist hopes—can move successfully through the preconditions into a well- established take- off within the orbit of the democratic world, resisting the blandishments and temptations of Communism. This is, I believe, the most important single item on the Western agenda (Rostow, 1960, p. 134)

But Pylak's thesis refutes Rostow's propositions on the ground that, "The results do not confirm a direct or linear relationship between the level of innovativeness and economic development, although they do reveal various configurations of innovativeness and development factors in regions" (Pylak, 2015; p. 57). Pylak draws a conclusion: it is important for policies for less developed regions to recognize the unique circumstances of those region.

Institutional Change

Institutional change and policy change are similar in many ways, albeit significant differences exist. Streeck and Thelen (2005) explain institutions as "formalized rules that may be enforced by calling upon a third party" (p.9). This has implications for the relationship between institutional change and policy entrepreneurship. Streeck and Thelen (2005) argue that in a scenario where "policies stipulate rules that assign normatively backed rights and responsibilities to actors and provide for their public, that is third party enforcement" (p.12), then, institutional change theories are essentially theories of policy change. This can be extended to the institutional versus policy entrepreneurship case described above.

While the theory of institutional change has broad applicability, as the name suggests, it's most direct relevance is in the context of institutions, except in situations where policies and institutions overlap. Policy reforms do not just happen; they often happen for several reasons. As a result of crises, economic shocks, and policy failures, new ideas and approaches are often sought to help inform public policies. McNamara (1998) adopts the constructivist institutionalists framework to offer insights into three channels through which policy reforms happen: policy failure, policy paradigm innovation, and policy emulation. The ramifications for this reasoning and the three channels are elucidated below:

First, a period of policy failure leads to the collapse of the old paradigm and the search for new solutions. While this policy failure may be accompanied by a crisis, the main feature is a period of greater uncertainty. Second, a new paradigm emerges offering a clear policy solution that is advocated by the epistemic community and implemented by politicians in a few states. Politicians in other states monitor the results of these test cases to judge whether the policy is effective or not. Third, politicians in other states proceed to emulate this policy, embedding the new paradigm in their own institutional framework (Glinavos, 2013; p.46).

Acemoglu et al. (2020) use a political economy framework to examine institutional stasis, or what some call extreme institutional persistence. To offer insights into the durability of institutions, two interrelated factors are used to explore the precise nature of this relationship. First, the incongruence between political and economic underpinnings, they argue, may constitute the basis of institutional persistence as corroborated below:

Stasis does not follow simply from the fact that power begets power; it also requires that those who are so empowered want to maintain the current institutional arrangements. But imagine that groups that are empowered under current institutions prefer a different set of institutional arrangements. This could be, for example, because of economic reasons: repressive institutions may create major economic costs, which even the group controlling political power may want to avoid (Acemoglu et al., 2020; p. 4).

These authors further opine that even if political elites do not benefit directly from "initiating institutional change, the threat of other political reactions from non-elites can induce them to do so," (Acemoglu et al., 2020; p. 5) based on political economy dynamics, particularly in nondemocratic political systems, "where the control of elites over the political system depends on the inability of the disempowered majority to organize and solve their collective action problem." (Acemoglu et al., 2020; p.5).

The implications of institutional reforms and the quest for economic growth under market-centric settings in the African context are unpacked after I discuss the transaction cost imperative below.

New Institutional Economics and Transaction Costs

Like property rights, governance, institutions, contracts, social capital, bounded rationality, etc., transaction costs are a core element of new institutional economics (NIE). From Williamson's (1975) transaction cost theory and Axelrod's (1984) cooperation theory to North's (1990) NIE and Coleman's (1990) social capital and trust, transaction costs are essentially about institutional design. A major proposition in Adam Smith's 1776 classic, *The Wealth of Nations*, is that low transaction costs are important for trade and wealth creation. For 2009 Nobel Laureate, Oliver Williamson, transaction costs are determined by five factors: frequency, asset specificity, uncertainty, bounded rationality, and opportunistic behavior (1981). In clear terms, the progress of humanity is essentially about lower transaction costs.

Whittington and Dowall (2006) explain contractual innovations, through the lens of Williamson's transaction cost theory, as varying modes of economic organization (e.g., market, hybrid, hierarchy).

Whether through incrementalism or the PET model described earlier in this chapter, when political or economic shocks occur, certain lessons are learned right from agenda-setting to policy actions. Policy actors can therefore minimize transaction costs by learning from the vantage point of history. Williamson argues that the steady state is, in essence, the one that achieves economic efficiency by minimizing the costs of exchange. Coase (1960) explores the nuances of transaction costs and property rights in the context of externalities and market failures, and how these diverge from mainstream neoclassical propositions.

In the NIE context, political economy issues related to distributional conflicts and weak enforcement capacity generate transaction costs that make it difficult to efficiently enforce property rights in developing countries. In simple terms, making private property rights a core part of the economic system resolves underlying collective action problems – e.g., free riding, moral hazard, and tragedy of the commons – which often constitute a fair share of the transaction costs from rentierism and other powerful political and economic interests in jurisdictions with weak governance and institutional frameworks.

Taken together, the discussion on institutional change and transaction costs above offers a lens from which Africa's efforts at democratization and political reforms to advance its development priorities in the 1980s can be understood. Towards the end of the 20th century, sweeping political and institutional reforms in the hitherto authoritarian regimes across the continent paved the way for more open economic and political systems. The end of one-party rules and military juntas – along with the neoliberal economic doctrines that received a big boost under Margaret Thatcher and Ronald Reagan – defined the emergence of Africa's contemporary mixed political economy architecture judging from how the neoliberal ideas, policies, and practices of the era ultimately recognized the key role of government in the economy.

In the same vein, the reforms triggered by the Reagan-Thatcher revolution, the Washington Consensus and its vestiges, and the adverse economic and social impacts of neoliberalism continue to influence the debate on the political economy of policy innovation dynamics in Africa till today. While the end of one-party rule meant the political space was opened for effective competition, the nuances of Africa's traditions, culture, history, socioeconomic dynamics, and development imperatives mean there is mixed evidence on the appropriateness of Western-style democracy, economic liberalism, and political pluralism as a model for policy innovation. Ghana and Rwanda offer classic examples and these case studies are examined in the latter chapters.

PRACTICAL IMPLICATIONS

Given the pace of digital disruptions in the global economy, innovation partnerships have become a must-have for productivity and efficiency gains. The spread of a policy innovation across governments is not new; countries learn from the effectiveness of policies in other regions and structure their own policies accordingly (Meseguer, 2006). However, the learning dynamic is often selective and influenced by political leanings. Gilardi (2010) contends that right-leaning political actors are often more concerned about the electoral implications of reforms, while their left-wing counterparts pay more attention to the policy effects.

Unlike in startups, where disruption is the way of life, traditional, large private corporations and public bureaucracies typically have policies and processes built around operational excellence, with little or no room for experimentation. As such, since these entities are not organized for innovation to seamlessly happen, it is not uncommon for them to collaborate with academia and startups to foster innovation and creativity by developing and testing new technologies and business models. In his 2019 book, *What It Takes: Lessons in the Pursuit of Excellence*, Stephen Schwarzman talks about how to achieve success through the relentless pursuit of excellence:

Eights just do the stuff you tell them. Nines are great at executing and developing good strategies. You can build a winning firm with 9s. But people who are 10s sense problems, design solutions, and take the business in new directions without being told to do so. Tens always make it rain (Schwarzman 2019; p. 99).

What if Schwarzman's sentiment were the case in the world of policymaking? Like the business world where driving innovation requires entrepreneurs, being successful at policy innovation requires policy entrepreneurs. In many ways, it is akin to value and wealth creation in business entrepreneurship. Policy innovation is a complicated process with many moving parts. It is a dynamic process that involves the capacity and willingness to develop ideas, organize, and manage multiple components along with risks of varying proportions.

Following the discussion under the MSF, in addition to Kingdon, the significance of institutional change and policy entrepreneurship in the public policy development process received extensive attention by American political scientist and communications theorist Harold Lasswell through the seven-stage policy process in 1956. Lasswell (1956) transformed policy sciences through his multidisciplinary approach to understanding the process of policymaking. Adapting the philosophy of pragmatism and functional psychology and allied reformers and pragmatists, Lasswell's work contributed immensely to erasing the lines that divide disciplines like economics, communications, law, philosophy, anthropology, psychology, and psychiatry. His thesis continues to drive the bi-directional model of knowledge creation around the policymaking process and the use of the knowledge so created to improve that process.

The lines between public sector innovation and policy innovation are blurry. This has implications for the discussion so far. Brookfield Institute (2018), through expert interviews, attempts to resolve the ambiguity in the literature and concludes that while the former integrates "a wider range of structural and capacity-building efforts to enable and accelerate innovation within government, which might include integration of new public sector technologies and services", the latter "has a narrower focus on the policy development process and the innovativeness of the resulting artifact or instrument."

TAKEAWAYS FOR AFRICA: AN INTEGRATIVE APPROACH

As noted above, and as will be further elaborated below, the theoretical insights and key political economy underpinnings in this chapter rest on contemporary history of Africa's industrial development, both before and after independence. While decolonization and the regaining of independence provided unprecedented opportunity for policy experiments to guide the continent's future economic trajectory, path dependence theory sheds light on how the evolution of institutions and economies depends on initial conditions. In the African context, from production and consumption to exchange and regulation, the continent's economic architecture was designed, through colonial institutional dynamics, to export primary commodities.

Sectoral Dynamics

In the context of sectoral analysis, agriculture remains the mainstay of most economies in Africa. However, low productivity and subsistence have perpetuated poverty and poor earning conditions of farmers. While governments on the continent have important roles in the context of removing barriers and paving the way for private sector investment to help unlock the potential of the sector, policy entrepreneurs also have a major role. From farm managers and warehouse aggregators to food processors and other farmer-facing individuals, policy entrepreneurs are change agents who abound in both the public and private sectors. For instance, extension services are a critical component of most interventions targeted at agricultural transformation in Africa. These change agents can, under the right incentive framework, contribute to transforming the sector.

A case in point. Boettiger et al. (2017) articulate that transforming the agricultural sector requires a range of multidimensional, interrelated, and dynamic factors. Based on over 30 country diagnostics, their analysis categorizes the drivers of agricultural transformation under three broad groups. The first captures political economy factors which traverse changes in institutions, governance, and political systems. The second group emphasizes the quality of the national agricultural strategy. The third, which is the most relevant in our context, emphasizes delivery mechanisms which are critical for effectively implementing agricultural plans. And in many ways, this echoes the role of the policy entrepreneur, since results depend largely on "the ways in which countries manage decision making and progress against targets as well as how they use change agents to support the large-scale behavior change among smallholder farmers that underpins a successful agricultural transformation." (Boettiger et al., 2017; para. 3).

Further, this analysis reveals that eight of the 13 national agricultural plans examined in Africa did not channel scarce resources to their most impactful channels; the authors argue that efforts targeted at transforming agricultural systems often prioritize volume rather than value and productivity across the value chain. In fundamental ways, which serve to reinforce the significance of the MSF, the role of policy entrepreneurs as change agents in the agricultural transformation drive of nations is underscored:

The success of any agricultural transformation relies on how well millions of smallholders and small- and medium-size enterprises can be helped to change farming practices as quickly and effectively as possible. The critical enabler, without which an agricultural transformation is likely to fail, is a frontline "change agent" that helps farmers modify their practices. Change agents are people who farmers trust and interact with regularly. The high-level objectives of a transformation are realized in practice only when they are effectively translated to smaller, on-farm shifts. For example, increased productivity in the dairy sector might be achieved through farmers accessing better animal health technologies and better cattle breeds or joining dairy cooperatives to sell their milk. Change agents provide the critical interface with farmers. To catalyze this, a change agent might be the person providing extension knowledge, offering financing for farming inputs such as fertilizer, aggregating crops, or facilitating marketing services. For example, a change agent can help farmers make the transition from growing wheat to more complicated but lucrative opportunities such as raising tomatoes, vegetables, and orchard crops. (Boettiger et al., 2017; para. 13)

Governance Dimension

To the extent that good governance and strong institutions are key drivers of prosperity and sustainable development, the underlying political economy context explains the pervasive sub-par performance of many countries on the continent on various socioeconomic indicators. For instance, the Ibrahim Index of African Governance (IIAG), produced by the Mo Ibrahim Foundation, measures and monitors governance[2] performance in African countries.

The 2019 IIAG results, available in the 2020 report, show that over the last decade, 36 countries saw improvements in their overall governance[3], which implies that in the last decade, governance performance has improved in over 60 percent of countries on the continent. The Gambia witnessed the biggest jump based on improvements in accountability and transparency and its participatory environment, while Mauritius remains in the top position for the 10th year in a row. However, more broadly, the IIAG reveals an unbalanced governance progress over the 2010-2019 period, with only eight countries witnessing improvements in all four categories. On regional comparisons, of the five geographical regions, Southern Africa recorded the highest score at 53.3, followed by Western Africa (53.1), Northern Africa (52), Eastern Africa (46.2), with Central Africa showing the weakest performance at 38.8 (Figure 2).

Agenda 2063 of the African Union "envisions a continent in which there is a universal culture of good governance, democratic values, gender equality, and respect for human rights, justice and the rule of law." (African Union,

Figure 2. Overall governance scores and trend classifications for African countries
Source: Mo Ibrahim Foundation: 2020 Ibrahim Index of African Governance

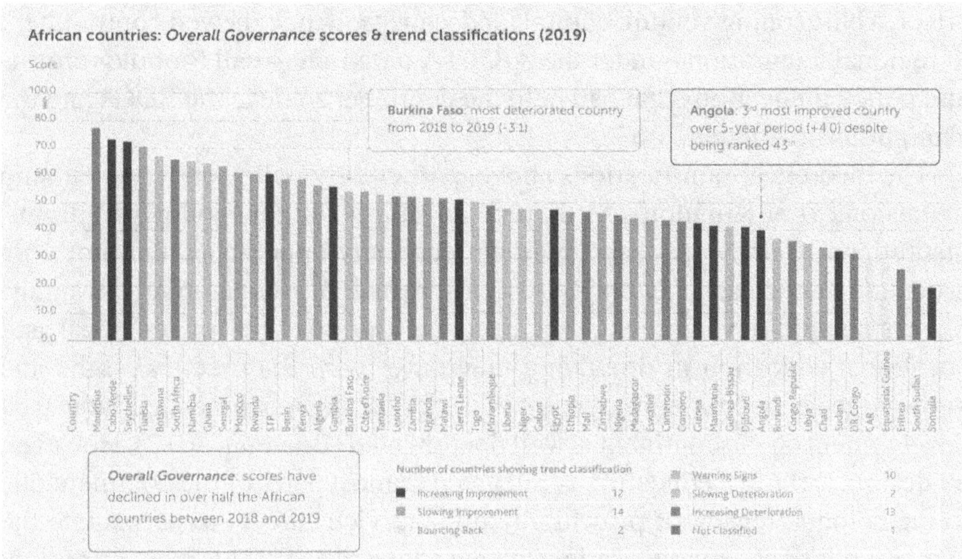

n.d.; para 1). This has implications for the continent's development discourse. While many countries have instituted policy reforms aimed at strengthening institutions in the last two decades, much work remains to be done.

Theory versus Reality

Economics always recognizes that history matters. The path dependence theory, discussed earlier, tells us that economic outcomes are largely informed by history. As discussed in the introduction chapter, in comparison to other regions of the world, on major economic and social progress metrics, Africa's post-colonial development performance has been disappointing. Many factors explain this, particularly in the context of the long-run influence of initial conditions and the highly exploitative institutions of slavery and colonialism on comparative current economic outcomes.

The post-colonial African experience reflects how past institutional forces exerted a persistent impact on economic outcomes long after colonialism, resulting in development paths characterized by a lack of policy capacity to institute major reforms needed for structural transformation and economic vitality. However, unlike how prevailing conditions in the past led to squandered development opportunities, Africa is well-positioned to reconfigure its economic system through a new development architecture that maximizes the benefits of the ongoing digital transformation. Among others, the leapfrog effect, a burgeoning venture capital landscape, and the renewed commitment to regional integration –under the AfCFTA paradigm – call for bold reforms and policy innovations that can help the continent achieve the SDGs and the aspirations of Agenda 2063.

The theoretical ramifications above, particularly policy entrepreneurship in the context of Kingdon's MSF, provide a basis for new policy paradigms, institutional frameworks, and political economy approaches that not only articulate but clearly leverage Africa's revealed comparative advantage for sustainable development. For instance, the potential of technical and vocational education in producing manpower with the practical skills and knowledge needed for employment in trades for the much-needed industrial development on the continent is well documented (Boateng, 2012). However, by design, technical education is relegated in most parts of the continent due to the colonial legacy of prioritizing civil service careers to perpetuate the colonial political economy order (Onyene et al., 2014). This is an important area that needs urgent policy innovation through incrementalism.

The PET, discussed earlier, has implications for the policy cycle discourse in Africa in the context of Agenda 2063. The notion of the African Renaissance is deeply rooted in Pan-Africanism, heralded largely in the 1960s. For instance, the literature on the social and political causes of civil war recognizes the importance of political systems in triggering or serving as a deterrent to conflicts. While the causes of political conflicts are often complex and difficult to unpack, the PET provides decent underpinnings by systematically linking policy learning and policy change. Rwanda is a case in point here.

During the Rwandan Civil War, an estimated 800,000 people were killed by Hutu militiamen, soldiers, and ordinary citizens over a period of about 100 days. In the economic analysis of the causes and consequences of the genocide, Malthusianism – vis-à-vis resource scarcity, famine, and mass migration – played a major role. In the years leading up to the genocide, Rwanda had grown poorer due to a wide range of factors, including the lack of sufficient land for farming, drought and famine, and a sharp drop in the world market prices for coffee – an important foreign exchange earner for Rwanda. In the aftermath of the genocide, the Government of Rwanda implemented a wide range of policy reforms in the hope of rebuilding the economy and society. While much work remains to be done, Rwanda has made significant progress in economic and structural reforms since the end of the genocide.

In the past, institutional constraints and the lack of political will by African leaders prevented policy coordination around regional integration on the continent. The contrarian disposition of incrementalism to the more broad-based, rational comprehensive model of policymaking is reminiscent of the trends in liberal intergovernmentalism during the initial discussions on African regional integration under the AfCFTA framework. While most of the countries in Africa embraced the idea, concerns around nationalism reverberated in a few countries at the onset. Nigeria, for example, delayed signing the pact and opted for an incremental approach by engaging in consultations with policy actors. By ensuring her final decision was politically expedient, and not perceived as being a fundamental policy shift, this country succeeded in reducing the risks and costs of uncertainty in trade policymaking.

A major pitfall in the application of incrementalism in the African context is the entrenched assumption of social stability, which, in turn, guarantees incremental policy improvements. While this holds true in many Western industrial societies, the nuances are more complicated in much of the Global South. To assume that the status quo is stable in Africa – where sub-Saharan African countries dominate the list of the least developed countries (LDCs) of the world – is an oversimplification that hinders an open conversation and pragmatic correction of a development path orchestrated by a colonial past that makes it difficult to break the vicious cycle of inequality and poverty.

Lane (2000) summarizes the implications:

For all its simplicity maybe incrementalism is too crude in relation to the complexity of the policy process. The idea that policies are heavily constrained by past commitments, that policy-making is the application of mechanical rules – standard operating procedures – that reduce complexity, calculation and uncertainty, and that policy-making never touches the base of its programmes may satisfy data for certain periods of decision-making in some countries. However, its general validity is doubtful and its theoretical appeal is decreased by the obvious voluntaristic aspect of action, including collective action. It may be the case that public policy-making could not consider all the alternatives and rank all the outcomes as incrementalism predicts, but it does not follow that decision-making is bound to be of limited scope at the margin (Lane, 2000; p. 76).

Major regional industrial ecosystems in Africa are, by colonial design, a product of agglomeration economies and efficiency considerations considering the prevailing export economy. From major roads and ports to coastal cities and infrastructure and logistics arrangements, the vestiges of the colonial economy remain dominant in Africa's contemporary public policy development discourse. Despite the popularity of import substitution industrialization for self-sufficiency in many African countries immediately after independence, as articulated in the earlier chapters, the protectionist argument for infant industries failed largely because major industrial policies of the era produced bureaucratic inefficiencies, rent-seeking, corruption, and rising debt levels, resulting in macroeconomic imbalances. This led to the structural reforms of the 1980s and the marked increase in the market-oriented nature of African economies through neoliberal policies supervised by the BWIs to support fiscal austerity, privatization, deregulation, and free trade.

Despite offering a robust platform to unpack the reasons for the dismal socioeconomic records on the continent over time, it is important to be mindful of the many qualifications on the predictive ability of the path dependence model when used in political economy analysis. This means the constellation of economic, social, and political factors at the beginning must be separately analyzed for retrospective insights about the role played by the various colonial institutional structures and policies. In 2014, US President Barack Obama counseled 500 young Africans attending a leadership training in Washington, D.C. on the need to seek solutions within their countries rather than blaming the past:

As powerful as history is, and you need to know that history, at some point you have to look to the future and say, 'OK, we didn't get a good deal then, but let's make sure that we're not making excuses for not going forward. (Shearlaw, 2014; para.3)

While there are many unresolved debates around the structural adjustment economic management model, evidence on its adverse impacts on vulnerable populations – particularly in terms of outcomes in health, education, and child nutrition in developing countries – is robust. In their edited volume, *Adjustment with a Human Face*, Cornia et al. (1987) corroborate the need for interventionist policies to be anchored on microeconomic realities to support households which make up the private sector. At the end of the day, short-term structural adjustments and stabilization policies have implications for long-term development. Striking a right balance is key. Soludo and Mkandawire in *Our Continent, Our Future*, present a postmortem of the structural adjustment exercise in Africa; these authors succinctly explain why it is important to address household economic vulnerability by appropriately gauging the microeconomic consequences (intended or unintended) of macroeconomic policies:

Many of the microeconomic policies that are condemned were successfully used in the Asian economies. If African economies have failed, it was largely due to the lack of selectivity and flexibility in the use of these instruments and the absence of a coherent strategy for applying them. In the debate over policy, virtually every policy initiative — macro or micro — that was taken during the dirigiste era is condemned. The "guilty by association" condemnation of many central elements of industrial policy has led to the neglect of existing industry and to unnecessary waste. Even more ominous for Africa's future industrialization prospects is that the SAPs have left African governments with virtually nothing to do for industry except prepare it for privatization or closure (Soludo and Mkandawire, 1998; p.38)

The debates on policy change and reform in the post-structural adjustment era have focused largely on achieving an optimal outcome in this context. Macroeconomic stabilization and structural balance are important; however, they should not happen at a high social cost. Three decades after the structural adjustment exercise, not many in the African development policy domain realize that while one-off revolutionary changes may not have happened, several sweeping policy changes have occurred over time. The notion of incrementalism, through which many small policy changes result in a larger broad-based policy change, is instructive. There are clear metrics to assess this. The subsequent chapters offer insights in this regard.

Compared to the 1980s, democratization has spread rapidly across the African continent. Lessons from the import substitution and structural adjustment policies of the past six decades remain the very foundation upon which contemporary economic management and governance reform models across the continent are built. And it is obvious that as key believers in multilateralism and shared prosperity, in the context of the SDGs, the core values of social equity, environmental sustainability, and economic inclusion remain on the front burner as African countries navigate the complexities associated with sustainable development.

Where do we go from here? It is of no use to keep blaming Africa's economic underperformance and poverty on colonial imperialism. In the change management paradigm, in addition to inertia, sabotage, and rebellion, resistance to change happens in many ways and leaders are encouraged to explore the deterministic links of resistance to plan and achieve desired outcomes:

The ghosts of the past are always lying in wait to haunt us. As long as everything is steady state, they remain out of sight. But the minute you need cooperation for something new or different, the ghosts spring into action. Old wounds reopen, historic resentments are remembered — sometimes going back many generations. Leaders should consider gestures to heal the past before sailing into the future (Kanter, 2012; para. 10).

To conclude, crises often trigger reinvention and fundamental change. From the Great Recession of 2009 to the ongoing COVID-19 pandemic, crisis situations provide both an opportunity to reflect on the principles of disruption, as well as growth and reinvention possibilities. Several multi-billion-dollar startups were birthed after the Great Recession. From Uber and Airbnb to Instagram and WhatsApp, many of these businesses were pioneered by young entrepreneurs, who save for the recession, would likely not have pursued entrepreneurship. Like the Schumpeterian gale of creative destruction pattern discussed earlier, while the aftermath of the 2009 recessionary shocks consumed the likes of Blockbuster and Phones4U, due partly to complacency, those ahead of the reinvention envelope like Apple and Netflix continue to reap the benefits of nimbleness more than a decade after the downturn (The Economist, 2014).

As discussed under the various theories, institutional and policy settings underpin the governance infrastructure of a country. Policy innovation requires a systematic review of actions, players, and resources to drive inclusive and sustainable growth. A multi-stakeholder strategy is required to achieve the Africa we all want.

Insanity is doing the same thing over and over again and expecting different results

— Albert Einstein

REFERENCES

Acemoglu, D., Egorov, G., & Sonin, K. (2020). *Institutional change and institutional persistence*. National Bureau of Economic Research: Working Papers 27852. doi:10.3386/w27852

African Union. (n.d.). *Agenda 2063*. https://au.int/en/democracy-law-human-rights

Aghion, P., Hepburn, C., Teytelboym, A., & Zenghelis, D. (2014). *Path dependence, innovation, and the economics of climate change*. The New Climate Economy. https://www.lse.ac.uk/granthaminstitute/wp-content/uploads/2014/11/Aghion_et_al_policy_paper_Nov20141.pdf

Arthur, W. B. (1994). *Increasing returns and path dependence in the economy*. University of Michigan Press. doi:10.3998/mpub.10029

Axelrod, R. (1984). *The Evolution of Cooperation*. Basic Books.

Baumgartner, F., Green-Pedersen, C., & Jones, B. (2006). Comparative studies of policy agendas. *Journal of European Public Policy*, *13*(7), 959–974. doi:10.1080/13501760600923805

Baumgartner, F., & Jones, B. (1993). *Agendas and instability in American politics*. University of Chicago Press.

Boateng, C. (2012). Restructuring vocational and technical education in Ghana: The role of leadership development. *International Journal of Humanities and Social Science*, *2*(4), 108–114.

Boettiger, S., Denis, N., & Sanghvi, S. (2017). *Successful agricultural transformations: Six core elements of planning and delivery. How can countries increase their odds of a successful rural transformation?* McKinsey & Company. https://www.mckinsey.com/industries/chemicals/our-insights/successful-agricultural-transformations-six-core-elements-of-planning-and-delivery

Brookfield Institute for Innovation + Entrepreneurship. (2018). *Exploring policy innovation: Tools, techniques + approaches*. https://brookfieldinstitute.ca/wp-content/uploads/BrookfieldInstitute-PIP-Landscape-1.pdf

Cairney, P. (2012). *Understanding Public Policy: Theories and Issues*. Palgrave Macmillan. doi:10.1007/978-0-230-35699-3

Cairney, P. (2013). *Policy concepts in 1000 words: The advocacy coalition framework*. https://paulcairney.wordpress.com/2013/10/30/policy-concepts-in-1000-words-the-advocacy-coalition-framework/

Carayannis, E. G., Barth, T. D., & Campbell, D. F. (2012). The Quintuple Helix innovation model: Global warming as a challenge and driver for innovation. *Journal of Innovation and Entrepreneurship*, *1*(1), 1–12. doi:10.1186/2192-5372-1-1

Carayannis, E. G., & Rakhmatullin, R. (2014). The quadruple/quintuple innovation helixes and smart specialisation strategies for sustainable and inclusive growth in Europe and beyond. *Journal of the Knowledge Economy*, *5*(2), 212–239. doi:10.100713132-014-0185-8

Cerna, L. (2013). *The nature of policy change and implementation: A review of different theoretical approaches*. OECD. Retrieved from https://www.oecd.org/education/ceri/The%20Nature%20of%20Policy%20Change%20and%20Implementation.pdf

Coase, R. H. (2013). The problem of social cost. *The Journal of Law & Economics*, *3*, 1–44. doi:10.1086/466560

Coleman, J. S. (1990). *The Foundations of Social Theory*. Harvard University Press.

Cornia, G. A., Jolly, R., & Stewart, F. (1987). *Adjustment with a human face: Protecting the vulnerable and promoting growth: A study by UNICEF*. Oxford University Press.

David, P. A. (1985). Clio and the economics of QWERTY. *The American Economic Review*, *75*(2), 332–337.

David, P. A. (1987). Some new standards for the economics of standardization in the information age. In P. Dasgupta & P. Stoneman (Eds.), *Economic Policy and Technological Performance*. Cambridge University Press. doi:10.1017/CBO9780511559938.010

David, P. A. (2007). Path dependence: A foundational concept for historical social science. *Cliometrica*, *1*(2), 91–114. doi:10.100711698-006-0005-x

Deegan, J. (2021). *Rational &incremental policymaking: an analysis of rational and incremental approaches to policy development and implementation*. https://jasondeegan.com/rational-incremental-policymaking/

Etzkowitz, H., & Leydesdorff, L. (1995). The triple helix—University-industry-government relations: A laboratory for knowledge-based economic development. *EASST Review, 14*(1), 14-19.

Fowler, L. (2020). Using the multiple streams framework to connect policy adoption to implementation. *Policy Studies Journal.*

Gilardi, F. (2010). Who Learns from What in Policy Diffusion Processes? *American Journal of Political Science, 54*(3), 650–666. doi:10.1111/j.1540-5907.2010.00452.x

Glinavos, I. (2013). *Redefining the market-state relationship: responses to the financial crisis and the future of regulation.* Routledge. doi:10.4324/9780203718797

Greener, I. (2002). Theorizing path-dependency: How does history come to matter in organizations? *Management Decision, 40*(6), 614–619. doi:10.1108/00251740210434007

Greener, I. (2005). The potential of path dependence in political studies. *Politics, 25*(1), 62–72. doi:10.1111/j.1467-9256.2005.00230.x

Herweg, N., Zahariadis, N., & Zohlnhöfer, R. (2018). The Multiple Streams Framework: Foundations, Refinements, and Empirical Applications. In P. A. Sabatier & C. M. Weible (Eds.), *Theories of the policy process* (4th ed.). Routledge. doi:10.4324/9780429494284-2

Höglund, L., & Linton, G. (2018). Smart specialization in regional innovation systems: A quadruple helix perspective. *R & D Management, 48*(1), 60–72. doi:10.1111/radm.12306

John, P. (2012). *Analyzing Public Policy.* Routledge.

John, P. (2018). Theories of policy change and variation reconsidered: A prospectus for the political economy of public policy. *Policy Sciences, 51*(1), 1–16. doi:10.100711077-017-9297-x

Jones, B., Sulkin, T., & Larsen, H. (2003). Policy punctuations in American political institutions. *The American Political Science Review, 97*(1), 151–169. doi:10.1017/S0003055403000583

Jones, B. D., & Baumgartner, F. R. (2005). *The politics of attention: How government prioritizes problems.* University of Chicago Press.

Kanter, R. M. (2012). Ten Reasons People Resist Change. *Harvard Business Review.* https://hbr.org/2012/09/ten-reasons-people-resist-chang

King. (1985). John W. Kingdon, Agendas, Alternatives, and Public Policies, Boston: Little, Brown, 1984, xi + 240 pp., $9.95. *Journal of Public Policy, 5*(2), 281–283. doi:10.1017/S0143814X00003068

Kingdon, J. W. (2011). *Agendas, alternatives, and public policies* (2nd ed.). Longman. (Original work published 1984)

Kingdon, J. W., & Stano, E. (1984). *Agendas, alternatives, and public policies* (Vol. 45). Little, Brown.

Kriz, A., Bankins, S., & Molloy, C. (2018). Readying a region: Temporally exploring the development of an Australian regional quadruple helix. *R&D Management, 48*(1), 25–43. doi:10.1111/radm.12294

Krugman, P. (1991). History Versus Expectations. *The Quarterly Journal of Economics, 106*(2), 651–667. doi:10.2307/2937950

Lane, J. E. (2000). The public sector: Concepts, models and approaches. *Sage (Atlanta, Ga.).* Advance online publication. doi:10.4135/9781446220085

Lasswell, H. D. (1936). *Politics: Who Gets What, When, How*. New York: Whittlesey House.

Lasswell, H. D. (1956). The decision process: Seven categories of functional analysis. Bureau of Governmental Research, College of Business and Public Administration, University of Maryland.

Lawlor, E. F. (1996). Review of the book *Policy change and learning: An advocacy coalition approach*, edited by P. Sabatier and H. C. Jenkins-Smith (1993) Westview Press. *Journal of Policy Analysis and Management, 15*(1), 110–121. doi:10.1002/pam.4050150111

Leydesdorff, L. (2012). The triple helix, quadruple helix, …, and an N-Tuple of helices: Explanatory models for analyzing the knowledge-based economy? *Journal of the Knowledge Economy, 3*(1), 25–35. doi:10.100713132-011-0049-4

Lindberg, M., Lindgren, M., & Packendorff, J. (2014). Quadruple helix as a way to bridge the gender gap in entrepreneurship: The case of an innovation system project in the Baltic Sea region. *Journal of the Knowledge Economy, 5*(1), 94–113. doi:10.100713132-012-0098-3

Lindblom, C. (1959). The Science of "muddling through". *Public Administration Review*, *19*(2), 79–88. doi:10.2307/973677

Lindblom, C. (1979). Still muddling, not yet through. *Public Administration Review*, *39*(6), 517–526. doi:10.2307/976178

Lowe, C. U. (1982). The triple helix—NIH, industry, and the academic world. *The Yale Journal of Biology and Medicine*, *55*(3-4), 239–246. PMID:7180024

Lundgren, M., Squatrito, T. & Tallberg, J. (2018). Stability and change in international policy-making: A punctuated equilibrium approach. *Review of International Organizations*, *13*(4), 547-572. doi:10.1007/s11558-017-9288-x

McNamara, K. (1998). *The currency of ideas, monetary politics in the European Union*. Cornell University Press.

Meseguer, C. (2006). Rational Learning and Bounded Learning in the Diffusion of Policy Innovations. *Rationality and Society*, *18*(1), 35–66. doi:10.1177/1043463106060152

Mintrom, M. (2019). So you want to be a policy entrepreneur? *Policy, Design, and Practice*, *2*(4), 307–323. doi:10.1080/25741292.2019.1675989

Mo Ibrahim Foundation. (2020). *Ibrahim Index of African Governance*. Index Report. https://mo.ibrahim.foundation/sites/default/files/2020-11/2020-index-report.pdf

Moyson, S., Scholten, P., & Weible, C. M. (2017). Policy learning and policy change: Theorizing their relations from different perspectives. *Policy and Society*, *36*(2), 161–177. doi:10.1080/14494035.2017.1331879

Nohrstedt, D. (2009). Do advocacy coalitions matter? Crisis and change in Swedish nuclear energy policy. *Journal of Public Administration: Research and Theory*, *20*(2), 309–333. doi:10.1093/jopart/mun038

Nordberg, K. (2015). Enabling Regional Growth in Peripheral Non-University Regions—The Impact of a Quadruple Helix Intermediate Organisation. *Journal of the Knowledge Economy*, *6*(2), 334–356. doi:10.100713132-015-0241-z

North, D. C. (1990). *Institutions, institutional change, and economic performance*. Cambridge University Press. doi:10.1017/CBO9780511808678

Onyene, V., Salisu, R., Johnson, O., & Olusanya, O. (2014). Indigenous orientation in the technical and vocational education programme: Tool for a sustainable society. *International Studies in Educational Administration, 42*(1), 45-59.

Patton, C., Sawicki, D., & Clark, J. (2012). *Basic methods of policy analysis and planning*. Prentice Hall.

Pierson, P. (2000). Increasing Returns, Path Dependence, and the Study of Politics. *The American Political Science Review*, *94*(2), 251–267. doi:10.2307/2586011

Puffert, D. J. (2000). Path dependence, network form, and technological change. In *History Matters: Economic Growth, Technology, and Population*. Stanford University. https://citeseerx.ist.psu.edu/viewdoc/download?doi=10.1.1.197.7932&rep=rep1&type=pdf

Pylak, K. (2015). Changing innovation process models: A chance to break out of path dependency for less developed regions. *Regional Studies, Regional Science*, *2*(1), 46–72. doi:10.1080/21681376.2014.979433

Ranga, M., & Etzkowitz, H. (2013). Triple Helix Systems: An Analytical Framework for Innovation Policy and Practice in the Knowledge Society. *Industry and Higher Education*, *27*(4), 237–262. doi:10.5367/ihe.2013.0165

Robinson, J. A., & Acemoglu, D. (2006). *Economic origins of dictatorship and democracy*. Cambridge University Press.

Rostow, W. (1960). *The stages of economic growth, a non-Communist manifesto*. Cambridge University Press.

Sabatier, P. A. (1988). An advocacy coalition framework of policy change and the role of policy-oriented learning therein. *Policy Sciences*, *21*(2/3), 129–168. doi:10.1007/BF00136406

Sábato, J., & Mackenzie, M. (1982). *La producción de tecnología. Autónoma o transnacional*. Nueva Imagen.

Schienstock, G. (2011). Path dependency and path creation: Continuity vs. fundamental change in national economies. *Journal of Futures Studies*, *15*(4), 63–76.

Schumpeter, J. A. (1942). Capitalism, Socialism, and Democracy (3rd ed.). New York: Harper and Brothers.

Schwarzman, S. A. (2019). *What it takes: Lessons in the pursuit of excellence.* Avid Reader Press / Simon & Schuster.

Shearlaw, W. (2014). *Africa should stop blaming history for its economic problems – Is Obama right?* Guardian Africa Network. https://www.theguardian.com/world/2014/jul/30/-sp-obama-africa-colonial-excuses-poll

Smith, A. (2002). The Wealth of Nations. Bibliomania.com Ltd.

Soludo, C. C., & Mkandawire, P. T. (1998). *Our continent, our future: African perspectives on structural adjustment.* Africa World Press.

Streeck, W., & Thelen, K. A. (Eds.). (2005). *Beyond continuity: Institutional change in advanced political economies.* Oxford University Press.

The Decision Process. (1956). *Seven Categories of Functional Analysis, Harold D. Lasswell.* University of Maryland Press.

The Economist. (2014). *The collapse of phones 4u: Death of a salesman.* https://www.economist.com/britain/2014/09/20/death-of-a-salesman

Unger, R. M. (2019). *The knowledge economy.* https://www.oecd.org/naec/THE-KNOWLEDGE-ECONOMY.pdf

Whittington, J., & Dowall, D. E. (2006). *Transaction-cost economic analysis of institutional change toward design-build contracts for public transportation.* Working Paper, No. 2006-09. Institute of Urban and Regional Development, University of California at Berkeley. https://iurd.berkeley.edu/wp/2006-09.pdf

Williamson, O. (1981). The Economics of Organization: The Transaction Cost Approach. *American Journal of Sociology, 87*(3), 548–577. doi:10.1086/227496

Williamson, O. E. (1975). *Markets and Hierarchies: Analysis and Antitrust Implications.* Free Press.

Zahariadis, N. (1995). *Markets, states, and public policy: Privatization in Britain and France.* University of Michigan Press. doi:10.3998/mpub.13929

ENDNOTES

1 See Carayannis, Barth, and Campbell (2012), Carayannis and Rakhmatullin (2014), Nordberg (2015), Höglund and Linton (2018), and Kriz, Bankins, and Molloy (2018).

2 The Mo Ibrahim Foundation defines governance as the provision of political, social, and economic public goods and services that every citizen has the right to expect from their government, and that a government has the responsibility to deliver to its citizens.

3 Calibrated based on 237 variables that measure governance concepts from 40 sources, before they are combined to form 79 indicators: https://mo.ibrahim.foundation/sites/default/files/2020-11/2020-index-report.pdf

Chapter 4
Policymaking and the African Renaissance

ABSTRACT

Political economy analysis relies heavily on rationally justifiable assertions that lend themselves to logical proof. Why are major economic prescriptions rooted in classical physics expected to deliver outcomes that recognize the differing situations and challenges of the actors in our political and socioeconomic systems? This chapter questions why orthodox economists distort theory and logic to defend mainstream, neoclassical approach to economic analysis. Due to the pitfalls of conventional neoclassical doctrines, depicting the evolutionary behavior of economies with static models is a difficult exercise. The potency of pragmatism in relation to the connections between economic science, philosophy, and normative economics in making sense of the public policy development process is acknowledged. To break the shackles of poverty and address disturbing patterns of poverty, conflicts, and income inequality, policy innovations and reforms across the fabrics of Africa's political economy institutions are key.

I came to the conclusion that unless you are ruled properly, you cannot move forward. Everything else is second. Everything.

—Mo Ibrahim

DOI: 10.4018/978-1-7998-7383-9.ch004

ECONOMICS AND POLITICS are no strange bedfellows; this has implications for mainstream public policy analysis. Why does economics occupy a dominant position within the disciplines that make up the social sciences and yet economic policy advice is often at the mercy of politics? The pitfalls in mainstream economics – along with the policy prescriptions emanating from its predictive prowess – are obvious and well-documented. The foundational issues on this will be discussed extensively in this chapter, while the implications and evidence are covered in the subsequent chapters.

Economic theory and empirical evidence, through the marginal propensity to consume construct, support the notion that compared to low-income earners, the relatively well-off spend significantly lower shares of extra incomes on consumption. In the absence of government spending, economic underperformance in Africa is partly due to a shortfall of aggregate demand, relative to the economy's full potential. Bolstering aggregate demand through interventions that raise labor productivity and income-earning ability through participation in the formal economy can go a long way in reducing poverty and creating a more equitable economic society.

Due to fragmentation, structural constraints, and a plethora of political economy and institutional factors, most African economies operate below their productive capacities. Also, as discussed in the preceding chapters, economic inequality is pervasive in Africa. From both a demand and supply perspective, this constitutes a major drag on growth. Keynesian economics posits that increase in aggregate demand – whether anticipated or unanticipated – has beneficial impacts on short-run output and employment. Gains from economic growth can help address income inequality if properly harnessed.

On the supply side, income inequality and limited spending can affect capital accumulation. To the extent that investments in health, education, and infrastructure are productivity drivers that enhance socioeconomic mobility, policy innovations targeted at increasing and sustaining aggregate demand not only address structural imbalances but also serve as a key economic stabilizer when exogenous shocks derail an economy from its growth path – in contrast to new classical theory which argues that markets can fix a downturn through downward adjustments in prices. These ramifications have major implications; I cover this in detail in this chapter.

How do economists affect policy? In a political context, among the social science disciplines, economics is perhaps the most influential, largely because of its inherent ability to use scientific methods in theory formulation to explain individual, household, and aggregate outcomes. From climate change and social equity to industrial policy and trade policy, politics always supersedes economics in the policymaking process. In the exact words of Hirschman and Berman (2014), "Every sociologist, anthropologist and political scientist knows that economics is the most politically influential social science" (p. 779). To offer a nuanced insight into the inherent limitations in the ability of economists to influence the policymaking process through their paradigms and analytical capabilities, Hirschman and Berman examine a diverse range of literatures focused on the role of economists in policymaking. Their symmetric approach relies on the success and failure of certain economic interventions, while discounting the effect of current perceptions of the accuracy of such interventions.

Hirschman and Berman (2014) disentangle definitional issues that may obscure key insights along three key nomenclatures in two domains: individual economists, ideologically unified networks of economists, or the profession versus economic ideas, economic data, or economic models. They offer three important suggestions on how economists and economics can more effectively influence policy: increase in professional authority, acquiring positions of institutional power, or reshaping the cognitive infrastructure of policymaking with reasoning styles or policy devices. This is expatiated below:

Economists can have effects by achieving a certain level of professional authority, and then drawing on that authority in various ways. They can have effects by acquiring particular institutional positions within the policymaking apparatus, which may mean formal organizational roles or influential locations in social networks. And they can reshape the cognitive infrastructure of policymaking, either by spreading an economic style of reasoning—that is, by teaching policymakers to think about problems as economists do—or by helping to establish economic policy devices—the sociotechnical tools that allow policymakers to see the world in certain ways (like GDP, or the unemployment rate) or assist them in making decisions (like cost–benefit analysis) (Hirschman & Berman, 2014; p. 790)

Fourcade et al. (2015) describe economists in terms of their firm belief in the ability of economics to fix the world's problems. In their analysis of the 25 most respected publications in each of economics, politics, and sociology, they conclude that 40 percent of the citations in the articles published between 2000 and 2009 in the American Economic Review referenced the other 24 major economic publications. This compares with 0.8 percent and 0.3 percent citations in political science and sociology peer-reviewed publications, respectively. As Fourcade et al. capture it, most of the citations appear in books or publications not included in the 25 top publications. This tells us one thing: economists do not hide their belief in the supremacy of their discipline among the social sciences. These authors add that "these traits help to define and account for the intellectual self-confidence of economists and in turn for their assertive claims on matters of public policy." (Fourcade et al., 2015; p. 91).

Political economy analysis relies heavily on rationally justifiable assertions that lend themselves to logical proof. And when this notion is extrapolated to mainstream neoclassicism, then, scientific methods in the form of mathematical proof require quantification – and need positivism – as a basis. This explains why, for instance, positivism as a style of reasoning will be more complex – and much more preferred – in economic policy analysis than religion or metaphysics. In this sense, logical positivism provides a wide array of possibilities for economic analysis to include reasoning, theory, econometric modeling, testing, and inferences as valid means to formalize theories, quantify impacts, and influence policy. This, again, explains why economists always "sit on the fence" in the face of complicated moral and ethical issues.

It is important to pay closer attention to the interactions between politics, economics, policy, technology, and society – and how the interdependence among these disciplines shapes the public policy development process. And pragmatism – particularly in relation to the connections between economic science, philosophy, and normative economics – has never been more important (Defalvard, 2005).

THE LIMITS OF CONVENTIONAL NEOCLASSICISM

Do orthodox economists distort theory and logic to defend mainstream, neoclassical approach to economic analysis? Why are major economic prescriptions rooted in classical physics expected to deliver outcomes that recognize the differing situations and challenges of the actors in our political and socioeconomic systems? Physical laws have useful applications in economic phenomena, but it is a fallacy to think that economies and society obey mechanical rules in strict terms. The assumption of perfectly rational economic agents paves the way for abstract mathematical models – that ignore the often unexpected and unpredictable changes in human behavior – to lump the enormous complexity of economic processes in simplistic parameters that help to simulate reality.

Due to the pitfalls of conventional neoclassical doctrines, depicting the evolutionary behavior of economies with static models is a difficult exercise. Existing theoretical frameworks of neoclassical economics are heavily reliant on static optimization and classical mechanics. Even in dynamic models, it is difficult rationalizing the fact that mathematical equations are reported in measurement units that are not defined, while economics needs real-world units consistent with dimensional quantities. Newton's law of universal gravitation states that the gravitational attraction between two bodies is directly proportional to the product of their masses and inversely proportional to the square of the distance between them, and Tinbergen (1962) extends this physical construct to trade policy by modeling the bodies as exporting and importing countries, while their masses represent economic sizes. And then, a problem arises. The model is unable to account for the barriers to trade that a region faces with all its trading partners – the so-called multilateral trade resistance.

Since countries with varying sizes react differently to changes in border barrier-type trade costs, removing the border produces a stronger reallocation effect for small countries, creating a disproportionately larger impact on their price index (Olayele, 2019). To address this oversimplification of spatial economic reality, additional rounds of general equilibrium counterfactuals crafted with the aid of advanced econometric specifications are deployed to fix the identified biases. The modeling process is always in a state of flux as characterized below:

A characteristic feature that distinguishes economics from other scientific fields is that, for us, the equations of equilibrium constitute the center of our discipline. Other sciences, such as physics or even ecology, put comparatively more emphasis on the determination of dynamic laws of change. In contrast, we have hardly mentioned dynamics. The reason, informally speaking, is that economists are good (or so we hope) at recognizing a state of equilibrium but are poor at predicting precisely how an economy in disequilibrium will evolve. Certainly, there are intuitive dynamic principles: if demand is larger than supply then the price will increase, if price is larger than marginal cost then production will expand, if industry profits are positive and there are no barriers to entry, then new firm will enter, and so on. The difficulty is in translating these informal principles into precise dynamic laws (Mas-Colell et al., 1995; p. 620)

Perhaps if economics were based on immutable laws like physics, it would be much easier for policymakers to take advice from economists at face value. However, since economies are run by people and politics, different schools of thought and doctrines in economics have major implications for the policy trajectories in different jurisdictions. Rather than relegating these complexities to the background, perhaps for the umpteenth time, the limitations of equilibrium theory – and the notion that some unobservable market force will help match demand and supply – and its ability to foster desirable outcomes through the private property exchange system should be laid to rest. One of the most compelling illustrations on how the evolution of the discipline ultimately shapes policy outcome and society is summarized below:

Individuals are not born as economists; they are molded through formal and informal training. This training shapes the way they approach problems, process information and carry out research, which in turn influences the policies they favor and the role they play in society. The economics profession changes as cohorts with older-style training are replaced with cohorts with newer-style training. In many ways, the replicator dynamics of graduate school play a larger role in determining economists' methodology and approach than all the myriad papers written about methodology (Colander, 2005; p. 175)

POLICYMAKING UNDER DISRUPTIONS

What major policymaking lessons did we learn from the 2008 GFC? Not much. Despite the agelong inadequacies of policy frameworks, approaches, and tools, 12 years after, the COVID-19 pandemic found economics and policymaking in an arguably much worse situation than 2008. As discussed above, the capitalist mode of income distribution continues to worsen inequality, complicate the climate crisis, and trigger social discontent in the face of technological advances and prosperity. To avert a major catastrophe and a breakdown of the political and socioeconomic systems, it is no longer enough to improve modern capitalism.

The notion in economic theory that firms and consumers are perfect and rational decision makers who can achieve optimal behavioral outcomes under well-defined problems in an equilibrium system is nothing but wishful thinking. Of course, agents do differ indeed, and due to information asymmetries, decision-making happens under a much more complex situation. In many ways, this underscores the urgent need for an injection of new methods, paradigms, and assumptions about human behavior.

Again, the pitfalls of standard neoclassical economics, in the context of accounting for real world problems, are well-documented. Economic theory is largely based on assumptions that are not founded in reality – and the inherent weaknesses associated with this have resulted in many of the crises around us today. Given the increasingly disruptive global geopolitical landscape and the economic fallout from COVID-19 – particularly the disparate impact of the pandemic on certain industry sectors and demographic groups – the case for overhauling the current global economic system vis-à-vis the analytical frameworks, models, devices, and paradigms that underpin its workings is compelling. Colander's (2005) proposition above on the evolution of the economics discipline – in terms of methodology and approach – merits further analysis. I explore this further in this chapter.

While the rise of new variants of the discipline – such as behavioral economics, evolutionary economics, experimental economics, new institutional economics, new information economics, social choice theory, new information economics, neuroeconomics, and complexity economics – has helped to improve policy analytics by addressing many of the pitfalls associated with elegant, but often restrictive and unrealistic equilibrium systems, neoclassical economics remains the workhorse of policy analysis and the public policy development process. This has implications for policy, business, and society.

Complexity Economics

Like most systems, the economy is in a state of flux. Complexity economics,[1] in the Austrian tradition, offers some insights here. Arthur (1999) describes this from the lens of complexity economics, based on the notion that the economy is not a system in equilibrium, but one that is in motion with constantly emerging structures, unfolding patterns, and ongoing renewal. The economy is in a non-equilibrium natural state, with constantly changing interactions and strategies among agents due to two factors: uncertainty and technological innovation (Arthur, 2013).

In a 2021 article, *The Coming Revolution in Complexity Economics*, Richard Vodra summarizes the key takeaways from the 2019 Fall Symposium of the Santa Fe Institute – focused on examining the problems with mainstream economics and how complexity economics can improve the status quo. The following criteria for validating a system of thought and policy, within a framework accounting for the following conditions, were on the front burner of the agenda:

1. Fails to predict major financial crises, or even upcoming recessions;
2. Has led to climate change and massive environmental degradation;
3. Creates massive social discontent in the face of "prosperity;"
4. Allows slavery, child labor, and other forms of exploitation;
5. Undermines government actions and other forms of collective decisions;
6. Cannot explain the absence of inflation in the face of the policies of the last decade;
7. Has no satisfactory theory of change or economic growth;
8. Has no way to properly encourage or enforce long-term commitments;
9. Does not deal with fear, hope, sharing, art, or many other "non-economic" influences; and
10. Does not incorporate the importance of energy and entropy in economic activity. (Vodra, 2021; para. 7)

A rational and reasonable staring point is to admit that the complexity of economic and social systems has been grossly underestimated. Existing models and frameworks are not adequate, and insofar as neoclassical axioms and doctrines remain the benchmark for most policy debates, as former OECD Chief of Staff and Sherpa to the G20, Gabriela Ramos, puts it, "A complexity approach allows us to look at systems of systems consisting of vast numbers of individual elements that interact in complicated ways, such as ecosystems, financial markets, and energy networks, or societal phenomena such as urbanization and migration." (OECD, 2017; p.4).

COVID-19 and the Economic Redesign Imperative

More than a decade after the GFC, some of the scars left over from it are still clear and present today. From labor market polarization and wage stagnation to the huge shift in the geography of prosperity and the decline in manufacturing clusters (DePillis, 2019), the Great Recession led to a wide range of economic shocks that heralded notable differences in the vulnerability of regions, firms, and households. While economies and societies are still living with the effects of the crisis, questions on why economists could not foresee it or offer meaningful solutions persist till today (see Olayele, 2021). Even so, given the scale of the unfolding COVID-19 pandemic, an exogenous shock, the economics profession has come under the spotlight again.

COVID-19 has disrupted economic systems with disproportionate impacts on marginalized populations, and already precarious industries and occupations. The unprecedented magnitude of the decline in jobs and production triggered by the pandemic has exposed the deep flaws in existing social and economic structures. Like never before, this situation shows the limits of conventional neoclassicism and its premise of "a strict adherence to the holy trinity [of] rationality, selfishness, and equilibrium" (Colander et al., 2004; p. 485).

The pandemic is now in its third year, and the exact degree of economic damage caused is yet to be ascertained. This will take time because there are second order, long-term disruptions that will occur as the economic recovery gathers steam. The disproportionate impacts of the pandemic have made global headlines, with many upper-income households and superstar firms in the high-tech, e-commerce, and financial services industries reaping huge gains from capital appreciation and increased automation, while vulnerable and historically marginalized populations – who are overrepresented in high contact-based service industries and low-wage jobs – bear higher-than-average losses across key economic, health, and social dimensions. This continues to exacerbate income inequality, with implications for the economic recovery, and more importantly, the long-term post-pandemic economy in the context of demand side structural dynamics.

Historically speaking, the COVID-19 pandemic is the worst viral outbreak the world has seen in more than a century. The pandemic exposed fundamental flaws in current economic thinking, and the limitations of existing tools for structural analysis. The neoclassical school of economic thought has informed the global economic order and policymaking for over a century, but COVID-19 has revealed the gross inadequacy of the current global neoliberal capitalist architecture, along with the neoclassical paradigms that have informed much of the systematic and scientific arguments put forward to validate this school of thought. Perhaps there is no better time than now to rethink tools, paradigms, and methodological frameworks that inform what criteria are used by the next generation to evaluate productive, resilient, equitable, and sustainable economic systems. Among others, adequately accounting for social provisioning, climate justice, informality, conflicts, caregiving, and public health will go a long way. The case for looking at economic policy with more critical and fresh approaches is compelling.

Technology, Marxism, and Pareto Optimality

Why is technology so distant from policymaking? Clearly, the accelerating pace of technological innovation calls for a new economic policymaking architecture. The ongoing digitization in the global economy is affecting every facet of humanity, with disproportionate impacts in the Global South. In many ways, it is now obvious that technology should be an inherent pillar in the policymaking process. Many of the greatest challenges of our era need actors in the policy and technology domains working together to find win-win solutions. In many ways, the greatest impetus for updating the current economic policymaking architecture comes from a fundamental and undeniable realization: while certain policy goals may not have changed significantly over time, policy tools and the settings under which those policies are crated often do vary when more information becomes available.

As discussed in the preceding sections, the assumptions of rational, self-interested, and forward-looking agents operating in economic spaces with no adjustment lags and inertias are nothing but a pure hallucination. Since such idealized settings are unrealistic, why then is much of contemporary real-world policymaking based, at least partly and by implication, on the dictates of these predictive and prescriptive scenarios? As described by Austrian economist, Friedrich Hayek, the first staunch supporter of free markets to win the Nobel Prize in Economics, the market system is an information processing mechanism characterized by spontaneity. As events unfolded, Hayek later abandoned economics to study political and legal philosophy to gain a deeper understanding of the foundations of society, culture, and institutions. Even so, the Swedish Academy of Sciences split Hayek's Nobel Prize with Swedish socialist economist, Gunnar Myrdal, a fierce advocate of welfare state and radical government reforms.

Gunnar Myrdal was one of the pioneers of the Swedish welfare state anchored on social equality and universal rights. He also wrote extensively on the social and economic dynamics of race relations in the US. The Swedish Academy of Sciences underscores Hayek and Myrdal's work as a "...penetrating analysis of the interdependence of economic, social and institutional phenomena." (The Royal Swedish Academy of Sciences, 1974; para. 3). Myrdal later called for the Nobel Prize in Economics to be abolished because economics was an inexact, "soft" science loaded with value judgments, adding that in hindsight, he should not have accepted the prize. Myrdal clearly saw things ahead, judging, at least, from his Nobel Prize Lecture published in 1975:

Among things which, at that time, besides defects in our theoretical approaches, contributed to our common over optimism in regard to planning for development in underdeveloped countries, was that only gradually, toward the censuses around 1960, did we have reasons to worry much about a population explosion, as population increases as known up till then had not been proceeding at too alarming a rate. Also, the anxiety emerging in more recent years about depletion of not renewable resources had not then drawn our attention to the tremendous inequality in the use of resources. The challenge was not apparent of the virtual necessity of bringing down the consumption of these and other resources in the developed countries, if development should be possible in the underdeveloped ones. (Myrdal, 1975; p. 421)

While the ongoing disruptions portend a gradual decimation of the old sociopolitical economic order, there are no signs that a new order is about to be birthed. After wars of conquest, colonialism, and imperialism during the Age of Discovery from the 15th century to the 18th century, modern capitalism emerged from an international economic regime that resulted in the European colonization of the Americas after Christopher Columbus' voyages to the West Indies, Central and South America, and other islands of the Caribbean starting in 1492. This led to the discovery of the New World and the trans-Atlantic economy, colonial and interstate systems, and deepened East-West trade (Mark, 2020). After this came the Industrial Revolution in Britain and the ascendancy to power of the bourgeoisie – before the American and French Revolutions of 1776 and 1789, respectively.

In the latter part of the 19th century, the rise of country-level corporate capitalism heralded a new wave of imperialist conquest, which manifested through the consolidation of industrial financial corporations, nation-states, and national markets under one global system. This ultimately led to the oil and fiscal crises of the 1970s, and the eventual demise of the gold window, Keynesian economics, and a unified and fixed exchange system which, combined, triggered the collapse of the Bretton Woods system and the global financial system. The latter part of the 20th century, particularly the late 1980s and early 1990s, saw waves of privatizations and market deregulations. The interplay between economic and policy factors ultimately altered the industrial architectures of many economies.

Karl Marx's work in economics laid the foundation for contemporary discourse on labor and its relation to capital. In the context of the European colonization of the Americas, the early form of capitalism practiced in Europe was based on mercantilism, with limited market systems, which later allowed influential ruling classes, collectively known as the bourgeoisie in Marxist tradition, to thrive. The bourgeoisie amassed enormous power and influence that enabled them to control the means of production, while the proletariat, otherwise called the working class, sold their labor-power in return for wages (Marx & Engels, 1848). Marx's depiction of the power relationship between capital and labor remains critical for understanding and advancing policy innovation to address some of the pitfalls of modern capitalism.

Due to the many pitfalls of the neoclassical paradigm, some strands of modern public economics and public choice theory advocate, indirectly, an economic governance model in which production and income distribution will occur in the absence of private property rights and the markets (Bowles, 2018). However, Marx's extensive analysis of the domination of labor by capital, even under private perfectly competitive and liberal arrangements, makes it more appealing in contemporary policymaking to explore policy changes that can address the shortcomings outlined by Marx in the labor theory of value where labor exploitation is a necessary condition for profits. This complicates the potential for analytical possibilities since the notion of subjective preferences is more fashionable in the context of mainstream, orthodox economics.

In the tradition of Walras (1874), a market with many sellers and buyers trading one good for another offers a good model of a global economy with a general equilibrium that accounts for the actions of all agents. Such notion of subjective value determination has implications for policy design. James Bernard Murphy and Graeme Garrard in their 2019 book, *How to Think Politically*, blend the views of "ancient and modern, Western, Chinese and Islamic thought, religious, and seculary thinkers" to answer some fundamental questions on the future of politics and what is at stake through the lenses of "a diverse group of the 30 greatest political thinkers who have ever lived" as expressed in their introduction:

It is fashionable today to describe politics as a swamp. For many it has become nothing more than a vulgar spectacle of deceit, ambition, and opportunism. Trust in our political institutions and leaders has sunk to new lows, and politicians are held in greater contempt than for generations. Voter anger and disenchantment are growing at an alarming rate. Distracted by all the unseemly squabbling of politics, we end up allowing markets and bureaucrats to make decisions for us, leaving citizens resigned and alienated from politics-as-usual. It is very hard to imagine that ideas, let alone ideals, could play any part in all of this (Murphy & Garrard, 2019; p. 1).

Adam Smith in his 1776 *Wealth of Nations* contends that the invisible hand is the best regulator of economic activity as it guides resources to their most valued use. But market failures are not going away anytime soon. Self-interest and competition are fundamental to the workings of the market system, since self-interested behavior inevitably produces an outcome that is good for the whole of society. Lindblom (1959) describes the helplessness of policymakers because of sub-optimal level of information in the form of both partial information and too much information.

In the face of too many choices, Yale political scientist, James Scott, in *Seeing Like a State*, sheds light on how central planners try to simplify the seemingly complex nature of human societies by narrowing their array of choices to arrive at a decision. Scott argues that states often like to simplify reality by accommodating complexities under their own administrative categories, thereby ignoring local knowledge which is fundamental to addressing complex socioeconomic, political, and environmental systems. Citing various examples in the context of East African agriculture, he describes below how interventions aimed at fixing society or the natural environment often result in counterproductive, and in some cases, disastrous outcomes:

But "fiasco" is too lighthearted a word for the disasters I have in mind. The Great Leap Forward in China, collectivization in Russia, and compulsory villagization in Tanzania, Mozambique, and Ethiopia are among the great human tragedies of the twentieth century, in terms of both lives lost and lives irretrievably disrupted. At a less dramatic but far more common level, the history of Third World development is littered with the debris of huge agricultural schemes and new cities (think of Brasilia or Chandigarh) that have failed their residents. It is not so difficult, alas, to understand why so many human lives have been destroyed by mobilized violence between ethnic groups, religious sects, or linguistic communities. But it is harder to grasp why so many well-intended schemes to improve the human condition have gone so tragically awry (Scott, 1998; p.4).

Furthermore, this becomes a little complicated in the context of explaining how certain policy ideas yield varying results depending on local political, economic, and social contexts. This is important considering the debate on how and why advice and robust ideas by economists often do not resonate in the political decision-making process. To the extent that distributional conflicts are inherent in political decision-making, economic policymaking is often not grounded in the principles and predictions of theory.

Ray Fair, in *Predicting Presidential Elections and Other Things*, asks why an incumbent party tends to do well when the state of the economy is good and poorly when the economy is bad. To unpack this, he builds a theory around what voters expect on their future well-being, using both economic growth rate and inflation. Growth rate is seen as a proxy for the state of the economy, while the rate of inflation helps voters gauge the effect of overheating on their financial well-being. In other words, voters' expectations are influenced by the recent performance of the economy during the election. Voters interpret good economic performance under the incumbent party as a positive sign about their own future well-being, while poor economic performance is predictive of a negative future economic outcome in well-being, thereby tilting voters towards the opposition party.

Fair adds other non-economic variables like media attention and the duration of the incumbent party in power as good predictors in the theory of voting behavior. A major conclusion in the book is that since strong economic performance during an election year may help the electoral prospects of the party in power, the notion of a "political business cycle" is commonplace. The incumbent party has an incentive to stimulate the economy as part of its re-election strategy. To achieve this, the economy may be deliberately slowed down in the few years before the election, to pave the way for stronger growth towards the end of a four-year term. Such deliberate manipulation of the economy for political gains has major implications, and this resonates in the sentiment below:

I have often been asked if I really believe that many voters know the actual values of the growth rate and inflation when they enter the voting booth on election day. How many people really look up the numbers in their newspapers before voting? (This is usually a hostile question.) It is surely unlikely that many voters know the exact numbers. They form their opinions about the economy by looking at the conditions around them – how their friends and neighbors and employers are doing – not by looking at the numbers themselves. They may also be influenced by the media, especially radio and television commentators. The numbers, however, are likely to be related to the conditions that people are observing. If the growth rate is negative, for example, it is likely that the conditions that people see around them are not so good and that commentators are saying bad things about the economy. It is thus not necessary that voters know the exact numbers as long as the numbers accurately reflect what the voters are actually paying attention to (Fair, 2002; pp. 57-58)

Italian economist, engineer, sociologist, and philosopher, Vilfredo Pareto (1848-1923), was part of the Walras-Lausanne tradition – a precursor to the neoclassical school of thought. Pareto improved upon and advanced the general equilibrium theory after Walras. Arguably the most prominent mathematical economist of the latter part of the 19th century and the first in the 20th century, Pareto's thesis argues that an economic system is in a Pareto Optimal state when no further configurations can yield an equilibrium state in which further changes can make one person better off without leaving another person worse off at the same time (Mas-Colell et al., 1995). This implies that the initial allocation was Pareto-non-optimal. Essentially, this construct – known as Pareto Optimality – is an exchange efficiency argument in which no redistributive regime for a given bundle of goods can increase welfare of one consumer without reducing the welfare of another. Or production efficiency in which factor inputs cannot be reallocated to raise the output of one product without lowering that of the other product. Or efficiency in product-mix or composition of output.

At the heart of the Pareto efficiency proposition is the possibility of evaluating all tradeoffs among optimal combinations under multiple equilibria (Mas-Colell et al., 1995). But here is a reason why the proposition above may be an oversimplification of reality: to attain Pareto Optimality, three marginal conditions must be satisfied: efficiency in production, efficiency in consumption, and efficiency in product-mix or composition of output. And to pave the way for mathematical derivations of the marginal conditions, we must necessarily assume that there are only two consumers, two factor inputs, and two commodities. Indeed, this is far from reality.

Practical policy implementation recognizes this pitfall and navigates the contours by ensuring that a policy that raises overall societal welfare, but creates winners and losers, is still a good policy – if losers are compensated and winners are taxed. On paper, this is good and simple. Not exactly in politically polarized environments. Much like bounded rationality allows us to satisfice rather than optimize when making decisions with limited information, time, and cognitive capacity, heuristics allow for mental shortcuts to allow generalizations and rules-of-thumb to aid in decision-making by bypassing redundancies. As always, qualifications are in order. Unlike what positivism stands for, issues such as race, religion, gender, metaphysics, and other important socioeconomic and demographic dynamics cannot be discarded in the policymaking arena.

Normativism is largely about good or bad, and not so much about right or wrong. And much of the controversies in economic policy derive from the ideological underpinnings and political philosophies under which economics is applied in statecraft. Again, in the world of policymaking, normativism and value judgments are at the opposite end of the spectrum from positivism. In essence, readers should distill the key takeaways by succinctly capturing the reasons adduced, which offer a path as the conclusion of the argument in this book. By the time readers get to the latter chapters of this book, they would have a deeper understanding not only of the topics covered, but also how the motivation behind a specific policy matters just as much as its effectiveness – both in the context of value judgment and moral ethics.

RETHINKING PUBLIC POLICY ARCHITECTURE

The rapid pace of technological and disruptive innovations that has come to define the current digital global economy has led to an interdependence marked by a seamless globalization process that is driving the Fourth Industrial Revolution and its concomitant effect on growth and development. This has led to structural changes that make it difficult for traditional economic models to effectively explain trends and patterns in contemporary analysis. Such reality provides a compelling reason for policy experimentation in a bid to deploy innovative approaches to policy development to move the needle on some of the most pressing issues of our time.

In search of pragmatic answers to the pressing policy issues of the moment, based on the notion of "entrepreneurial government," Osborne and Gaebler in their 1992 book, *Reinventing Government: How the Entrepreneurial Spirit is Transforming the Public Sector*, examine the bureaucracy-laissez faire nexus and itemize eight principles that should guide programmatic interventions in addressing societal needs:

1. Programs are driven by constituencies, not customers
2. Programs are driven by politics, not policy

3. Programs create turf, which public agencies defend at all costs
4. Programs tend to create fragmented service delivery systems
5. Programs are not self-correcting
6. Programs that are obsolete rarely die
7. Programs rarely achieve the scale necessary to make a significant impact
8. Programs normally use commands, not incentives

Government does not have the financial war chest to fulfill all that society needs. Yet, implicit in its social contract is the assumption that through the invisible hand, government can create an environment conducive enough for market forces to unleash the entrepreneurial spirit that drives economic agents to find a way to meet these needs. Efficient information exchanges and price signaling remain key. Osborne and Gaebler argue that to dismantle administrative bureaucracies, entrepreneurial governments can leverage policy to harness the decisions and behavior of individuals for win-win outcomes in both markets and community. In the context of regional ecosystems, they argue that cities are markets with "vast, complex aggregations of people and institutions, each constantly making decisions and each adjusting to the other's behavior based on the incentives and information available to them" (Osborne & Gaebler, 1992; p. 282).

From happiness and fairness to equity, social justice, and diversity to climate change, parental leave, childcare access, and the gender pay gap, it has become obvious that mainstream economics is not set up to succeed as a useful compass for tackling complex, non-linear public policy challenges. In the synopsis of her 2017 book, *Doughnut Economics: Seven Ways to Think Like a 21st-Century Economist*, Kate Raworth does not hold back on how mainstream economics has failed humanity:

Economics is broken. It has failed to predict, let alone prevent, financial crises that have shaken the foundations of our societies. Its outdated theories have permitted a world in which extreme poverty persists while the wealth of the super-rich grows year on year. And its blind spots have led to policies that are degrading the living world on a scale that threatens all of our futures. (Financial Times Business Book of the Year, 2017; para. 1)

Yet, economics and public policy are inseparable. The logic of economic science has made it the corner stone of public policy. And as the debate on redesigning sociopolitical and economic systems to make them fairer and more equitable rages, the limits of mainstream economics, particularly the gold standard assumption of rationality, must be reevaluated. Much like how the original version of prospect theory published in 1979 was modified[2] in 1992 by Kahneman and Tversky as an alternative to the neoclassical doctrine of expected utility theory, the public sector and policy innovation landscape needs a rejig.

I lend my voice, in *Age of Economics*, to the debate on the changing view on the place of economic science in public policymaking. I argue that unlike how economics allows for experimentation in the quest for novelty in economic inquiry – which tends to be framed in narrow terms – such luxuries cannot be afforded in the realm of policymaking because of the grave consequences that come with certain policy mistakes, with long-lasting effects that may traverse generations:

And by implication, that means you have to bring many actors, stakeholders, and vested interests to a common ground. It is very important to achieve consensus. You have to consider trade-offs, which often mean compromises, consultations, polling, concessions, politicking, and what have you. All of those things are involved. (Olayele, 2021; para. 18).

The call for a new approach to policymaking is gaining momentum (OECD, 2017). The global economic order is in a state of flux, and it is dangerous to oversimplify things when interpreting history. Pritchett and Summers (2014) warn policymakers about the dangers inherent in mischaracterizing mean reversion in GDP growth as "middle-income trap."[3] The authors opine on the need for lower-middle-income countries to prepare for creative destruction as part of the recipe for sustaining rapid economic growth:

......one of the factors that makes sustaining rapid growth so difficult is that growth depends on both parts of creative destruction, but only one is popular with governments and economic elites. Everyone loves the 'creative', as it brings new investments, new industries, and new profits. But sustained economic growth typically relies on continued structural transformation in which new industries arise, but also old industries shrink – sometimes just relatively, but sometimes absolutely. While essential to sustained economic growth, neither governments nor existing firms like destruction – with its geographic shifts, employment shifts, and firm exits that are a necessary part of weeding out uncompetitive industries. This makes it much harder to sustain rapid growth (which few do) than to get it going (which many do). While this happens at 'middle-income' levels, it is also a part of economic

transformation at every stage – from the challenges posed by the threat of new industrialists to the landed aristocracy in the Industrial Revolution to the difficulties facing the most advanced countries today. Sustaining growth is not a 'middle-income' problem – it is the fundamental challenge of progress at all stages. (Pritchett & Summers, 2014; para, 19)

Public policy remains a powerful tool for economic development. The purpose of economic science is to help decision-makers understand complex realities and predict outcomes. But under the new digital economy, where disruptions and innovations have become the new normal, the models, tools, techniques, and approaches of policy analysis need to be re-examined. Policy innovation has a role in helping put things into perspective, whilst addressing some of the pitfalls in a reinvigorating way. This has a major significance for policy paradigms, tools, and frameworks in the African context –given how informality, fragmentation, subsistence, cultural affinity, weak institutions, and low productivity drive the continent's contemporary political economy outcomes. The literature on substantive and procedural tools for public policy is somewhat non-systematic, and such disparate situation has unintended consequences. In addition to using the right tools for policy formulation, policymakers need a good understanding of available tools and toolkits in the policy design process.

Bali et al. (2021) argue that policy instrument choices are often viewed through a binomial ideological lens based on a 'one size fits all' stereotype that includes "good versus evil", "market versus state", or "competition versus monopoly." The authors caution that such dichotomous, zero-sum rigid choices reduce creativity and the ability of policy instruments to be responsive to the differing social, political, and economic dynamics that characterize both policymaking and the decision-making process on policy tool choices.

Since information asymmetries and non-linearity characterize much of real-world policymaking, it is important to deploy a multipronged approach that accounts for possible policy incongruence and its implications. Temporary shocks often produce persistent effects, and both theory and empirical evidence caution that if the context is not right, policy interventions may produce unintended consequences. To the extent that such interventions have long lasting effects, with major implications for intergenerational equity and justice, policy mistakes have huge costs. This becomes even more important in the context of low-income, fragile states in Africa where disruptions and market failures arising from externalities could create a more persistent crisis.

In many ways, this corroborates stylized facts that differing complexities and pitfalls hamper evidence-informed policy formulation.

ECONOMIC REBASING IN AFRICA: A POLICY INNOVATION LESSON

The United Nations Statistical Commission recommends governments rebase their national accounts system every five years to account for price dynamics. GDP rebasing replaces an old base year with a more recent one to account for the evolution in prices. Apart from improving estimation methods and statistical classifications, rebasing is beneficial for planning and policymaking because once constant prices are estimated in terms of the prices of the new base year, the new reference point for future GDP estimates gives a more accurate representation of the size and structure of the economy.

Under this regime, important policy and programmatic interventions around key activities like domestic resource mobilization, fiscal allocation, revenue-sharing formula determination, capital budgeting, and debt management can be benchmarked so they are comparable with other jurisdictions. Also, rebasing can have a major impact on policymaking, through macroeconomic transmission channels like GDP per capita, debt-to-GDP ratio, and tax-to-GDP ratio. This can provide insights as governments contemplate a plethora of industrial policy options. Of particular importance is the fact that rebasing often provides an opportunity to incorporate new activities not captured in the computational framework deployed in previous exercises, thereby giving potential investors useful insights upon which to base their investment decisions. In the African context, rebasing is a major opportunity to expand the coverage of economic activity by capturing much of the informal sector.

In 2014, Nigeria, Tanzania, Kenya, Uganda, and Zambia rebased their economies, producing relatively large changes in their respective sizes. Nigeria rebased its 2013 GDP from $270 billion to $510 billion (an increase of about 90 percent), and in the process, overtook South Africa to become Africa's biggest economy. The Nigerian statistical authorities attributed the significant change to years of underreporting of growth in emerging economic sectors like banking, telecommunications, Nollywood, and the informal economy – sectors that were largely not captured in previous official statistics. Notwithstanding the recommendations for rebasing to be a five-yearly exercise, prior to 2014, the last time Nigeria rebased its economy was in 1990. In the same year, Kenya's economy expanded by 25 percent after it was rebased, leading to a change in its status from low- to lower-middle-income status.

For the most part, the poorest countries in the world are agriculture-based subsistence economies, with low labor productivity since a disproportionately large share of labor spends time on simple automatable tasks. Knowing how African economies have reinvented their industrial structures over time will be key to policy experimentations targeted at addressing the two often inseparable problems of poverty and inequality – which not only restrict socioeconomic mobility of the poor, but also constrain further growth opportunities. What does the rebasing exercise portend for Africa's future economy, particularly the digital services economy? This piece by the Brookings Institution makes a compelling case for rethinking Africa's services economy:

These rebasing exercises have helped to clarify the diversity within select African economies, providing policymakers with a better fundamental understanding of the structural changes their economies are undergoing. But revised statistics alone will not ignite economic growth across the continent—they must be integrated into the ongoing development policy debates occurring in these countries. In particular, the rise in the services sector's share of GDP together with gradual or no increases in the shares of industrialization and agriculture may have significant implications for sustaining the region's growth. (Sy, 2015; para. 14)

As discussed in the earlier chapters, fixing underlying structural economic issues that perpetuate widening inequality and its concomitant effect on aggregate demand is fundamental to building an inclusive and sustainable economy. Keynesianism contends that moving players in the underground economy to the formal sector can increase the earning potential of individuals at the bottom end of the income distribution, thereby unlocking growth through higher spending. Much like GDP rebasing can help policymaking efforts in a wide range of areas, a reimagining of policy paradigms, tools, and analytical frameworks can help propel Africa's economy as Sy, yet again, succinctly captures it:

Keeping these changes in mind, policymakers must now focus on the sectors that are most poised for transformation and consider how they can provide targeted support. A consensus seems to be forming policies that can draw more labor into and reinvigorate manufacturing including through agro-

processing activities, boost agricultural productivity through the use of high-value crops, and develop labor force skills to improve productivity in services. (Sy, 2015; para. 16)

However, under the ongoing digital transformation, new industries are driving growth and new products and technological developments continue to shift consumption patterns. As rural societies in Africa gradually embrace the digital economy, policymaking must embrace new policy tools, paradigms, and analytical frameworks that recognize the appropriate "speed of adjustment" required to account for incremental gains vis-à-vis the formalization of activities in the subsistence economy.

PAN-AFRICANISM AND THE RENAISSANCE

Pan-Africanism is an ideology anchored on unleashing the collective power, endowments, and expertise of Africa and Africans to promote inclusive and sustainable social, economic, and political development of the continent (African Union, 2015). Africa's quest for economic integration dates back to the establishment of the Organisation of African Union (OAU) in 1963. In 1991, through the Treaty of Abuja, the African Economic Community (AEC) was finalized as a framework for an integrated economy among continental African nation states – with the AEC comprised of a six-stage roadmap to full economic integration, including a customs union, a single market, and a monetary union.

In May 2013, African Heads of State and Government signed the 50th Anniversary Solemn Declaration as an affirmation of their commitment to transforming the continent into a global powerhouse of the future (African Union, 2015a). Agenda 2063 is the blueprint and shared strategic framework of the African Union for attaining inclusive and sustainable economic growth and development in Africa. A long-term, 50-year development trajectory for the continent, Agenda 2063 is based not only on the notion of Pan-Africanism and the African Renaissance, but also on economic, legal, social, and political systems conducive for rapid and robust economic and social development. Given past efforts at driving socioeconomic development on the continent, Agenda 2063 builds on past and existing initiatives, and as such, it is "a continuation of the pan-African drive over centuries, for unity, self-determination, freedom, progress, and collective prosperity pursued under Pan-Africanism and African Renaissance…. (African Union, 2015b; p. 2).

As a framework, Agenda 2063 is intended "to build an integrated, prosperous and peaceful Africa, driven and managed by its own citizens and representing a dynamic force in the international arena" (African Union, 2015b; p.2) through the following seven aspirations (Figure 1):

Aspiration 1: A prosperous Africa based on inclusive growth and sustainable development—Africa will by 2063 be a continent of shared prosperity, which finances and manages its own growth and transformation.

Aspiration 2: An integrated continent, politically united based on the ideals of Pan Africanism and the vision of Africa's Renaissance—By 2063 Africa will have emerged as a united, strong, sovereign, independent and self-reliant continent that realizes full economic and political integration.

Aspiration 3: An Africa of good governance, democracy, respect for human rights, justice and the rule of law—By 2063, Africa will have undergone a deepening of the culture of good governance, democratic values, gender equality, respect for human rights, justice and the rule of law.

Aspiration 4: A peaceful and secure Africa—By 2063, Africa will emerge as a peaceful and secure continent, a conflict-free continent with harmony and understanding among communities at the grassroots level.

Aspiration 5: An Africa with a strong cultural identity, common heritage, values and ethics—Africa, as the cradle of human civilization, is custodian of a cultural patrimony that has contributed enormously to human progress. African cultural identity, values and ethics as a critical factor in Africa's re-emergence on the global stage in the decade of the 2010s, will be promoted and strengthened by 2063.

Aspiration 6: An Africa whose development is people-driven, relying on the potential of African people, especially its women and youth, and caring for children—By 2063, Africa will be a continent where all citizens will be actively involved in decision-making in all aspects of development, including social, economic, political and environmental. Africa will be a continent where no child, woman or man will be left behind.

Aspiration 7: Africa as a strong, united, resilient and influential global player and partner—Africa will emerge as a strong, united, resilient and influential global player and partner with a bigger role in world affairs. (African Union, 2015b; pp. 6-7)

Figure 1. African union's agenda 2063 framework
(Credit: African Union)

Like the European Renaissance, contemporary discourses on the African Renaissance sometime depict a similar pathway to economic sufficiency, social progress, and political emancipation; this account is untrue because the African situation is different and more nuanced (Earle & Lowe, 2005). While the Renaissance in Europe from the 14th to the 17th century was preceded by the Middle Ages, it ushered in major shifts in European thought and worldview. The Renaissance was the most significant period of development in European history, with dramatic changes in European architecture, art, literature, mathematics, music, philosophy, politics, religion, and science (History Crunch. n.d.).

In the case of Africa, the struggles for political independence and self-rule triggered the birth of several nation states without the accompanying economic and cultural emancipation needed to succeed. This political economy arrangement, for instance, saw roads and railways built by European imperialists for the sole purpose of exporting primary commodities, thereby depriving the newly independent countries the ability to add value to raw materials and raise productivity. This also perpetuated distorted economic structures characterized by import dependence. In their 2020 work, *The Political Economy of Pan-Africanism*, Abu Girma Moges and Mammo Muchie espouse why this configuration is not permissive for sustainable economic and social development:

Pan-Africanism was motivated and driven by political imperatives and it was a response to the urgent demands for liberation of Africa from European colonialism. The political liberation was the most urgent objective of Pan-Africanism and yet the movement had objectives beyond political liberation. The central and enduring theme of the movement has remained to be the total economic, social, cultural, racial, and political liberation and development of the African Nation. The organized movement was born among the African diaspora. However, the center of gravity of the movement was and remains to be at its home land in Africa while the diaspora remains an active and progressive agent of the process. The challenge has been how to effectively use the massive but fragmented human, natural, innovative, entrepreneurial, intellectual, and social capital of Africa to promote sustainable and inclusive development that consolidates the power of Africa (Moges and Muchie, 2020; p.60).

To break the shackles of poverty and address disturbing patterns of poverty, conflicts, and income inequality, policy innovations and reforms across the fabrics of Africa's political economy institutions are key. Lansana Gberie, Sierra Leone's Permanent Representative to the United Nations in Geneva and Ambassador to Switzerland, aptly summarizes this:

The African Renaissance, an idea popularized by Mandela's successor Thabo Mbeki and one that Mandela fully supported, has certainly not yet been realized. There are still petty wars and petty tyrannies, not to mention an unequal global economic and political system, holding the continent back. But Mandela's life and work for the continent suggested that it is possible. (Gberie, 2021; para. 14)

To conclude this chapter, it is imperative for Africa's public policy architecture to strike a right balance vis-à-vis the preferences of policymakers and other policy actors to ensure the specificities of the differing regional- and country-level institutional dynamics are accounted for in the overarching policy frameworks underpinning Agenda 2063's Pan Africanism. This will ensure the capacity to innovate contributes to economic stability.

Finding sustainable policy solutions to the myriad of challenges facing Africa will involve paying attention to the various stages of political decision-making. In the context of John Kingdon's MSF (discussed under theories of policy change in chapter 3), this will involve systematic and modern applications of policy paradigms and devices across the three streams of actors and processes in the policy cycle – i.e., a data-driven approach in the problem stream, solutions in the policy stream, and influencing political decision-making in the politics stream.

With these considerations in mind, one would think that insofar as real-world policy implementation often involves pragmatic communication and public enlightenment, the policy design and analysis phases should equally be an interactive process under a framework that incorporates the reality of the influence of technology in our modern, hyphen-tech economy.

When Henry Ford made cheap, reliable cars people said, 'Nah, what's wrong with a horse?' That was a huge bet he made, and it worked.

—Elon Musk

REFERENCES

African Union. (2015a). *Overview - Agenda 2063: The Africa We Want.* https://au.int/en/agenda2063/overview

African Union. (2015b). *Agenda 2063: Background Note.* https://au.int/sites/default/files/documents/33126-doc-01_background_note.pdf

Arthur, W. B. (1999). Complexity and the economy. *Science*, *284*(5411), 107–109. doi:10.1126cience.284.5411.107 PMID:10103172

Bali, A. S., Howlett, M., Lewis, J. M., & Ramesh, M. (2021). Procedural policy tools in theory and practice. *Policy and Society*, *40*(3), 295–311. doi:10.1080/14494035.2021.1965379

Bowles, S. (2018). *Marx and modern microeconomics.* VOX[EU] Centre for Economic Policy Research. Retrieved from https://voxeu.org/article/marx-and-modern-microeconomics

Colander, D. (2005). The Making of an economist redux. *The Journal of Economic Perspectives*, *19*(1), 175–198. doi:10.1257/0895330053147976

Colander, D., Holt, R., & Rosser, B. Jr. (2004). The changing face of mainstream economics. *Review of Political Economy*, *16*(4), 485–499. doi:10.1080/0953825042000256702

Defalvard, H. (2005). Pragmatism and Institutionalism in Economics: A Tool-Based Approach. *Revue de Metaphysique et de Morale*, (3), 375–389. doi:10.3917/rmm.053.0375

DePillis, L. (2019). 10 years later, America's booming economy still bears scars of the great recession. *CNN Business*. https://www.cnn.com/2019/06/24/economy/great-recession-us-economy/index.html

Earle, T. F., & Lowe, K. J. P. (Eds.). (2005). *Black Africans in Renaissance Europe*. Cambridge University Press.

Fair, R. (2002). *Predicting presidential elections and other things*. Stanford University Press.

Financial Times. (2017). *FT Business Book of the Year*. https://ig.ft.com/sites/business-book-award/books/2017/longlist/doughnut-economics-by-kate-raworth/

Fourcade, M., Ollion, E., & Algan, Y. (2015). The superiority of economists. *The Journal of Economic Perspectives*, *29*(1), 89–114. doi:10.1257/jep.29.1.89

Garrard, G., & Murphy, J. (2019). *How to think politically: Sages, scholars and statesmen whose ideas have changed the world*. Bloomsbury Publishing.

Gberie, L. (2013). Mandela's Struggles for Peace and Justice in Africa. *Africa Renewal Online*. https://www.un.org/africarenewal/web-features/mandela%E2%80%99s-struggles-peace-and-justice-africa

Hirschman, D., & Berman, P. E. (2014). Do economists make policies? On the political effects of economics. *Socio-economic Review*, *12*(4), 779–811. doi:10.1093er/mwu017

History Crunch. (n.d.). *Causes of Renaissance*. https://www.historycrunch.com/causes-of-the-renaissance.html#/

Kahneman, D., & Tversky, A. (1979). Prospect theory: An analysis of decision under risk. *Econometrica*, *47*(2), 263–291. doi:10.2307/1914185

Lindblom, C. (1959). The Science of "muddling through". *Public Administration Review*, *19*(2), 79–88. doi:10.2307/973677

Mark, J. (2020). European colonization of the Americas. *World History Encyclopedia.* https://www.worldhistory.org/European_Colonization_of_the_Americas/

Marx, K., & Engels, F. (1848). *Manifesto of the communist party.* Retrieved from https://www.marxists.org/archive/marx/works/1848/communist-manifesto/index.htm

Mas-Colell, A., Whinston, M. D., & Green, J. R. (1995). *Microeconomic theory* (Vol. 1). Oxford University Press.

Moges, A. G., & Muchie, M. (2020). The political economy of Pan-Africanism. *Routledge Handbook of Pan-Africanism.* https://www.routledgehandbooks.com/doi/10.4324/9780429020193-3

Myrdal, G. (1975). The Equality Issue in World Development. *The Swedish Journal of Economics*, *77*(4), 413–432. doi:10.2307/3439336

OECD. (2017). *Debate the Issues: Complexity and policy making*. OECD iLibrary. . doi:10.1787/9789264271531-en

Olayele, B. F. (2019). Gravity, borders, and regionalism: A Canada–US sub-national analysis. *The International Trade Journal*, *33*(5), 416–443. doi:10.1080/08853908.2019.1628675

Olayele, F. (2021). *Age of Economics.* https://www.ageofeconomics.org/interviews/fred-olayele/

Osborne, D., & Gaebler, T. (1992). *Reinventing government: how the entrepreneurial spirit is transforming the public sector*. Addison-Wesley Pub.

Pritchett, L., & Summers, L. H. (2014). *Growth slowdowns: Middle-income trap vs. regression to the mean.* VOX[EU] Centre for Economic Policy Research. Retrieved from https://voxeu.org/article/growth-slowdowns-middle-income-trap-vs-regression-mean

Scott, J. C. (1998). *Seeing like a state: How certain schemes to improve the human condition have failed.* Yale University Press.

Smith, A. (1976). An Inquiry into the Nature and Causes of the Wealth of Nations. Oxford University Press. (Original publication 1776)

Sy, A. (2015). Are African countries rebasing GDP in 2014 finding evidence of structural transformation? In *Africa in Focus.* Brookings Institute. https://www.brookings.edu/blog/africa-in-focus/2015/03/03/are-african-countries-rebasing-gdp-in-2014-finding-evidence-of-structural-transformation/

The Royal Swedish Academy of Sciences. (1974, October 9). *The Sveriges Riksbank Prize in Economic Sciences in Memory of Alfred Nobel 1974.* https://www.nobelprize.org/prizes/economic-sciences/1974/press-release

Tinbergen. (1962). *Shaping the world economy: Suggestions for an international economic policy*. Twentieth Century Fund.

Tversky, A., & Kahneman, D. (1992). Advances in prospect theory: Cumulative representation of uncertainty. *Journal of Risk and Uncertainty*, *5*(4), 297–323. doi:10.1007/BF00122574

Vodra, R. (2021, March 29). The coming revolution in complexity economics. *Advisor Perspectives.* https://www.advisorperspectives.com/articles/2021/03/29/the-coming-revolution-in-complexity-economics

Walras, L. (1954). Eléments d'économie politique pure (W. Jaffé, Trans.). Allen & Unwin. (Original publication 1874)

ENDNOTES

1. While complexity economics developed roots from the heterodox approaches and insights of scientists at the Santa Fe Institute in the late 1980s, the premise is as old as political economy itself dating back to the era before Adam Smith. The Santa Fe Institute was established in 1984 to offer insights into complex adaptive systems, chaos theory, and allied issues in complexity science.
2. After its relative success in addressing the flaws in the expected utility theory – which due to the cognitive limitations on the part of a decision-maker does not allow for influences on choice selection – Kahneman and Tversky's (1979) prospect theory was revised in 1992 to not only account for uncertainty, but also risky prospects with unlimited number of outcomes. This version of the prospect theory, called cumulative prospect theory, is based on cumulative rather than separable decision weights.
3. The notion that economic growth becomes more difficult after countries reach an intermediate income threshold.

Section 3

The Political Economy of Policy Innovation

Chapter 5
The Political Economy of Modern Capitalism

ABSTRACT

This chapter revisits the debate on modern capitalism. While capitalism has many pitfalls, its unprecedented ability to create wealth through the invisible hand remains compelling. A missing piece in the discourse on the failure of capitalism and the ineffectiveness of regulations is that, while mainstream, neoliberal economic thinking puts a lot of trust in the ability of competitive markets to deliver efficient outcomes. The rise of the superstar firms has resulted in the birth of oligopolies in the private sector. This trend is exacerbated by the infusion of politics, which further weakens the purpose of a markets-based system, regarding helping guide incentives. Policymaking must reimagine the outcome of the interactive effects of markets with the digital economy as we seek ways to address the fundamental challenge of inclusive growth. To turn innovation from a paradigm to reality, the interplay of economics and politics is key.

There's not a single country that actually approaches economics in a pure, free market, capitalist way. I like the free market - but it very much exists only in textbooks. If I had a choice, and we could live in a very pure world, I would be a supporter of the free markets.

— Dambisa Moyo

DOI: 10.4018/978-1-7998-7383-9.ch005

WHAT HAPPENED to the theory of convergence? The decades-long rise in inequality is not abating. According to the 2020 *World Social Report,* global inequality is getting worse, with the richest one percent of the population increasing their share of global income between 1990 and 2015, while the 40 percent at the lower end of the income distribution earned less than a quarter of total income. The 2021 edition of the World's Real-time Billionaires, published by Forbes, shows that the world's 10 richest billionaires control over $1 trillion in combined wealth.

To put this into perspective, this is much higher than the GDP of every nation on earth, with a few exceptions. A 2019 analysis based on data from the World Bank by the financial literacy website, HowMuch.net, reveals that while the largest 15 economies in the world account for 75 percent of total global GDP – totaling $85.8 trillion in 2018 – the low-income countries with a combined population of about 705 million people represent only 0.6 percent.

The issue of income and wealth disparity has been on the front burner of the global policy debate for some time. It is not new. What is new, it appears, is the pace at which the interactive effects of the forces of globalization and digital disruptions are producing a more unequal distribution of capital and labor income – thereby exacerbating the fate of the marginalized. Oxfam's 2020 report, *Time to Care*, shows the flaws in the current economic system with the world's 2,153 billionaires having more wealth than 60 percent of the global population – about 4.6 billion people. The report takes a deep dive into the regional and gender distribution and provides further evidence that the 22 richest men in the world are wealthier than all the women in Africa.

The ongoing digital disruptions are reshaping markets, with distributional implications for technology deployment across nations, regions, firms, industries, and occupations, along with the concomitant impact on the distribution of rewards. In the same vein, state structures, rentier capitalism, globalization, tax havenry, conflicts, structural adjustment, Schumpeterian innovation, multilateralism in a multipolar world, transactionalism, and asymmetric shocks are all drivers of these global imbalances, with distortionary impacts on lives and livelihoods.

Much has been said about the deleterious impact of the 2008 financial crisis on the bottom 90 percent, but the scale of the long-lasting detrimental effects of the COVID-19 pandemic is yet to be ascertained. In the presence of still many unknowns, economic impacts are difficult to predict. However, we know one thing: the eventual overall damage will be huge. Much like how pre-existing medical conditions like hypertension, diabetes, or coronary heart disease can increase fatality risk for a patient infected with COVID-19, the economic systems of poor countries entered the pandemic with fragile health systems, food insecurity, financial exclusion, infrastructure deficit, decline in commodity prices, unreliable regional production chains, and weak institutions, among others.

While much progress has been made in terms of income inequality between countries during the past quarter century, due, partly, to rapid economic growth in emerging economies like China and India, significant between-country gaps remain. In the same vein, income and wealth are increasingly concentrated at the top of the distribution – with historically marginalized groups like Indigenous peoples, migrants and refugees, racial and ethnic minorities, women, and the disabled suffering[1] disproportionately (United Nations, 2020).

The COVID-19 pandemic is a global, once-in-a-century health crisis, but unfortunately, the world's most vulnerable people and communities will reel from the impacts for decades, long after it is a forgotten issue in much of the Global North. Building a more resilient economy after COVID-19 will be crucial to the billions of livelihoods that have been disrupted. The United Nations espouses the dangers in failing to address the existential threats this poses to human existence:

The measurements and impacts of inequality go far beyond income and purchasing power. Inequalities of opportunity affect a person's life expectancy and access to basic services such as healthcare, education, water, and sanitation. They can curtail a person's human rights, through discrimination, abuse, and lack of access to justice. In 2018, we saw the world's 12th consecutive year of decline in global freedom, with 71 countries suffering net declines in political and civil liberties. High levels of inequality of opportunity discourage skills accumulation, choke economic and social mobility, and human development and, consequently, depress economic growth. It also entrenches uncertainty, vulnerability and insecurity, undermines trust in institutions and government, increases social discord and tensions and trigger violence and conflicts. There are growing evidence that high level of income and wealth inequality is propelling the rise of nativism and extreme forms of nationalism. In addition, the evolution of issues such as climate change, technology, and urbanization raise urgent policy challenges. For example, climate change is exacerbating environmental degradation, increasing the frequency and intensity of extreme weather events, and by no means impacting people uniformly. If climate change continues unaddressed it will increase inequality within countries and may even reverse current progress in reducing inequality between countries. Meanwhile, technology can be a great equalizer – by enhancing connectivity, financial inclusion, access to trade and public services, for instance – but those yet to be connected may experience further marginalization as a result, especially as progress is slowing, even reversing, among some constituencies. With a global trend toward urbanization, cities are becoming a growing site for inequalities. They find high levels of wealth and modern infrastructure coexist with pockets of severe deprivation, often side by side. This makes gaping and increasing levels of inequality all the more glaring within cities (United Nations, 2020; para. 8-10)

THE COLLAPSE OF CAPITALISM

About 250 years ago, Adam Smith was in a vantage position to observe industrial capitalism, albeit he could not imagine the scale of transformation it would bring to society. No doubt, the pitfalls of capitalism are littered all around us, due, principally, to short-term profit maximization prioritization at the detriment of societal well-being and environmental sustainability. Yet, it is difficult to deny the improvements in standards of living and the impacts of the concomitant innovations from the capitalist mode of wealth creation.

Capitalism has evolved over the past centuries, and the rise of individualism – vis-à-vis greater civil liberties, economic freedom, and property rights – meant that the role of government and the social contract paradigm has also changed significantly. In their 2016 piece, *Rethinking Capitalism*, Jacobs and Mazzucato allude to the limitations of mainstream economics in explaining how modern capitalism works, as well as why it no longer does, in key ways. They contend that this does not mean the pitfalls in modern capitalism are irredeemable, but existing analytical paradigms and economic models are grossly inadequate, and in some cases, broken and unfit.

Palmer in his 2011 edited volume, *The Morality of Capitalism*, describes capitalism as a system based on cultural, spiritual, and ethical values, and by extension, an organized system that embraces equality of rights because of its basic structures of ethical norms and rules:

Capitalism is not just about people trading butter for eggs in local markets, which has gone on for millennia. It's about adding value through the mobilization of human energy and ingenuity on a scale never seen before in human history, to create wealth for common people that would have dazzled and astonished the richest and most powerful kings, sultans, and emperors of the past. It's about the erosion of long-entrenched systems of power, domination, and privilege, and the opening of "careers to talent. (Palmer, 2011; p.4)

Palmer argues that the capitalist mode of production is far from being amoral as often portrayed by different interest groups, for whatever reasons, but rather, it is indeed what has made our lives possible. And regarding its ability to foster innovation and creativity, he says in the introduction section of his edited volume, *The Morality of Capitalism*, "Indeed, capitalism rests on a rejection of the ethics of loot and grab, the means by which most wealth enjoyed by the wealthy has been acquired in other economic and political systems."

In essence, capitalism has many pitfalls, but its unprecedented ability to create wealth – through the invisible hand – by providing incentives for business enterprises to voluntarily organize and coordinate the factors of production should never be taken for granted. Perhaps a more important task for policy is to reimagine the outcome of the interactive effects of markets with the digital economy as we seek ways to address the fundamental challenge of inclusive growth. Only then can the current global economic waves help drive an inclusive growth agenda that recognizes those at the lower end of the income distribution deserve a better deal, while not shying away from the dictates of rational choice theory that the representative economic agent will always choose a course of action that maximizes expected utility. Afterall, the bottom 90 percent is also highly heterogenous. The devil, as the saying goes, is in the detail.

A major characterization of the neoclassical production function is a standard assumption of profit maximization by firms. Under this framework, changes in a firm's revenue are linked to changes in the costs of capital and labor, with implications for competition, efficiency, and transparency. The past few decades have heralded a decline in labor's share of income, due to the prevailing highly capital-intensive multinational system of production. In addition to the concentration of capital ownership, this mode of wealth creation generates varying returns to different categories of labor, with workers at the top of the income distribution reaping disproportionately large rewards over time.

One missing piece in the discourse on the failure of capitalism (and the ineffectiveness of regulations) is that while mainstream, neoliberal economic thinking puts a lot of trust in the ability of competitive markets to deliver efficient outcomes – in the form of lower prices and a wider choice spectrum

– the rise of the superstar firms has resulted in the birth of oligopolies in the private sector (and in the public sector, partly through industrial policy, and partly through legislation from the onset). This trend is exacerbated by the infusion of politics, which, as corroborated by Crouch (2013), outrightly defeats the purpose of a markets-based system, regarding helping guide incentives.

Crouch argues that while capitalism is the only complex system that can deliver an efficient and innovative economy, the 2018 GFC has validated the notion that without state intervention, capitalism could cause more harm. This manifestation is quite common in developing countries where the line between business and state can often get blurry due to weak institutions, making corporate lobbying a critical element of success in the field of enterprise. Again, Palmer aptly explains this by making a distinction between free market capitalism and crony capitalism in his 2012 interview:

It's important to distinguish free-market capitalism from crony capitalism, a system that has mired many nations in corruption and backwardness and is, sadly, on the rise. In many countries, if someone is rich, there is a very good chance that he (rarely she) holds political power or is a close relative, friend or supporter – in a word, a crony – of those who do hold power, and that his wealth came not from being a producer of valued goods and services but from enjoying the privileges that the state can confer on some at the expense of others. (Palmer, 2012; para 7).

Stiglitz (2016) examines inequality over a 30-year period from the lens of both mainstream economics and modern trends in capitalism. He finds that while the rewards that accrued to workers reflected the marginal productivity of labor, it is a different story for corporate executives, whose rewards had no correlation with productivity. Stiglitz's analysis supports the argument on the harmful effects of rentier capitalism on the economic system. This underscores the need for policy innovation to fix the pitfalls in the 20th century income distribution system – in which the share of labor in total output has shrunk steadily, leading to a stagnant middle class and vast wealth accumulation from rental income.

Christopher (2020) in *Rentier Capitalism* examines this issue from the perspective that the rise of neoliberalism in the early 21st century was not so much for free markets and competitive outcomes, buy for private ownership of scarce assets – such as land, intellectual property, natural resources, and digital platforms – through privatization and allied means for plutocrats. Using the UK economy as a case study, and in the hope that his work would offer useful lessons for other jurisdictions facing rentier dominance, he highlights how key strategic sectors – like finance, real estate, utilities, and pharmaceuticals – got infused with rentierism. Standing (2017), in *The Corruption of Capitalism*, opines that rising economic inequality is not necessarily the most fundamental sin of capitalism. Rather, he is more concerned, just like Christopher, about the rigging of global capitalism in favour of plutocrats and to the detriment of precariat. He also calls for a new, equitable income and wealth distribution system suitable for this era. In an edited extract of *The Corruption of Capitalism* titled *The Five Lies Of Rentier Capitalism*, the third lie is characterized thus:

The third lie of rentier capitalism is that the institutional structure of capitalism built in the globalization era is 'good for growth'. To the contrary: it has hindered growth and made what growth that has occurred less sustainable, with rising ecological costs that are partly the outcome of rentier mechanisms, notably trade and investment accords, of which there are over 3,000. There is no evidence that those promote investment. Most studies have found only weak or non-existent correlations between those treaties and investment flows. Nor is there much correlation between opening up to foreign investment and growth. Instead, the correlation is with financial instability. (Standing, 2016; para 12).

Surprisingly, perhaps, the trend on capitalism refutes John Maynard Keynes' sentiment in *The General Theory of Employment, Interest and Money* that ultimately, the spread of capitalism "would mean the euthanasia of the rentier, and, consequently, the euthanasia of the cumulative oppressive power of the capitalist to exploit the scarcity-value of capital." (Marxists.org, n.d.; para 9).

Keynes wrote his piece in 1936. I am writing this in 2022. Obviously, after 86 years, not much has changed. To put it more mildly, rentier capitalism is waxing stronger. But, perhaps, to be fair to Keynes, it should be said that there was no Internet in 1936. There was no Uber. And certainly, no Airbnb. We now enjoy the full complement of Industry 4.0. It is fair to acknowledge that times have changed, and technological innovations are driving growth and sparking productivity gains across a wide range of industries. As such, to the extent that fixing or replacing rentier capitalism is one of the defining challenges of our era, policy innovation has a major role. And to deliver effective and efficient outcomes, markets must be the transmission channels of policy innovation. This is not impossible.

Clearly, policy failures have contributed to the outcomes of unfair economic designs that perpetuated extreme wealth accumulation on the backs of marginalized populations – in both formal and informal economic societies – working under poor conditions. This is not acceptable. And humanity can do much better. But, wait a second before you lash wildly at the markets. There is still no alternative to capitalism. And to help our reasoning and ability to innovate policy as we navigate the uncharted waters of digital disruptions and structural change, it is important to understand that capitalism entails more than markets for the exchange of goods and services; it does cover an entire system of innovation, wealth creation, and social change. My point: it can be refined; it can be improved upon. Indeed, economic justice matters, but capitalism is the lubricant of democracy. It is easy to blame modern capitalism for the perils and delusions of society, but it is not easy to offer an alternative. Paul Krugman lends his voice: "Capitalism can run, even flourish, in a society of selfish cynics. But a non-market economy cannot," (Krugman, 1997; para. 9). Facts, events, and anecdotes sometimes intersect in a counterintuitive way. Tough to reconcile.

ESG and Rentier Capitalism

One wonders, based on the discussion so far, what role policy innovation could play in fixing the many ills associated with rentierism. Labor markets have witnessed significant shifts and polarizations in recent decades, with disproportionate impacts on the poor and marginalized. Such polarization and economic divergence have only exacerbated existing income inequality. It is therefore important to strike a better deal for workers in the bottom half of the income spectrum. Due to historically high global inequality, the increased flow of income and wealth to the top of the economic ladder in the aftermath of the COVID-19 pandemic has raised concerns on the potential for a "K-shaped" recovery – in which case divergent recovery trajectories exacerbate the economic conditions of marginalized groups.

Certainly, the ghost of Nobel Laureate, Milton Friedman, has not stopped hovering over the environmental, social, and governance (ESG) debate. While deliberate innovations to promote competition are in order, it is another matter entirely what such policy designs would look like, and the responsibilities of policy entrepreneurs in the design and execution phases. This, again, shows that there may be no proven, real alternative to capitalism, albeit there is no shortage of stark choices. In 1970, Friedman wrote his influential paper, *The*

Social Responsibility of Business is to Increase its Profits, which dwells on corporate social responsibility and shareholder primacy:

There is one and only one social responsibility of business—to use its resources and engage in activities designed to increase its profits so long as it stays within the rules of the game, which is to say, engages in open and free competition, without deception or fraud. (Friedman, 1970; p. 6)

While Friedman's take on shareholder value maximization is often mischaracterized in the ESG investing world today, it is important to understand that the central tenet of the paper is more about the need to abide by the rules of the game – to the extent that the primary objective of a corporation is to make money for its shareholders. Traditionally, ESG issues have not been of primary concern to investors, but the laser focus on fixing the ills of social inequality and tackling urgent challenges like climate change in the past two decades or so has triggered an exponential growth in ESG activities.

Due, partly, to the proliferation in technological innovations over the last decade and the increased attention on ESG in the international development and finance community, there is a growing political appetite to experiment with new paradigms to problem solving through policy innovation. The structural challenges, high inequality, and labor market polarization that accompanied the Great Recession have resulted in the recent global backlash against economic globalization, international migration, and other neoliberal economic policies. As a result, not only are governments hyperfocused on the costs, benefits, and distributional implications of public investments and policies across regions and sectors, corporate executives are also increasingly navigating the complex duality associated with business and philanthropy by simultaneously advancing corporate and social goals through impact projects that resonate with the broader society. Indeed, the ESG discourse, in a way, is a battle for the soul of modern capitalism.

Inequitable Systems and Their Second Order Effects

COVID-19 represents an unprecedented shock to labor markets, with low-wage, essential workers on the receiving end – given the labor market effects of the pandemic vis-à-vis changes in labor costs. While jobs are fully back to pre-pandemic levels in many jurisdictions – especially for the highest wage earners – many low-wage workers are still reeling from the aftermath. The social injustices perpetuated by rentier capitalism are not limited to wages and compensations alone. There are second order effects. For instance, transportation mobility and housing are key issues. The inequitable effects of transportation policies on underserved populations, especially in dense urban centers, are well documented. Moreso, due to the widening gap between housing cost and income, housing affordability remains a pervasive challenge, particularly for low-income earners whose housing and transport decisions are driven by these nuances.

Policy decisions on congestion pricing, emission standard, highway capacity, and highway pricing depend largely on household preferences. Public parks and green space have major impacts on the physical, psychological, and social well-being of urban residents. In many ways, congestion and pollution externalities associated with automobile use have implications for location choices and leisure time; creating a more efficient, sustainable, equitable, and integrated transportation network that improves mobility is key. These issues cannot be addressed outside of the policy innovation-market nexus.

The cyclicality of the labor share of output, especially following a recession, has received considerable attention in the literature (Elsby et al., 2013). Among others, uncertainty and structural factors perpetuate wage depression in the aftermath of a recession. And, due to their largely labor-intensive mode of wealth creation, small businesses are a vulnerable group. As such, rentier capitalism, which favors economic activity reallocation with asymmetric and distortionary impacts on labor's share of output, can only exacerbate existing gaps. Policy interventions must prevent a further erosion of labor's share of GDP, and the concomitant increase in inequality.

In terms of innovation, the shift in economic activity from small, and often labor-intensive businesses, to large, capital-intensive ones, merits the attention of policy. While this is part of the broader analysis of the rentier system – to the extent that it is one of the key drivers of income and wealth inequality over the years – the fact that the fall is often not within a typical firm, but a steady reallocation in favor of the big, capital-intensive ones, makes it a major policy issue. Research shows this is one of the reasons for the emergence of "superstar firms" with market power in key sectors of the economy.

In the broader context of the inclusive development paradigm, the notion that growth just for the sake of growth is no longer enough continues to dominate the development literature. And this explains, at least partly, why inclusive growth has become extremely popular in recent times. Inclusive growth basically calls for more segments of society to participate in the economy, since the benefits of economic growth have not accrued to those at the bottom end of the income spectrum. From climate change and parental leave to wellness, happiness, gender pay gap, and equitable workplace practices, policy innovation has a major role in addressing the current flaws in our economic system. Indeed, under the appropriate incentive frameworks, policy innovation can help move the needle on issues like happiness, fairness, equity, and social justice.

IMPLICATIONS FOR AFRICA'S STATE-BUSINESS RELATIONS

By all accounts, the discussion above deserves further analysis in the African case. This is especially important given that except for in recent times, political leaders on the continent have typically come from the military, academia, or the law profession – making the predominant occupation of government the provision of social justice and public goods, albeit the more ambitious and interventionist regimes occasionally make forays into industrial policy and other state-led market coordination efforts.

Dani Rodrik in *Institutions for High-Quality Growth* espouses the role of institutions, through political incentives, on policy outcomes. Rodrik (1999) argues that countries with strong institutions tend to benefit from the resource economy, due to the minimization of perverse political incentives. In other words, until institutional arrangements are conducive enough to offer incentives for entrepreneurs to take risk and create value, the potential of the private sector cannot be fully harnessed. Credible commitment of the state to policies, deals, or arrangements is a key element of an effective state-business relations because:

Trust in state-business relations is an outcome of repeated interactions between bureaucrats and politicians on the one hand and private sector actors on the other, and can occur both through formal mechanisms (such as periodic meetings of a Joint Economic Council) and informal mechanisms (such as through networks of friendship and contacts that state and private actors may have). (Sen, 2015; p. 9)

State-business relations – whether collusive or collaborative – are a core part of the political economy dynamics of countries. Te Velde (2006) explains four key drivers of state-business relations: (i) how the private sector is organized compared to the public sector, (ii)) how the public sector is organized compared to the private sector, (iii) how the state interacts with the private sector, and (iv) frameworks to avoid collusion. A fundamental failure of the current socioeconomic system lies in its inability to explain or correct the inequitable, and often arbitrary, distribution of wealth and income. The political economy of development discourse recognizes the important role of effective state-business relations in harnessing the necessary resources and collaborations required for structural transformation and institutional reform, albeit the dichotomy may blur under certain circumstances:

Both collusive and collaborative state-business relations are an outcome of close, and often personalised, interactions between the state and the business sector so, in practice, it is often difficult to distinguish between the two types of relations in many country contexts. Collaborative state-business relations can turn collusive if economic and political elites find larger gains in short-run rent-seeking, rather than through cooperation and coordination that delivers increased growth, innovation and capability development only in the long term. (Sen, 2015; p. 6).

Bhagwati (1993), in *India Transition: Freeing the Economy*, places the political economy of India and its development trajectory in context from when it gained independence in 1947 through is centrally planned economy model, including the 1960s and 1970s when state-business relations produced rent-seeking outcomes and cartel-type dynamics. While democratic socialism shaped policy in India, in much of this era, the adoption of a market-based economy in the early 1990s rekindled the importance of credible commitments of the state to policies. In a way, this reinforces why entrepreneurs and investors, both local and foreign, need an assurance that the state will not change the rules of the game midway.

The business-politics nexus in Africa's political economy is in a flux, with implications for rent-seeking and its deleterious effects, on the one hand, and synergistic outcomes on the other hand. In contemporary analysis of the democracy-plutocracy nexus, Leftwich (2009) puts into perspective how a collusive state-business setting may lead to the capture of state agencies by powerful political and economic elites, who, in turn, directly profit from their political connections, thereby destroying value through unproductive rent-seeking. A nuanced analysis of well-functioning state and market institutions also involves how institutions affect actors – and the ways economic agents and political actors shape institutions. It is not all bad news; Maxfield and

Schneider (1997) allude to instances where state-business collaborations produce synergistic outcomes for the benefit of society.

A good understanding of the political economy barriers posed by ineffective state-business relations will offer insights into the appropriate policy innovations that can help move the needle. To turn innovation from a paradigm to reality, the interplay of economics and politics is key. On the ability of innovation to raise societal welfare, KnowledgeHub, an online website maintained by the United Nations Industrial Development Organization says:

Innovation is integral to a country's performance as enhanced productivity ultimately results in higher social welfare. The large disparities in income and social development between developed and developing countries are often rooted in considerable differences in their industrial development and use of technology, and the resulting gaps in their productivity. These gaps may grow with the shift towards the new industrial revolution, summarized in the concept of industry 4.0. However, effective utilization of innovation enables sustainable solutions for inclusive economic development and environmental challenges. Therefore, to achieve transformative changes and to transfer and deploy technology for entrepreneurship, innovation needs to be scaled-up and spread globally (United Nations Industrial Development Organization, n.d.)

Harrison et al. (2013) in a World Bank paper reveals that while infrastructure and access to finance are a major constraint on business competitiveness in Africa, political monopoly – with manifestations of weak institutions like corruption, nepotism, and uncertainty caused by the absence of the rule of law – portends great danger. This fosters a plutocratic model of capitalism because of the failure, not of capitalism itself, but of politics. The wealthy and powerful circumvent the income and wealth distribution system by paying little attention to the actual production of goods and services but are hyperfocused on scarce assets ownership through a skillful mastery of the politics-business dynamics that allow the economy to be run by the rich and for the rich.

For instance, the pervasive concentration of wealth and opportunities at the top of the ladder has often contributed to the perennial civil unrests in some parts of Africa (Ighobor, 2018). In the absence of a guaranteed pathway to economic security, leading to worse economic outcomes in later life, people tend to have less trust in institutions and the concomitant sense of injustice can breed other ills. Anne Case and Angus Deaton underscore this in their 2020 book, *Deaths of Despair and the Future of Capitalism*: "In the past two decades, deaths of despair from suicide, drug overdose, and alcoholism have risen dramatically." Helping marginalized and impoverished groups to build wealth and acquire income-generating skills is a starting point. Policy innovation, with the digital revolution acting as a catalyst, can help in this regard.

REGIONAL INTEGRATION AND DIGITIZATION

After the China Miracle,[2] Africa has long been cited as the final frontier for global growth and investment. But considering the recent lackluster growth – due, partly, to the commodities supercycle, crash in global energy prices, weak private capital inflows, and other structural and institutional constraints – the dynamics of its economic system do not seem to align with this expectation. Nonetheless, Africa continues to grow in importance, as well as the strategic commercial opportunities on the continent. The March 7, 2019 edition of The Economist alludes to the new scramble for Africa: "Governments and businesses from all around the world are rushing to strengthen diplomatic, strategic, and commercial ties."

Compared to regions like Europe and North America, intra-African trade is low; this reflects, partly, a relatively lower level of integration and development than in other regions (Allard et al., 2016). About 1.3 billion people live in Africa, with a collective GDP of roughly $ 3.4 trillion. In comparison, the US has a population of 328 million, with about $20 trillion in GDP. The low intra-regional trade on the continent can be explained by, among other factors, limited market size, fragmented economic space, and both demand- and supply-side constraints (Ancharaz et al., 2011).[3] The continent's poor performance on the intra-regional trade metric poses a substantial challenge for development. Deepening economic integration is key to accelerating progress towards the SDGs.

In many ways, the continent's future appears to depend critically on harnessing innovations and the opportunities offered by the current bourgeoning global digital economy to create opportunities for entrepreneurs and its growing youth population. Technological progress is a major driver of trade, financial integration, investment opportunities, increased knowledge transfer, and development (World Bank & WTO, 2019). This underscores the importance of harnessing the benefits of technology and economic integration to defragment markets, reduce efficiency, and boost productivity.

The AfCFTA was adopted in March 2018 when 44 African countries signed a framework to establish a single continental market for goods and services, in addition to a customs union with free movement of capital and business travellers. The AfCFTA brings together 1.3 billion people in a $3.4 trillion economic bloc that is the largest free trade area since the establishment of the WTO in 1994. The pact is expected to raise intra-African trade by as much as 52 percent above the baseline by 2022 (United Nations Economic Commission for Africa, 2018). On January 1, 2021, African countries officially began trading under the new continent-wide pact, which is expected, among other things, to foster industrialization and create jobs.

Like never before, the COVID-19 pandemic has moved digitalization to the front burner of the global trade, finance, and sustainable development agenda, and the case for increased economic integration and intra-African trade has never been stronger. Intra-African trade has the potential for building sustainable economic development and integration; working with key private, public, and development stakeholders, the continent can leverage PPPs to innovate policy in key sectors and domains to help businesses and communities bounce back stronger from the pandemic.

THE POLITICAL ECONOMY OF AFRICA'S INDUSTRIAL TRANSFORMATION

Agricultural transformation in Africa has not advanced as predicted by the consensus development orthodoxy of the 1950s and 1960s. Due to digitalization and structural shifts in the global economy, industrialization prospects through the traditional progression from agriculture to manufacturing to services in many developing economies are fading fast. While a thorough inspection of the facts matters, much of the available evidence supports the view that Africa's industrialization prospects are still alive, albeit it may not happen in a linear fashion predicted by theory. What does this mean for policy? Often referred to as the last frontier in the global economy, the continent's young population, huge resource endowments, low-cost labor availability, and other important demographic shifts have major implications.

The role of manufacturing in economic growth and development is unambiguous in the development discourse; the premise for industrialization as a sine qua non in the quest for growth is richly grounded in theory. From Lewis' surplus labor paradigm and Rostow's five stages of economic growth model to Kuznet's (1973) dual economy and the switch from agriculture to industry propositions and Linder's focus on supply conditions as a basis for exchange, the link between industrial productivity and economic growth is clear.

Despite its many flaws, the role of theory in much of the literature in explaining trade patterns in terms of productivity differences, remains compelling (Olayele, 2019). In addition to the important role it plays in fostering structural adjustments, the tradable sector allows for productivity improvements that foster higher wages, profits, and capital investments. This underpins how industrial diversification in tradable sectors can catalyze greater efficiency and productivity, which in turn, drive innovation and higher incomes.

From the capitalist class and working class to trade unions and pressure groups that triggered major political and socioeconomic transformations, the modern global economy is a product of industrialization. The world over, dynamic modern sectors that absorb workers from agrarian and subsistence sectors of the economy remain critical for wealth creation and socioeconomic mobility. Advances in the modern knowledge economy, driven largely by technologies and innovation, continue to foster the reallocation of workers from traditional, low-productive sectors to high-productivity, often digitally enabled activities. Not only is this trend generating prosperity and increased efficiencies in production processes, but it is also driving competitiveness and trade openness as rightly predicted by economic theory.

The agrarian, pre-industrial age operated under social, political, and cultural systems with limited means of production. Following the mapping of the global economy in the aftermath of the Age of Discovery and European exploration, industrial development lies at the heart of the sustained economic prosperity the world has seen. Much of the innovation and increase in living standards in modern history – particularly in the late 1700s and early 1800s – was possible because of the shift from agrarian and handicraft paradigms to models where economy activity prioritized industry as witnessed during the Industrial Revolution in Britain. From Europe and the U.S. to Asia and the emerging economies of the world, industrialization is a common denominator in the growth accounting process.

The Second Industrial Revolution, which ended on the eve of World War I, heralded the rise in the role of technology in society. This led to the unprecedented growth in cities, immigration, and factories from the late 19th to early 20th centuries – along with the emergence of wealthy entrepreneurs and a burgeoning middle class. Then came the Third Industrial Revolution, and the internet, which revolutionized business and society through the pivotal role of digital communications technology. Amid the ongoing Fourth Industrial Revolution, humanity is witnessing a fusion of innovations in artificial intelligence, 3D printing, quantum computing, robotics, autonomous vehicles, biotechnology, the Internet of Things, and other technologies (Niler, 2019).

Of course, beyond these theories, history, political factors, and other institutional dynamics are crucial to understanding the patterns that we see in economic systems that are different in structural compositions vis-à-vis the Western industrialized economies these models were designed for. This is particularly important in the political economy of policy innovation discourse in Africa – the primary preoccupation of this book. I argue that policy innovation is a complex, non-linear process; this offers a fresh perspective for examining richer dynamics by which the political economy nuances of countries pave the way for accounting for the effects of other interactive outcomes on the overall economy and society.

For a long time, industrialization has been touted as the panacea to the myriad of issues hampering wealth creation, prosperity, and socioeconomic progress in Africa. Despite consistently featuring on the front burner of the development agenda in many countries on the continent, Africa's failure to industrialize despite the myriad of policies deployed by governments across the continent to help factor reallocation efforts remains a concern.

In the context of the growth and industrialization debate, this calls into question, in a way, the effectiveness of policy interventions targeted at altering production structures in favor of promising sectors with high growth, innovation, and structural transformation prospects. Signe (2020) alludes to how "structural adjustment reforms like privatization of state-owned enterprises and trade liberalization, along with foreign aid, restarted African manufacturing in the 1990s," (p.99) as well as the effect of Achilles' heel – increased competitive pressures from foreign products and African currencies – on the eventual decline of the sector. Rodrik (2016) explains the dangers inherent in premature deindustrialization in both economic and political terms, while noting that the low- and middle-income countries are at a greater risk of "running out of industrialization opportunities", compared to the advanced, industrialized countries. He argues that the contemporary trend in deindustrialization is driven by the forces of globalization and automations due to technological innovations, with countries in Asia relatively insulated – while those in Latin America have remained vulnerable.

While Rodrik's economic argument that deindustrialization reduces the potential for growth potential "and the possibilities for convergence with income levels of the advanced economies" due to the highly dynamic nature of the manufacturing sector is in order, the leapfrog hypothesis makes it somewhat contentious. Rodrik's premise remains that deindustrialization at income levels significantly lower than the threshold at which advanced economies began to deindustrialize may produce a situation in which "These developing countries are turning into service economies without having gone through a proper experience of industrialization." Perhaps the political ramification of Rodrik's thesis is more relevant in the industrial development discourse of Africa. Rodrik presents the dangers of premature deindustrialization in the context of its potential in constituting a drag on democratization, in addition to making it more fragile:

Mass political parties have traditionally been a by-product of industrialization. Without the discipline and coordination that an organized labor force provides, the bargains between the elite and non-elite needed for democratic transitions and consolidation are less likely to take place (Rodrik, 2016; p. 5)

Nonetheless, some other scholars contend that it may be too soon to conclude that industrialization has eluded Africa (see Nguimkeu & Zeufack, 2019; and Kruse et al., 2021). To corroborate this, Kruse et al. (2021) find that while the level of manufacturing employment in sub-Saharan Africa is low, the continent witnessed a reversal in deindustrialization in the early 2000s (see Table 1). This is not without a caveat though.

Table 1. Share of manufacturing in GDP and labor force

	Employment			Nominal value added			Real value added		
Region	**1990**	**2010**	**2018**	**1990**	**2010**	**2018**	**1990**	**2010**	**201**
Advanced Asia	26.1	15.4	13.9	24.5	19.9	19.7	17.9	19.7	19.
Developing Asia	10.0	11.9	13.4	16.3	19.0	18.2	14.2	18.1	18.
Latin America	14.1	11.0	10.3	22.0	16.5	14.9	18.7	17.1	15.
MENA	15.9	15.0	14.5	20.5	16.8	17.5	15.9	17.4	16.
Sub-Saharan Africa	7.2	7.2	8.4	15.4	11.4	10.4	12.7	11.4	10.

Note: manufacturing share (%) in employment, nominal GDP, and real GDP by region, unweighted averages.

Source: Kruse et al. (2021)

While differences in research design and methods are attributed to the divergence of Kruse et al.'s results from Rodrik's findings, it is important to note that before the renaissance witnessed in the manufacturing economy of the 2000s, disappearing textile factories and ceramics plants in Nigeria, redundant industrial parks in Ethiopia, and non-existent footwear industry in South Africa were becoming commonplace on the continent (de Vries et al., 2021). This confirms that while manufacturing jobs grew during the period under review, manufacturing productivity remained stagnant. This trend is consequential, with major implications for fixing existing structural constraints that limit Africa's economic modernization potential through manufacturing.

Clearly, fragmentation, informality, and demand- and supply-side constraints – which continue to hamper large-scale economic transformation in Africa – are key issues that come to mind. While economies of scale and productivity gains from larger scale operations are key to unlocking industrial development, institutional dynamics in the context of state-business configurations capable of creating competitiveness-enhancing business environments are equally important.

The analysis so far has major political economy implications, especially in the context of the import substitution industrialization (ISI) in Africa. Home-grown ISI became commonplace on the continent during the second half of the 20th century, partly because having just gained independence, not only did many African governments embrace nationalism, but they were also reticent to neoliberalism. This meant that much of the economic policy prescriptions from the Western industrialized nations were shunned. Another contributing factor was that ISI became part of the tools employed by the colonial powers "to right the wrongs of colonization by industrializing newly independent African countries" (Julian, 2021, para. 1)

Due to a combination of state-led interventions and protectionist policies, the manufacturing sector witnessed growth in the immediate post-independence era. However, by the middle of the 1980s, "a series of external shocks—including oil price increases, commodity price decreases, real interest rate rises, withering public coffers, and the limitations of domestic markets—were major factors in industrial decline in the region." (Signe, 2020; p. 99)

Page (2014) attributes Africa's failure to industrialize to both bad policy and bad luck. Bad policy because most African countries in the ISI era had similar industrial policies with a dominant role for the state in structural and investment climate reforms. This led to a situation in which, as Page explains, "Import substitution sowed the seeds of its own destruction." (para. 7). While the analysis alludes to the beneficial outcomes of policy interventions in terms of overall macroeconomic management and growth performance, it characterizes the downsides in the context of the associated deadweight loss that often stifles productivity and competitive outcomes thus:

The tendency of many African governments to assign a leading role to the state in creating and operating manufacturing firms simply made the problem worse. Investments were often made with little regard to efficiency, and the managerial capacity of the state was badly overstretched (Page, 2014; para 7).

Just like serendipitous encounters are not uncommon in policy outcomes, bad luck is also not a rarity. To the extent that ISI was aimed at enhancing the prospects of self-reliance and self-actualization – considering the strong argument in favor of industrialization in the context of job creation and its productivity-enhancing power – the fact that Africa is less industrialized today (Julian, 2021) than it was almost five decades ago remains unacceptable. This becomes even more worrisome when analyzed in the context of the state-led economic transformation in China and the Asian tigers.

In the 1950s, Taiwan, South Korea, Hong Kong, and Singapore all shared similar economic features – in terms of output, structure, and quality – with many African countries. But over time, through an industrial policy that struck a right balance between infant industry protection and large-scale investment and subsidization – thereby paving the way for global competitiveness –these economies rapidly transitioned from rural, agricultural economies to global leaders in manufacturing. Again, Page espouses the role of bad luck in Africa's failure to industrialize:

The terms of trade shocks and economic crises of the 1970s and 1980s brought with them a 20-year period of macroeconomic stabilization, trade liberalization and privatization. Import competition forces inefficient firms, both public and private, out of business. Uncertainty with the outcome of the adjustment process and low or negative economic growth meant that there was little private investment overall and practically none in industry. Political instability and conflict also caused investors to hold back. When Africa emerged from its long economic hibernation around the turn of the 21st century, African industry was no longer competing with the high-wage industrial "North," as it had in the 1960s and 1970s. It was competing with Asia. From the point of view of industrial development the timing of the region's economic recovery was unlucky to say the least (Page, 2014; para 6).

ISI as an industrial policy is anchored on the dependency theory-type Prebisch–Singer hypothesis and the notion that infant industry protection and inward-looking policies that provide local substitutes for foreign goods imports can foster industrial diversification. This produces an economic structure with key local industries accounting for a significant share of the domestic economy, with the attendant nationalistic tendencies. Due to the rent-seeking behavior often associated with protectionism, the deleterious effects of SAPs in the 1980s, and the debt crisis, ISI became a colossal failure (World Bank, 1994).

Of the several reasons that led to the dominance of the SAP as the economic management paradigm in developing economies in the 1980s, Mkandawire and Soludo (1998) attribute the loss of faith in neoKeynesianism in the late 1970s and the rise of the new classical economics school of thought as a fundamental rationale. By the same token, the political characterization of big government as being incompatible with efficient economic management – as evidenced by the collapse of the Soviet system – led to the ascendancy of neoclassicism as the prevalent economic doctrine. With deregulation and privatization becoming the dominant political economy doctrines across much of the industrialized world, leaders of Western industrial nations like Margaret Thatcher in Britain, Ronald Reagan in the U.S., and Helmut Kohl in Germany became fierce advocates of neoliberalism. In its 1994 report on the impact of SAP on the Nigerian economy, the World Bank concludes that:

Under the Structural Adjustment Program (SAP) introduced in 1986, Nigeria reformed its foreign exchange system, trade policies, and business and agricultural regulations. This success notwithstanding, per capita income is still only US$320 and consumption and income are little higher (in real per capita terms) than they were in the early 1970s before the oil boom. Because over 90 percent of Nigeria's export earnings are from oil, growth in agriculture and manufacturing could offset little of the large drop in purchasing power that resulted from the collapse of oil export revenues that had prompted the adoption of the SAP. For Nigeria to break its vicious circle of excessive public spending, inflation, and exchange rate depreciation, and to reach the virtuous circle achieved by these other developing countries, it will need to adopt a package of stabilization and structural measures that ensures the efficient use of resources (by both the public and private sectors) and the provision of basic social services. This path offers Nigeria the best prospects for sustaining economic growth and poverty reduction. (p. iii)

African countries were disproportionately affected by SAP because compared to other economies in the transition phase, high debt levels already put economies on the continent in a precarious position. When examined in the context of the differing socioeconomic and cultural systems in Africa and much of the Western world, this, again, calls to question the wisdom in extending the application of economic management models in industrial countries to traditional, agrarian economies – where the philosophy of Ubuntu prioritizes shared humanity and collective consciousness over liberal individualism that permeates much of the West.

Collier and Gunning (1999) and Mkandawire and Soludo (1998) explain the role of "internalist" and "externalist" perspectives on policy outcomes in Africa. Collier and Gunning argue that domestic destiny is not as important as domestic policy factors; Mkandawire and Soludo maintain that the initial conditions and history in the context of both internal and external factors are key. Debt and poverty levels in many developing countries rose sharply after the implementation of SAP (Shah, 2013). If the notion of development is fundamentally about improving well-being, then, almost four decades after implementing SAP in Africa, the prescription has yet to yield any significant results. To put it mildly, SAP failed Africa. Almost a quarter century after, Mkandawire and Soludo's assessment remains valid:

For almost two decades, countries in sub-Saharan Africa (SSA) have implemented structural-adjustment programs (SAPs), and at the threshold of a new millennium, Africa may be graduating from being a region with "lost development decades" to becoming the world's "forgotten continent." After more than a decade of acrimonious debates and tonnes of evaluation reports, there is an increasing convergence of views that SAPs have not worked and that, as designed, they are grossly defective as a policy package for addressing the endemic poverty and pervasive underdevelopment of the region (Mkandawire & Soludo, 1998; p. xi).

Signe (2018) corroborates the role of regional bodies and governments on the continent in "breaking down trade barriers, improving financial structures, and investing public resources in much-needed infrastructure" in a way that echoes Nurkse's (1971) sentiment in his seminal work on balanced growth theory. Of the many theoretical justifications for addressing the issue of market fragmentation, Nurkse's balanced growth model provides one of the most compelling arguments in support of the AfCFTA. Nurkse contends that the size of the market is both determined and defined by the volume of production.

Nurkse argues for simultaneous, large-scale public-sector investments in key sectors to fix the challenge of market fragmentation, thereby raising productivity and paving the way for increased private sector participation in the economy. He contends that output expansion in both the agricultural and manufacturing sectors is key for intersectoral balance; this thesis succinctly captures the imperative of the African case in terms of explaining market size in the context of productivity:

The limited size of the domestic market in a low-income country can thus constitute an obstacle to the application of capital by any individual firm or industry working for the market. In this sense the small domestic market is an obstacle to development generally (Nurkse, 1971; p. 118).

Signe (2018), again, itemizes how recent gains on the continent can drive further growth in manufacturing, given the rise in intra-African trade in manufactured goods from 10 percent of total trade in 2000 to 16 percent in 2014. And when analyzed in the context of the AfCFTA, the importance of state-business relations – as discussed earlier in this chapter – in fostering growth and structural transformation becomes obvious. Ample evidence abounds on the linkages among state-business relations, growth, investment, and investment productivity (Te Velde, 2013; Te Velde & Lemma, 2017).

Agriculture remains the mainstay of most economies across Africa; most of the citizens are farmers, and those who are not farmers earn a living in the informal, subsistence economy. Therefore, while the debate on the leapfrog effect continues, policymakers must prioritize investments in agriculture and the rural economy to build capacity and create pathways for players in the sector to earn higher incomes and transition into the formal economy. This is further corroborated below:

Although rural families often make their living from many different types of work, improvements in farming have proved to be the path toward widespread, poverty-reducing growth in the rural economy. Successful agricultural transformations have focused on the farming household, providing opportunities for farmers to earn a better income (Boettiger et al., 2017; para. 5)

DEMOGRAPHIC IMPLICATIONS

Talks about the demographic dividend have dominated the socioeconomic development discourse in Africa for some time now. The decline in Africa's fertility is extremely slow; this has key policy implications. Apart from a few

Southern African countries and island nations, sub-Saharan Africa has some of the highest total fertility rates in the world.

Based on 2018 data from the World Bank, the global average fertility rate[4] is 2.4 children per woman, with high variability across regions of the world. Africa accounts for the top 23 countries with the highest fertility rates in the world. While Niger tops the list at 6.9 children per woman, Tunisia has the lowest fertility rate in Africa at 2.1. Sub-Saharan Africa has, on average, the highest fertility rate at 4.7. For context, the fertility rate in the Euro area is 1.5, with France accounting for the highest at 1.9, while China and India have fertility rates of 1.7 and 2.2, respectively. Fertility rate in Australia, Brazil, UK, and the US stands at 1.7. Although this trend is generally the result of a combination of cultural, economic, and country-specific policy-related factors, it does have major implications for poverty, future educational attainment, fragility, political instability, productivity, and labor market outcomes (Mueni, 2016).

Canning et al. (2015) in *Africa's Demographic Transition* define the demographic dividend as "the interplay between changes in a population's age structure due to the demographic transition and rapid economic growth" (p. 1); they unpack the potential effect of demography on economic growth prospects, poverty, inequality, health, fragility, and human development. According to them:

But demography need not lead to disaster. If the focus shifts from population numbers to population age structures, the prospects for Africa may be positive. Declines in fertility automatically raise income per capita in the short run and have the potential to bring further gains in savings and investments in the long run. With prudent policies, African countries can reap the benefits of this demographic dividend. Policy choices and actions can transform the population of a nation into a healthy, educated, empowered labor force that can contribute to real and sustained economic growth that lifts people out of poverty. As a bonus, a demographic dividend can even accelerate economic growth in ways that spread prosperity across society. (Canning et al., 2015; pp.1-2)

Unlike in the industrialized countries, part of the motivation for having children in much of Africa's subsistence society is for economic security in old age. African parents expect their children to take care of them when they are old, with diminished capacity to engage in active income-earning activities. However, with a miniscule underground economy in the Western world, state-run social security and other assistance programs targeted at economic security for seniors provide viable alternatives to dependency on children. This, partly, explains why the economic incentive to have children is low in this part of the world.

CONCLUDING REMARKS

Structural and institutional constraints in Africa, which manifest through volatility in economic growth and subsistence economies, continue to limit industrial diversification potentials and the ability to develop resilience to shocks. It is hard for economic justice to thrive and accommodate incrementalism when resources, wealth, media, technology, political power, business capital, and other institutional arrangements – that perpetuate the wealth gap and relegate egalitarianism – disproportionately benefit plutocrats and oligarchs. For context, in many of the conflict-ridden countries in Africa, radical policy shifts and revolutionary approaches to policymaking are highly sought after.

Therefore, policy innovation efforts on the continent must recognize the long-term negative impacts of colonialism, as well as the pitfalls in Pan-Africanism as a political economy ideology with conflicting underpinnings on how economic, social, and political emancipation can be achieved. Of particular importance is the need to leverage Africa's favorable demographic position to achieve productivity gains. Through a multipronged approach that prioritizes private sector development, increased productivity can accelerate structural transformation and economic diversification. This can, in turn, help trigger incremental policy changes – through active involvement of John Kingdon-type policy entrepreneurs –who can move the needle in important socioeconomic spheres, with minimal disruptions in economic and social systems. The realization of the huge potential for Africa's development needs policy changes that can help to mainstream digital transformation in the informal economy.

To feel much for others and little for ourselves; to restrain our selfishness and exercise our benevolent affections, constitute the perfection of human nature.

— Adam Smith

REFERENCES

Allard, C., Iván, J., Kriljenko, C., Chen, W., Gonzalez-Garcia, J., Kitsios, E., & Treviño, J. (2016). *Trade integration and global value chains in sub-Saharan Africa: In pursuit of the missing link*. International Monetary Fund. https://www.imf.org/external/pubs/ft/dp/2016/afr1602.pdf

Ancharaz, V., Mbekeani, K., & Brixiova, Z. (2011). *Impediments to regional trade integration in Africa*. Africa Economic Brief: African Development Bank. https://www.afdb.org/fileadmin/uploads/afdb/Documents/Publications/AEB%20VOL%202%20Issue%2011_AEB%20VOL%202%20Issue%2011.pdf

Bhagwati, J. (1993). *India in transition: Freeing the economy*. Clarendon Press. doi:10.1093/acprof:oso/9780198288473.001.0001

Boettiger, S., Denis, N., & Sanghvi, S. (2017). *Successful agricultural transformations: Six core elements of planning and delivery. How can countries increase their odds of a successful rural transformation?* McKinsey & Company. https://www.mckinsey.com/industries/chemicals/our-insights/successful-agricultural-transformations-six-core-elements-of-planning-and-delivery

Canning, D., Raja, S., & Yazbeck, A. S. (2015). *Africa's demographic transition dividend or disaster?* International Bank for Reconstruction and Development / The World Bank., doi:10.1596/978-1-4648-0489-2

Case, A., & Deaton, A. (2020). *Deaths of despair and the future of capitalism*. Princeton University Press.

Christopher, B. (2020). *Rentier Capitalism: Who owns the economy, and who pays for it?* Verso Books.

Collier, P., & Gunning, J. W. (1999). Why has Africa grown slowly? *The Journal of Economic Perspectives*, *13*(3), 3–22. doi:10.1257/jep.13.3.3

Crouch, C. (2013). *Making capitalism fit for society*. Polity Press.

de Vries, G., Mensah, E. B., Kruse, H., & Sen, K. (2021). Many African countries had a surprise manufacturing surge in 2010s – it bodes well for the years ahead. *The Conversation*. https://theconversation.com/many-african-countries-had-a-surprise-manufacturing-surge-in-2010s-it-bodes-well-for-the-years-ahead-155405

Elsby, M. W. L., Hobijn, B., & Sahin, A. (2013). *The decline of the U.S. labor share*. Brookings Papers on Economic Activity, Fall 2013. https://www.brookings.edu/wp-content/uploads/2016/07/2013b_elsby_labor_share.pdf

Forbes. (2021). *The World's Real-time Billionaires*. https://www.forbes.com/real-time-billionaires/#7a0f75473d78

Friedman, M. (1970). The social responsibility of business is to increase its profits. *The New York Times Magazine*. http://umich.edu/~thecore/doc/Friedman.pdf

Harrison, A. E., Lin, J. F., & Xu, L. C. (2013). *Explaining Africa's (dis) advantage: The curse of party monopoly*. World Bank Policy Research Working Papers. https://elibrary.worldbank.org/doi/abs/10.1596/1813-9450-6316

HowMuch.net. (2019). *The World's $86 Trillion Economy Visualized in One Chart*. https://howmuch.net/articles/the-world-economy-2018

Ighobor, K. (2018). Closing Africa's wealth gap. *Africa Renewal*. https://www.un.org/africarenewal/magazine/december-2017-march-2018/closing-africa's-wealth-gap

Jacobs, M., & Mazzucato, M. (2016). *Rethinking Capitalism*. Political Quarterly Monograph Series. John Wiley & Sons, Incorporated.

Julian, S. (2019). *Understanding failed industrialization in Africa*. The Borgen Project. https://borgenproject.org/understanding-failed-industrialization-and-fighting-poverty-in-africa/

Keynes, J. M. (1936). *The General Theory of Employment, Interest and Money*. Retrieved from https://www.marxists.org/reference/subject/economics/keynes/general-theory/ch24.htm

Krugman, P. (1997). *Capitalism's Mysterious Triumph*. http://www.pkarchive.org/theory/Russia.html

Kruse, H., Mensah, E., Sen, K., & de Vries, G. (2021). *A manufacturing renaissance? Industrialization trends in the developing world (No. wp-2021-28). World Institute for Development Economic Research*. UNU-WIDER.

Kuznets, S. (1973). Modern economic growth: Findings and reflections. *The American Economic Review*, *63*(3), 247–258. https://www.jstor.org/stable/1914358

Leftwich, A. (2009). *Analysing the politics of state-business relations: A methodological concept note on the historical institutionalist approach.* Institutions and Pro-Poor Growth (IPPG) Discussion Paper Series 23 A. www.ippg.org.uk/papers/dp23a.pdf

Lemma, A., & Te Velde, D. W. (2017). State–business relations as drivers of economic performance. *The Practice of Industrial Policy: Government-Business Coordination in Africa and East Asia*, 63-79.

Maxfield, S., & Schneider, B. R. (Eds.). (1997). *Business and the state in developing countries*. Cornell University Press.

Mueni, E. (2016). Changing the Narrative on Fertility Decline in Africa. *New Security Beat.* Retrieved from https://www.newsecuritybeat.org/2016/04/changing-narrative-fertility-decline-africa/

Nguimkeu, P., & Zeufack, A. (2019). *Manufacturing in Structural Change in Africa.* World Bank Policy Research Working Paper (8992). https://papers.ssrn.com/sol3/papers.cfm?abstract_id=3440368

Niler, E. (2019). How the second industrial revolution changed Americans' lives: The rapid advancement of mass production and transportation made life a lot faster. *History*. https://www.history.com/news/second-industrial-revolution-advances

Nurkse, R. (1971). The theory of development and the idea of balanced growth. In A. B. Mountjoy (Ed.), *Developing the underdeveloped countries.* John Wiley & Sons. doi:10.1007/978-1-349-15452-4_9

Olayele, B. F. (2019). Gravity, borders, and regionalism: A Canada–US sub-national analysis. *The International Trade Journal*, *33*(5), 416–443. doi:10.1080/08853908.2019.1628675

Oxfam International. (2020). *Time to Care: Unpaid and underpaid care work and the global inequality crisis.* https://oxfamilibrary.openrepository.com/bitstream/handle/10546/620928/bp-time-to-care-inequality-200120-en.pdf

Page, J. (2014). Africa's failure to industrialize: Bad luck or bad policy? In *Africa in Focus.* Brookings. https://www.brookings.edu/blog/africa-in-focus/2014/11/20/africas-failure-to-industrialize-bad-luck-or-bad-policy/

Palmer, T. (2011). *The morality of capitalism: What your professors won't tell you*. Jameson Books.

Palmer, T. (2012). *At home and abroad, we all need to be reminded of the moral virtues of capitalism* [Interview]. City A.M. https://www.cityam.com/home-and-abroad-we-all-need-be-reminded-the-moral-virtues-capitalism/

Prebisch, R. (1950). *The economic development of latin America and its principal problems.* United Nations Department of Economic Affairs: Economic Commission for Latin America (ECLA). https://archivo.cepal.org/pdfs/cdPrebisch/002.pdf

Report, W. S. (2020). *Inequality in a rapidly changing world.* United Nations Department of Economic and Social Affairs. https://www.un.org/development/desa/dspd/wp-content/uploads/sites/22/2020/02/World-Social-Report2020-FullReport.pdf

Rodrik, D. (1999). *Institutions for high-quality growth: What they are and how to acquire them.* International Monetary Fund. https://www.imf.org/external/pubs/ft/seminar/1999/reforms/rodrik.htm

Rodrik, D. (2016). Premature deindustrialization. *Journal of Economic Growth, 21*(1), 1–33. doi:10.100710887-015-9122-3

Sen, K. (2015). *State business relations: Topic guide October 2015.* Governance and Social Development Resource Centre. https://gsdrc.org/wp-content/uploads/2015/10/State-BusinessRels.pdf

Shah, A. (2013). Structural Adjustment—a Major Cause of Poverty. *Global Issues.* https://www.globalissues.org/article/3/structural-adjustment-a-major-cause-of-poverty

Signe, L. (2018). *The potential of manufacturing and industrialization in Africa trends, opportunities, and strategies.* Africa Growth Initiative. Brookings Institute. https://www.brookings.edu/wp-content/uploads/2018/09/Manufacturing-and-Industrialization-in-Africa-Signe-20180921.pdf

Signé, L. (2020). *Unlocking Africa's business potential: Trends, opportunities, risks, and strategies*. Brookings Institution Press.

Singer, H. (1950). The distribution of gains between investing and borrowing. *The American Economic Review, 40*, 473–485.

Soludo, C. C., & Mkandawire, P. T. (1998). *Our continent, our future: African perspectives on structural adjustment*. Africa World Press.

Standing, G. (2017). *The corruption of capitalism: Why rentiers thrive and work does not pay*. Biteback Publishing.

Stiglitz, J. E. (2016). Inequality and Economic Growth. *The Political Quarterly*, *86*(S1), 134–155. doi:10.1111/1467-923X.12237

Te Velde, D. W. (2006). *Measuring state business relations in sub-Saharan Africa.* Institutions and Pro-Poor Growth (IPPG) Discussion Paper No. 4. Retrieved from https://assets.publishing.service.gov.uk/media/57a08c51ed915d3cfd0012ec/IPPGDP4.pdf

Te Velde, D. W. (2013). *Future Directions in Aid for Trade.* doi:10.14217/9781848591646-19-en

The Economist. (2019). The new scramble for Africa: This time, the winners could be Africans themselves. *Leader, Geopolitics*. https://www.economist.com/leaders/2019/03/07/the-new-scramble-for-africa

The World Bank & the World Trade Organization. (2019). *Global value chain development report 2019: Technological innovation, supply chain trade, and workers in a globalized world (English).* World Bank Group. https://documents.worldbank.org/curated/en/384161555079173489/Global-Value-Chain-Development-Report-2019-Technological-Innovation-Supply-Chain-Trade-and-Workers-in-a-Globalized-World

United Nations. (2020). Rising inequality affecting more than two-thirds of the globe, but it's not inevitable: New UN report. *UN News: Global Perspective Human Stories*. https://news.un.org/en/story/2020/01/1055681

United Nations Economic Commission for Africa. (2018). *Continental free trade area deal set to boost intra-African trade, says Ambassador Quartey.* UNECA. https://archive.uneca.org/stories/continental-free-trade-area-deal-set-boost-intra-african-trade-says-ambassador-quartey

United Nations Industrial Development Organization. (n.d.). *The Knowledge Hub* [Innovation Section]. https://tii.unido.org/section/innovation

World Bank. (1994). *Nigeria structural adjustment program: Policies, implementation, and impact.* Western Africa Department. Country Operations Division. https://documents1.worldbank.org/curated/en/959091468775569769/pdf/multi0page.pdf

ENDNOTES

1 This trend is pervasive across developing and developed countries, and is not tied to income.

2 The China Miracle is a term in the economic development literature describing how policy reforms in China resulted in exceptionally strong economic growth performance for three decades.

3 To put this into perspective, Africa is the second-largest continent in the world; bigger than China, India, the U.S., Japan, and most of Europe, combined.

4 OECD defines the total fertility rate as the total number of children that would be born to each woman if she were to live to the end of her child-bearing years and give birth to children in alignment with the prevailing age-specific fertility rates.

Chapter 6
State Structures and Economic Modernization

ABSTRACT

This chapter examines institutional structures and a comparative assessment of national and subnational fiscal systems in a bid to gauge policy effectiveness around redistribution and stabilization in Africa. The social, political, and economic ramifications are expected to offer a glimpse into the policy innovation imperative of the dichotomy between decentralized governance and centralized fiscal architecture. If the gains from regional innovation ecosystems are to be maximized, political economy nuances around state structures, fiscal regimes, executive-legislative financial autonomies, and allied matters must be appropriately situated. While most of the countries in Africa are unitary states—with all the powers of government vested in the central government—only Ethiopia and Nigeria are fully federal, with some features of federalism present in countries like South Africa and the Democratic Republic of the Congo. The discussion concludes that constitutional dynamics—whether in unitary or federal systems—are complex..

DOI: 10.4018/978-1-7998-7383-9.ch006

Development consists of the removal of various types of unfreedoms that leave people with little choice and little opportunity of exercising their reasoned agency. The removal of substantial unfreedoms, it is argued here, is constitutive of development.

— Amartya Sen

WHILE GLOBALIZATION has intensified technology diffusion globally, leading to increased productivity in EMDEs, the extent of income convergence predicted by economic theory has not been realized. This is due, partly, to changes in the patterns and processes of capital accumulation during the post-World War II economic boom, and the concomitant highly dynamic nature of the capitalist mode of production. The past few decades have heralded a decline in labor's share of income, due to the prevailing highly capital-intensive multinational system of production.

In addition to the concentration of capital ownership, this mode of wealth creation generates varying returns to different categories of labor, with workers at the top of the income distribution reaping disproportionately large rewards over time. A major characterization of the neoclassical production function is a standard assumption of profit maximization by firms. Under this framework, changes in a firm's revenue are linked to changes in the costs of capital and labor – with implications for competition, efficiency, and transparency.

In a way, this explains why the innovation discourse has transitioned from its purely scientific and technical focus to include digital opportunities and the evolution of new business models. For instance, economic diversification is often associated with higher levels of productivity because structural transformation leads to factor reallocation within and between sectors. However, due to institutional and structural constraints like informality, limited access to technology, and poor infrastructure, this is far from the case in many countries in the Global South. While the role of the state in creating incentives and reducing inequality is clear, a nuanced understanding of contemporary social policy requires a firm grasp of the role of markets. Again, this underscores why innovation is critical for transforming a wide range of policy initiatives by creating win-win outcomes in traditionally mutually exclusive competitive markets and public sector operations. It is important to examine what we know and do not know about the role of business, government, academia, and society in innovating policy. Only then can we focus on important reforms that can help drive competitiveness and economic growth, while addressing the root causes of rising poverty and inequality in society.

In this chapter, I examine institutional structures and conduct a comparative assessment of national and subnational fiscal systems in a bid to gauge policy effectiveness around redistribution and stabilization. Looking at the social, political, and economic ramifications will offer a glimpse into the policy innovation imperative around the dichotomy between decentralized governance and centralized fiscal architecture.

CONTEXTUALIZING FISCAL DECENTRALIZATION

In a theoretical context, there is no consensus on the precise role of fiscal policy, especially fiscal transfers and taxation, in the growth process (McCracken, 2006). Public finance theorists have long cited the fairness and efficiency concerns associated with regional fiscal disparities as something policymakers should worry about. Nonetheless, the importance of fiscal policy in achieving redistribution and stabilization remains undisputed.

Fundamentally, all transfer programs involve a flow of resources among the various units in a federal system. Whether intended or not, this has redistributive consequences. For instance, Ma (1999), argues that the need to correct vertical fiscal imbalances, horizontal fiscal imbalances, and inter-jurisdictional spillover effects provide economic justification for intergovernmental transfers. Fiscal transfer programs in many federal systems try to equalize differences in the tax capacities of regional jurisdictions.

While equity considerations have a way of making regional redistribution appear as a pro-growth policy, economic efficiency ramifications often reject such arguments based on the deadweight loss generated when equilibrium for a good or service is not Pareto optimal. Policymakers therefore constantly face the dilemma of balancing equity arguments against the distortionary effects of fiscal transfers on net payers and net recipients. This highlights why despite the economic justice imperative, the fundamental role of capitalism as the lubricant of democracy remains undisputed.

An important function of fiscal policy in a federal system is the capacity to make income transfers from richer to poorer regions; such transfers play different roles though. And while the recent backlash against social, cultural, and economic globalization has put additional pressures on policymakers to restructure the roles of various levels of government, the balance of power between the central and subnational levels of governments remains the priority for countries organized along federalist grounds (Fraser Institute, 2013).

To put things into perspective, a comparative analysis of the Canadian and US systems shows stark differences – despite the similarities between both countries along several institutional, cultural, and political economy grounds. Through the Equalization program, Canada allows its provinces and territories to provide public service at reasonably comparable levels of taxation. The US, unlike Canada, has no formal framework to transfer resources from prosperous states to less prosperous ones. Instead, the federal government uses the Grants-in-Aid – a subsidy-type program that is accompanied by federal regulations – to extend aid to enable states and local governments finance certain areas of their budgets (Olayele & Soo, 2020).

The literature on fiscal federalism provides three rationales for fiscal transfers. First, in countries where national governments have control over the major tax bases, leaving subnational governments with insufficient fiscal resources to cover their expenditure needs, vertical fiscal imbalances result. Fiscal transfer is therefore required to meet the resulting shortfall; it could also help to bridge differences in fiscal capacities because of horizontal fiscal imbalances (Ma, 1999). For instance, while a resource-endowed jurisdiction may have more than enough to provide public goods for its residents and care less about fiscal inflows from other levels of government, another region with a relatively higher proportion of poor, old, and young population may be fiscally incapacitated without such transfers. In this case, Equalization payments will be required to close the gap between the fiscal capacity and fiscal need of the jurisdiction in question.

In other words, a minimum standard of public service is required in all the federating units, and to avoid increasing the tax burden of residents, subsidies will be required from the central government by regions without sufficient resources to reach such minimum level. In Canada, provinces that are deemed to be eligible for Equalization receive monies while those designated as contributors do not receive any payments. It is worth mentioning that compared to other federalist developed countries, the intensity with which conditional grants are used is more pronounced in the US.

Under the assumption of perfect factor mobility, it may not be necessary for government to play the role of equalization as the market itself will reallocate resources to achieve this end. The reality, however, is that perfect factor mobility is unattainable due to information issues, relocation costs, and employment constraints, among other things. Thirdly, the need to internalize inter-jurisdictional spillover effects is also key. Due to concerns around free ridership by mobile residents and neighboring jurisdictions, a subnational government may underinvest in important public goods with positive externalities such as education, health, and interregional highway. In this case, the central government will have to address such suboptimal provision by providing subsidies or other incentives.

As Romer (1994) argues, through the endogenous growth theory, constant or increasing returns to capital may limit the ability of the so-called convergence in per capita income to address some of these gaps without policy intervention. The positive externalities of a knowledge-based economy in the growth accounting process, rather than some exogenous technological factors, will offer useful insights to help innovate the policy development process. While theory provides only a partial guide on the interrelationships between income, redistribution, and growth, Ostry et al. (2014) argue that the link between all three is a complex one (Figure 1).

Figure 1. Interrelationships between inequality, redistribution, and growth
(Credit: Redistribution, Inequality, and Growth in Ostry et al., 2014)

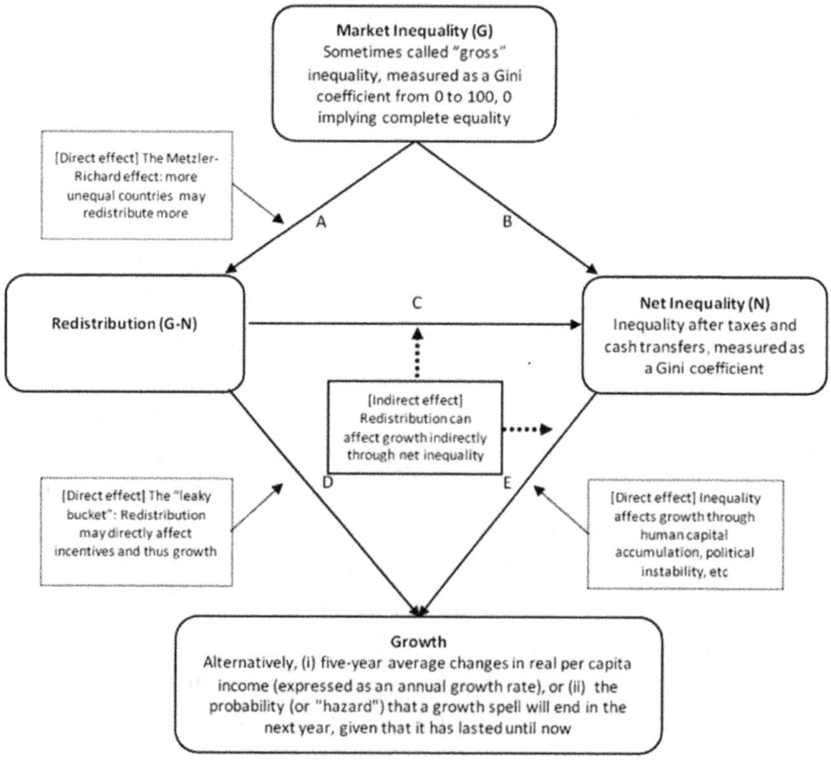

Figure 1 shows the direct effects of redistribution (line D) and net inequality (line E), while in each case, the value of the other variable is held constant. Ostry et al. calculate the "total effect" of redistribution on growth based on the assumption that "redistribution does not affect market inequality, so redistribution affects net inequality one-for-one." They add that the total effect is the sum of the estimated direct effect (line D) and the indirect effect, which is a combination of the effect of redistribution on net inequality (line C) and the estimated direct effect of net inequality on growth (line E). Several other directions of causality abound, in addition to possible channels for the income-inequality-redistribution nexus.

Clearly, inequality has the capacity to undermine growth. The growth-inequality dynamic can assume varying degrees of complexity. Arthur Okun in his popular 1975 book, *Equality and Efficiency: The Big Tradeoff*, points out that economic efficiency is achieved at a cost. The trade-off between an efficient economy or an egalitarian society implies that fixing fiscal disparities may end up weakening the efficiency of the economic system because of negative production incentives. While fiscal disparity may be bad for growth, policy designs that focus on taxes and transfers may even cause more harm than good. Drawing specific conclusions on the negative effect of redistributive policies is indeed a dilemma.

Bleaney et al. (2001) posit a benign solution to Okun's dilemma is to invest in public goods with the ability to produce pro-growth and pro-equality effects, simultaneously. In the same vein, Checherita et al. (2009) suggest in addition to fiscal transfers, governments can foster regional convergence through investment in infrastructure, human capital formation, and corporate subsidies differentiated by region.

These theoretical underpinnings, while based largely on Western approaches to studying political economy developments, are helpful in recognizing the limits of generalizations in the African context. However, the notion of European models of society as the only feasible pathway to modernization is deficient. As discussed in the preceding chapters, in conceptualizing the resonances in the development trajectories of countries in the Global North and Global South, the central tenet in development orthodoxy that low-income countries must pass through specific capitalist development phases as a precondition for achieving economic modernization has many pitfalls. To the extent possible, the pros and cons of the manifestations of Eurocentrism must be balanced against the realities of the traditional African philosophy of Ubuntu.

THE DIVERSIFICATION-SPECIALIZATION DEBATE

Economic diversification remains a recurring theme in public policy debates; it is believed to be the cure to the "resource curse" challenge. The benefits of diversification, as well as the importance of key economic, demographic, geographic, and institutional factors that explain it, remain widely acknowledged. However, explaining the specific reasons why diversification helps some economies to succeed where others fail remain a mirage. To further complicate things, most empirical investigations of the relationship between economic growth and diversity provide inconclusive evidence (see Attaran, 1986; Attaran & Zwick, 1987; Bishop & Gripaios, 2010; and Frenken et al., 2007).

The resource economics literature extensively discusses the far-reaching effects of commodity price shocks on resource-dependent economies (United Nations Conference on Trade and Development, 2019). To the extent that volatile prices drive government revenues, output, and capital investment, the policy debate on whether economic diversification can help jurisdictions escape the resource curse will continue to generate interests.

Gelb (2014) asks two important questions? "Why diversify in the first place?" "Why try to move away from a sector with a strong comparative advantage?" To which he, in turn, answers:

.....the motive may simply reflect the proposition, which is supported by evidence, that export diversification is associated with higher long-run growth. However, resource exporters differ from one another in many respects, including population, labor force and skills, location, levels of income, reserves, and the potential for other resource-based activities. These differences will shape diversification priorities and policies (Gelb, 2014; p. 57).

Regional economic diversification is a potent tool for advancing technological progress, innovation, positive technology externalities, and other sources of agglomeration economies – and as Porter (1990) puts it, this prompts firms to compete for scarce resources, and in the process, promotes innovation. Hoover and Giarratani (1984) agree that industrial clusters benefit from agglomeration economies due to specialization and regional competitive advantages, giving rise to the popular location theory, based on spatial economics and clusters.

Smith and Gibson (1988) argue that too much attention on diversification – at the detriment of specialization – could hurt a region's ability to exploit existing comparative advantages, which may in turn impact negatively on regional economic growth prospects. This is premised on the notion that basing policymaking on sequalization in factor endowments and market area could be counterproductive. Larger regional economies tend to be more economically diversified; economists believe that metropolitan cities succeed because agglomeration economies raise productivity and economic growth (Porter, 1995; Glaeser, 2011).

CONTEMPORARY SOCIAL WELFARE POLICY IMPLICATIONS

The efficiency and distributional implications of innovation policies continue to generate debates given how recent advances in technology have created polarizations and high inequalities between high-and low-tech sector workers (Basu & Getachew, 2020). Essentially, a high-performing government is one that tackles the challenges of our time heads on and simultaneously in an efficient, innovative, and responsive manner. Considering the ongoing digital transformation, public-private collaborations have become an efficient tool for harnessing new business models, process improvements, and technological breakthroughs. They have become recipes for success in the new economy.

Dani Rodrik in his 1997 book, *Has Globalization Gone Too Far*, unpacks the good and bad of globalization. His work sheds light on the impact of globalization shocks on the market-society nexus, where governments are caught in the middle of a polarized economic system in which "losers" are dissatisfied with their woes – which manifest through socioeconomic immobility and a declining quality of life – while "winners" with the right dose of education and skills are seamlessly climbing the economic ladder in an unfettered world market.

Rodrik explains the three major sources of tension under such global economic architecture: the transformation of the employment relationship, conflicts between international trade and social norms, and the pressures brought to bear on national governments in maintaining domestic cohesion and social welfare systems. He cautions on the potential symmetric impact of the possible consequences of social instability on both "winners" and "losers." In his words, "Social disintegration is not a spectator sport—those on the sidelines also get splashed with mud from the field. Ultimately, the deepening of social fissures can harm all." (Rodrik, 1997; p.7)

Martin Sandbu's 2020 book, *The Economics of Belonging*, cautions everyone to step back, take stock, and rethink the root causes of grievances and society's current challenges. The author contends that globalization is only partly responsible for the rise in populism due to high levels of poverty and inequality; instead, technological change and flawed but avoidable domestic policies are the drivers of our winner-take-all economic system. While not opposed to increased economic integration, Sandbu believes dramatic reforms – where productivity gains, support for SMEs, increased worker representation, and a revitalized regional development model become prioritized – are needed to fix the friction between globalization and social stability for society's overall benefit.

A classic example of the unintended consequences of the innovation economy is the fallout of Amazon's year-long process of establishing its second headquarters. The Amazon HQ2[1] outcome offers a glimpse of how sociopolitical and economic factors impact economic development programming. Its growth and welfare outcomes – through its impact on the efficiency–inequality trade-off – has become a textbook case study. The social welfare ramifications corroborate the arguments in the preceding chapters that economic empiricism is not adequate in assessing quality of life and socioeconomic equality.

While mainstream neoclassical models may have captured the benefits of the HQ2 project through macroeconomic metrics such as employment, capital investment, and tax revenue, the backlash underscores why nominal economic achievements are inadequate. As seen in the aftermath of the Great Recession, labor market polarization and rising cost of living in the face of aggregate growth outcomes generated adverse socioeconomic impacts which further exacerbated inequality. This has major implications for the urban-rural divide, to the extent that agglomeration economies drive the innovation ecosystem. In Sandbu's words, "But knowledge-based services thrive in the concentration of people and activities found in the big cities, whose bubbling human diversity and greater potential for serendipitous interaction make them the richest cauldrons of ideas." (Sandbu, 2020; p.29).

The discussion above, yet again, echoes Sandbu's sentiment that the winner-take-all dynamic in which markets disproportionately reward capital at the detriment of labor can only produce the same outcome. This informs my major takeaway in this section: economic development policy and programming must balance both economic growth and social welfare ramifications. This is not always an easy task; it is the core issue in public policy innovation.

STATE STRUCTURES AND POLICY DYNAMICS

State structures have implications for the ability to innovate and transform economic systems. A central debate in the political development process in EMDEs with decentralized federations is how to achieve near-Pareto outcomes in their economic systems (de Figueiredo & Weingast, 2002). To move the needle on developing effective, coherent, and relevant policies for industrial innovation, a good understanding of the public-private collaboration process is a necessity (Atkinson, 1991). This requires an unambiguous model of power distribution between the central and subnational governments in countries organized along federalist grounds. What does this mean for Africa?

Fiscal federalism and political decentralization remain a huge challenge in Africa due to governance failures – like authoritarianism, conflict, and social inequity – and economic and structural problems like fragmentation, excessive dependence on natural resources, and informality (Suberu, 2015). For context, public sector economics explains the pros and cons of fiscal decentralization in terms of its efficacy in increasing the degree of efficiency in the allocation of resources (Olayele & Soo, 2020).

One of the major goals of fiscal transfers from central governments is to promote equalization of basic public services through narrowing of fiscal disparities across subnational regions. In the fiscal transfers literature, the macroeconomic approach to measuring subnational fiscal capacity is based on the notion that the level of economic activity within a region represents the ability of the regional government to raise revenues (Schroeder & Smoke, 2003). The federal system is basically about shared rule, and the philosophy behind this political economy and constitutional arrangement is the notion of "unity in diversity."

The academic literature notes the following three terms are distinguishable in the explanation of federal system: federalism, federal political systems, and federations (Watts, 1996). Watts defines federalism:

Federalism is basically not a descriptive but a normative term and refers to the advocacy of multi-tiered government combining elements of shared-rule and regional self-rule. It is based on the presumed value and validity of combining unity and diversity and of accommodating, preserving and promoting distinct identities within a larger political union. The essence of federalism as a normative principle is the perpetuation of both union and non-centralization at the same time. (p.6)

Kenneth Wheare in his 1946 book, *Federal Government*, gives a classic summary of the basis of the federal government in terms of the federal principle which he defines as "the method of dividing powers so that the general and the regional governments are each, within a sphere, co-ordinate and independent" (Wheare, 1946; p.11). In essence, in a federal system, each level of government can exercise its autonomous sphere of power independently of the other. This means the powers of the national government are not exercised indirectly through the regions, but directly over individual citizens. This distinction is important. While Wheare's definition is not perfect, it does a good job in distinguishing federal from other government forms.

The institutional conditions that inform the public policy development process vary significantly across federal systems. For instance, under the constitutional history of the US, two key manifestations of the federal principle are seen in both "dual" and "cooperative" federalism. This holds true for countries with federal systems – e.g., Argentina, Belgium, Canada, Brazil, the US, Nigeria, Ethiopia, South Africa[2], Germany, India, Malaysia, Pakistan, and Spain. While the goal of these governance structures and institutional arrangements is to enable governments fulfil their social contracts of creating shared prosperity, dual federalism emphasizes that both the federal and regional governments are co-equals with each level legislating in a separate sphere, while cooperative federalism advances the principle that both levels of government legislate in the same sphere.

THE FEDERALISM-POLICY INNOVATION DILEMMA

Dual federations do advance policy innovation, but the incentives to stabilize coordinated policies dissipate over time; cooperative federations, on the other hand, support incremental evolution, making it hard for policy innovation to thrive (Benz & Broschek, 2020). To shed some light on this, Benz and Broschek's policy experimentation in the energy sector uses case designs comparing policy developments in two federal systems: Canada and Germany. In Canada's case, its dual federalism status permits unilateral actions of federal or provincial governments. In the German scenario, the need for the federal government to negotiate critical elements of transformative policy directly with corporate interests, without the need to invest time in intergovernmental relations, produces an outcome marked by a divergence from the incrementalism associated with joint decision-making.

Huddleston (2018) explains, in *Federalism and Tech Policy*, how states are better positioned than the federal government in creating new technological solutions by experimenting with different governance mechanisms. Weingast's (1995) seminal work on market-preserving federalism contends that in addition to a well-designed economic system, efficient markets require a political arrangement that ensures the state can fulfil its fundamental objective of honoring economic and political rights.

Weingast's initial work investigated the role of federalism in economic transformation of England in the 18th century, the US in the 19th and early 20th centuries, and China in contemporary times. His latter collaborations also examined Russia's unique type of federalism and how its many shortcomings have prevented it from advancing policy innovation to achieve inclusive development that can create prosperity across Russia's vast regions.

In many ways, subnational units are effective policy laboratories or, as Blythe (2015) calls it, "laboratories of democracy." This is because many successful policy innovations at the regional level can become adopted nationally through policy learning or policy diffusion. For instance, what is today known as Medicare was birthed in 1962 in the Prairie province of Saskatchewan in Canada (Brown & Taylor, 2012). In North America, Saskatchewan was the first jurisdiction to adopt a universal, publicly-funded comprehensive single-payer health care model. Within 10 years, this version of state medicine became a nationalized public health care model, with all of Canada covered by a medical insurance system based on the Saskatchewan model.

In the same vein, the state of Massachusetts in the US adopted a quasi-public health insurance model in 2006, leading to increased access in health care for less well-off citizens. And while the US does not yet have a fully nationalized public health model, some parts of the Affordable Care Act of 2010 are modeled after the Massachusetts plan (Semro, 2012). As such, healthcare policy deliberations in the US often involve a nuanced analysis of the state medicine model in Massachusetts, to the extent that this serves as a potential template for incremental national reforms (Herzlinger, 2006; Long et al. 2012).

In the global digital economy context, policy innovation must be grounded in models and practices that recognize that digital innovation and disruptions will often outpace regulatory and legislative arrangements and mechanisms (Evans, 2018). This is important, at least to the extent that strategic policy choices are dictated, directly or indirectly, by the balance of horizontal and vertical separation of powers (Comisso, 1986). Policy innovation efforts are driven largely by these ramifications.

FEDERALISM IN AFRICA: ETHIOPIA AND NIGERIA IN PERSPECTIVE

In this section, I focus on the inequality, conflicts, and institutions dimensions in Ethiopia and Nigeria – along with the implications for long-term divergent political economy outcomes. One of the major reasons countries adopt fiscal federalism is the gains that accrue from a more efficient resource allocation and mobilization regime from a public sector performance perspective.

While the benefits of fiscal decentralization over centralized fiscal systems have been discussed extensively in the theoretical and empirical literature (Olayele & Soo, 2020), the implications of the political economy of fiscal federalism in multi-ethnic, low-income federations are examined here.

Nigeria and the Quest for True Federalism

At 202 million people, Nigeria is the most populous country in Africa, followed by Ethiopia with 112 million people. While both countries are democracies with many economic, political, and ethno-linguistic similarities, significant differences exist in their political economy institutional arrangements – from rights and laws to regulations and policy processes to resource allocation and other nuances pertaining to state-society and state-economy dynamics. A multi-ethnic and culturally diverse federation, Nigeria is Africa's largest economy and biggest oil exporter with the largest natural gas reserves.

The country accounts for about half of West Africa's population and one of the largest youth populations in the world (World Bank, 2020). Nigeria's development challenges are largely related to its inability to diversify its economy away from oil, weak institutions, governance issues, and public financial management systems. Due to high poverty and inequality levels – which also continue to fuel social and political unrest – public expenditures in the last few years have been devoted to pro-poor initiatives.

Though a federal system by design, decades of military rule have resulted in the centralization of the Nigerian federation, and in many ways, turning a multi-ethnic and culturally diverse federation with 36 autonomous states and a Federal Capital Territory into a centralized system of federalism with all elements of absolute fiscal centralism and unitarism. After decades of military rule, Nigeria transitioned to a multiparty democracy in 1999. While governance situations have improved, broadly speaking, since the return of civil rule in 1999, the country faces serious security challenges ranging from the war against Boko Haram terrorist group in the northeast since 2011, criminality and militancy in the oil-rich Niger Delta, ethno-religious tensions, and political corruption.

In recent times, under the administration of President Muhamadu Buhari, there have been violent clashes between pastoralists and farmers in the northwest, southwest, and across the country's Middle Belt. This has exacerbated the precarious security conditions, manifesting in cattle rustling, kidnapping, ethnic massacres, and emergent Islamist extremist activity (Blanchard & Husted, 2020). Suberu (2009) reasons that contrary to the portrayal of Nigeria in global terms as a dysfunctional and failed state, the country has been relatively successful in dealing with the forces of state disintegration that have plagued other comparatively large multi-ethnic states on the continent. Despite all the challenges, his premise is that federalism in Nigeria "has helped to cross-cut major ethnic identities, foster inter-regional integration, promote inter-group equilibrium and generally cauterize potentially destabilizing centrifugal challenges to Nigeria's continuity and survival as a single political community." (Suberu, 2009; p. 67).

Nonetheless, Suberu's thesis acknowledges the corruption in the system, along with its manifestations of disappointing metrics on all major socioeconomic development indices, thereby making Nigeria a tough sell as a conflict management and diversity governance model in other parts of the continent. Suberu (2010) warns that electoral and anti-corruption reforms are a necessity "in mitigating potentially disintegrative ethno-political conflicts and to assuage current agitations for the wholesale restructuring or dismantling of the federal system" (Suberu, 2010; p. 459). As corroborated in Campbell and Rotberg (2021), 11 years after his admonition, Suberu's argument remains true, and even more compelling today.

Ethiopia and Regional Cleavages

Ethiopia is a diverse, multi-ethnic, and multi-religious nation. Unlike Nigeria, which adopted the federal system upon independence, Ethiopia embraced a decentralized, federal governance model to address many of the challenges associated with its century-old centralized unitary system –which started under a monarchy before the military took over. Before the COVID-19 pandemic, Ethiopia experienced strong, broad-based growth and was one of the fastest growing economies in Africa. In the decade before the pandemic, annual economic growth in the country averaged 9.4 percent (World Bank, 2021).

Development constraints in Ethiopia are principally related to political disruptions and social unrest, which make it hard to translate growth to poverty reduction. Limited competitiveness, due to an underdeveloped private sector, is also hampering its ability to weather economic and trade shocks. Despite overseeing unprecedented reforms from transitioning the economy to a more market-oriented model and increasing women's representation in government – all within a relatively short period of time – Ethiopian Prime Minister Abiy Ahmed won a Nobel Peace Prize in October 2019 for ending the 20-year conflict with Eritrea only to face, as the BBC (2021) puts it, "a rapid reversal" in a matter of months due to the war in the northern Tigray region of the country (para. 3).

The reformist Prime Minister is focused on consolidating the achievements of his government by addressing the issues of regional cleavages and ethnic antagonisms in the multicultural governing coalition, which is backed by a federal constitution that grants autonomy to the country's nine ethno-geographic regions. The Tigray People's Liberation Front on the other hand prefers a federal governance model where regional ethnic autonomy supersedes a centralized system of federalism where the source of authority lies at the center.

Paradoxically, the former model resembles a Nigeria-type federalism marked by increased contemporary ethno-religious conflicts and nationwide agitation for greater regional autonomy under the constitution. Such is the complex nature of the centralization-decentralization debate in federal systems, with major implications for national cohesion, especially in low-income countries with weak institutions, poverty, corruption, and fragility.

While Ethiopia's current federal structure is enshrined in the constitution of the Federal Democratic Republic of Ethiopia which was adopted in December 1994 (Gedamu, 2019), modern Ethiopia was shaped by the various strands of monarchical, military, and technocratic leaders at the helm in the 20th and 21st centuries. In the contrary, Nigeria became a federation immediately upon independence in 1960, and while federalism has helped to shape its multicultural and multi-ethnic heritage, with tangible progress, the country also navigated a brutal civil war between 1967 and 1970 leaving over a million people dead, with scars that linger till today. Nonetheless, after a series of repressive military regimes took a toll on the economic, governance, and social fabric of the country, it would be hard to question the appropriateness of a federal constitution, with multicultural and multi-ethnic governance provisions supposedly designed to address a myriad of issues associated with a complex entity like Nigeria.

POLICY INNOVATION FOR TRUE FEDERALISM

The preceding section underscores how the political economy challenges of Ethiopia and Nigeria are similar, yet different, on many fronts. The federal constitutions in both countries are derivatives of their multicultural, multi-ethnic, multi-religious, and multi-linguistic configurations. And while the quest for the "optimal dose" of federalism lies at the heart of the impasse in Ethiopia, the question of how the dose should be administered, if in fact such exists, seems to be more important in the case of Nigeria. Can policy innovation move the needle in both countries?

Harrison (2013) does a good job explaining the inherently contradictory nature of the federalism-public policy nexus. On the one hand, there are inefficiencies associated with crafting state/regional policy solutions due majorly to capacity. On the other hand, by giving room for subnational jurisdictions to develop policies to meet their own needs, federalism can promote policy experimentation and innovation.

Bulmer (2017) explains that while federalism has helped some countries to overcome conflicts or improve governance, it can also exacerbate things and generate deeper conflicts. The author cautions that "Federalism is also a complicated, often legalistic, form of government, which can be expensive and can hinder the coherent development and application of policies." (Bulmer, 2017; p.3). In essence, federalism is a flawed governance model that does not have answers to many contemporary complicated questions in multi-ethnic federal societies. Bulmer suggests that one or a combination of desirable features of macro-decentralized or quasi-federalism models could become an alternative to federalism.

The above analysis raises an important question for policy innovation and policy diffusion in Nigeria and Ethiopia. Like the Schumpeterian tradition of evolutionary growth and endogenous innovation, where the entrepreneur willing to make things happen through market dynamics, profit expectations, and long-run growth expectations is the vital force behind capitalism, where are Ethiopia and Nigeria's John Kingdon-type policy entrepreneurs who "could be in or out of government, in elected or appointed positions, in interest groups or research organizations"? As posited in Suberu (2010), electoral and anti-corruption reforms remain the solution to "mitigating potentially disintegrative ethno-political conflicts and to assuage current agitations for the wholesale restructuring or dismantling of the federal system" (Suberu, 2010; p. 459).

Kingdon identifies the defining characteristic of the policy entrepreneur as the willingness to invest personal resources – time, energy, reputation, and sometimes money – in the hope of a future return. Obviously, civil society has a role here, but this is beyond them. National and regional parliaments have a role, but this, too, is beyond them. Ethiopia and Nigeria need policy innovation to reimagine, redesign, and deliver an innovative federal system that advances their respective political economies.

Since many incremental innovations often happen across federal systems, perhaps it is more appropriate to streamline the quest for innovation in the policy development process to a specific situation: policy innovation in a federal system based on regional ethnic autonomy. Faguet et al. (2014) offer useful insights in this regard. Based on how decentralization affects state strength, they suggest a level of decentralization below that of "major ethnic, linguistic, or other identity groups" as the optimal solution (Faguet et al., 2014; p. 8).

Faguet et al. outline specific reform paths that can help strengthen four specific elements of state strength: (i) authority over territory and conflict prevention, (ii) policy autonomy and the ability to uphold the law, (iii) responsive, accountable service provision, and (iv) social learning. The logic behind this being that the regional specificity of elite interests matters because if they sense that they will be worse off under a fragmented arrangement, the likelihood of opposing secessionism and separatism becomes high. The authors succinctly identify the underlying issue: when decentralization happens below the level of social cleavages, secessionist tendencies are weakened because the preferences of moderate citizens diverge from those of radical leaders.

By weaving policy innovation into their thesis, these authors imply that when citizens become active in the political space "in their own right", such involvement in "small scale of local politics" will indirectly form the basis for strengthening advocacy and political legitimacy. This is another classic example that echoes Kingdon's recommendation that policy entrepreneurs are like business entrepreneurs because they are willing to "invest their resources – time, energy, reputation, and sometimes money – in the hope of a future return".

A major lesson from this chapter is that constitutional dynamics – whether in unitary or federal systems – are complex; if the gains from regional innovation ecosystems are to be maximized, political economy nuances around state structures, fiscal regimes, executive-legislative financial autonomies, and allied matters have implications for economic stability and prosperity. While most of the countries in Africa are unitary states – with all the powers of government vested in the central government – only Ethiopia and Nigeria are fully federal. Some features of federalism are present in countries like South Africa, the Democratic Republic of Congo, Somalia, the Comoros, Sudan, and South Sudan. Nonetheless, for non-federal states on the continent, to the extent that conflicts and other political and economic shocks warrant negotiations around power-sharing arrangements, a multi-stakeholder approach which gives room for incremental innovation is always in order.

Fairness does not require the redistribution of wealth; it requires the creation of wealth, geared to an economy that can provide employment for everyone able and willing to work.

— Felix Rohatyn

REFERENCES

Atkinson, R. D. (1991). Innovation policy making in a federalist system: Lessons from the states for U.S. federal innovation policy making. *Research Policy*, *20*(6), 559–577. doi:10.1016/0048-7333(91)90046-S

Attaran, M. (1986). Industrial diversity and economic performance in US areas. *The Annals of Regional Science*, *20*(2), 44–54. doi:10.1007/BF01287240

Attaran, M., & Zwick, M. (1987). The effect of industrial diversification on employment and income: A case study. *The Quarterly Review of Economics and Business*, *27*, 38–54.

Basu, P., & Getachew, Y. (2020). Redistributive innovation policy, inequality, and efficiency. *Journal of Public Economic Theory*, *22*(3), 532–554. doi:10.1111/jpet.12386

BBC News. (2021). Ethiopia's Abiy Ahmed: The Nobel prize winner who went to war. *BBC News*. https://www.bbc.com/news/world-africa-43567007

Benz, A., & Broschek, J. (2020). Transformative energy policy in federal systems: Canada and Germany compared. *Canadian Journal of European and Russian Studies*, *14*(2), 56–78. doi:10.22215/cjers.v14i2.2762

Bishop, P., & Gripaios, P. (2010). Spatial externalities, relatedness and sector employment growth in Great Britain. *Regional Studies*, *44*(4), 443–454. doi:10.1080/00343400802508810

Blanchard, L. P., & Husted, T. F. (2020). *Nigeria: Current issues and US policy.* Library of Congress, Congressional Research Service [RL33964]. https://crsreports.congress.gov

Bleaney, M., Gemmell, N., & Kneller, R. (2001). Testing the endogenous growth model: Public expenditure, taxation, and growth over the long run. *The Canadian Journal of Economics. Revue Canadienne d'Economique*, *34*(1), 36–57. doi:10.1111/0008-4085.00061

Blythe, H. (2015). Laboratories of democracy or machinery of death? The story of lethal injection secrecy and a call to the supreme court for intervention. *Case Western Reserve Law Review*, *65*(4), 15. https://scholarlycommons.law.case.edu/caselrev/vol65/iss4/15

Brown, L., & Taylor, D. (2012). The birth of Medicare: From Saskatchewan's breakthrough to Canada-wide coverage. *Canadian Dimension.* https://canadiandimension.com/articles/view/the-birth-of-medicare

Bulmer, E. (2017). *Federalism.* International Institute for Democracy and Electoral Assistance: Constitution-Building Primer 12. Retrieved from https://www.idea.int/sites/default/files/publications/federalism-primer.pdf

Campbell, J., & Rotberg, R. I. (2021). The giant of Africa is failing only Nigeria can save itself—but the United States can help. *Foreign Affairs.* https://www.foreignaffairs.com/articles/africa/2021-05-31/giant-africa-failing

Checherita, C., Nickel, C., & Rother, P. (2009). *The role of fiscal transfers for regional economic convergence in Europe.* Working Paper Series – European Central Bank. https://www.ecb.europa.eu/pub/pdf/scpwps/ecbwp1029.pdf

Comisso, E. (1986). Introduction: State structures, political processes, and collective choice in CMEA states. *International Organization*, *40*(2), 195–238. doi:10.1017/S0020818300027132

de Figueiredo, Jr. R. J. P. & Weingast, B. R. (2002, April). *Pathologies of federalism, Russian style: political institutions and economic transition* [Paper Presentation]. Fiscal federalism in the Russian federation: Problems and prospects for reform. Higher School of Economics, Moscow, Russia.

Evans, P. (2018). State structures, government-business relations, and economic transformation. In S. Maxfield & B. R. Schneider (Eds.), *Business and the State in Developing Countries* (pp. 63–87). Cornell University Press. doi:10.7591/9781501731976-005

Faguet, J. P., Fox, A. M., & Poeschl, C. (2014). *Does decentralization strengthen or weaken the state? Authority and social learning in a supple state.* Department of International Development, London School of Economics and Political Science. http://eprints.lse.ac.uk/60631/

Fraser Institute. (2013). *Federalism and fiscal transfers: Essays on Australia, Germany, Switzerland, and the United States.* https://www.fraserinstitute.org/studies/federalism-and-fiscal-transfers-essays-on-australia-germany-switzerland-and-united-states

Frenken, K., Van Oort, F., & Verburg, T. (2007). Related variety, unrelated variety and regional economic growth. *Regional Studies, 41*(5), 685–697. doi:10.1080/00343400601120296

Gedamu, Y. (2019). Explainer: why Ethiopia's federal system is deeply flawed. *The Conversation.* Retrieved from https://theconversation.com/explainer-why-ethiopias-federal-system-is-deeply-flawed-119313

GelbA. (2014). Should Canada worry about a resource curse? *The School of Public Policy Publications, 7*(2). Retrieved from https://ssrn.com/abstract=3078380

Glaeser, E. (2011). Triumph of the city [Excerpt]. *Scientific American.* https://www.scientificamerican.com/article/glaeser-triumph-of-the-city-excerpt/

Harrison, A. E., Lin, J. F., & Xu, L. C. (2013). *Explaining Africa's (dis) advantage: The curse of party monopoly.* World Bank Policy Research Working Papers. https://elibrary.worldbank.org/doi/abs/10.1596/1813-9450-6316

Herzlinger, R. E. (2006). Why innovation in health care is so hard. *Harvard Business Review.* https://hbr.org/2006/05/why-innovation-in-health-care-is-so-hard

Hoover, E. M., & Giarratani, F. (1984). *An Introduction to Regional Economics.* Knopf.

Huddleston, J. (2018). *What states and cities do right to promote innovation. Federalism and tech policy.* Mercatus Center – George Mason University. https://www.mercatus.org/bridge/commentary/what-states-and-cities-do-right-promote-innovation

Long, S. K., Stockley, K., & Nordahl, K. W. (2012). Coverage, access, and affordability under health reform: Learning from the Massachusetts model. *INQUIRY: The Journal of Health Care Organization, Provision, and Financing*, *49*(4), 303–316. doi:10.5034/inquiryjrnl_49.04.03 PMID:23469674

Ma, J. (1999). *Intergovernmental fiscal transfers in nine countries: Lessons for developing countries.* Policy Research Working Papers – World Bank Group. doi:10.1596/1813-9450-1822

McCracken, C. (2006). *Whether state fiscal policy affects state economic growth.* Economics Department: Stanford University.

Okun, A. M. (1975). *Equality and efficiency: The big tradeoff.* Brookings Institution Press.

Olayele, B. F., & Soo, K. T. (2020). Redistributive fiscal policies and regional economic disparities. *Cogent Economics & Finance*, *8*(1), 1853326. doi:10.1080/23322039.2020.1853326

Ostry, J. D., Berg, A., & Tsangarides, C. G. (2014). *Redistribution, inequality, and growth.* IMF Staff Discussion Note. https://www.imf.org/external/pubs/ft/sdn/2014/sdn1402.pdf

Porter, M. E. (1990). The competitive advantage of nations. *Harvard Business Review*. https://hbr.org/1990/03/the-competitive-advantage-of-nations

Porter, M. E. (1995). The competitive advantage of the inner city. *Harvard Business Review.* https://hbr.org/1995/05/the-competitive-advantage-of-the-inner-city

Rodrik, D. (1997). *Has globalization gone too far?* Institute for International Economics. doi:10.2307/41165897

Romer, P. (1994). The origins of endogenous growth. *The Journal of Economic Perspectives*, *8*(1), 3–22. doi:10.1257/jep.8.1.3

Sandbu, M. (2020). *The economics of belonging: A radical plan to win back the left behind and achieve prosperity for all.* Princeton University Press.

Schroeder, L., & Smoke, P. (2003). Intergovernmental transfers in developing countries: Concepts, international practices and policy issues. In P. Smoke & Y. H. Kim (Eds.), *Intergovernmental Fiscal Transfers in Asia: Current Practice and Challenges for the Future* (pp. 20–59). Asian Development Bank.

Semro, B. (2012). Comparing the affordable care act and the Massachusetts model. *HuffPost.* https://www.huffpost.com/entry/comparing-the-affordable-care-act_b_1974586

Smith, S., & Gibson, C. M. (1988). Industrial diversification in nonmetropolitan counties and its effect on economic stability. *Western Journal of Agricultural Economics*, *13*(2), 193–201.

Suberu, R. (2009). Federalism in Africa: The Nigerian experience in comparative perspective. *Ethnopolitics*, *8*(1), 67–86. doi:10.1080/17449050902738846

Suberu, R. (2010). The Nigerian federal system: Performance, problems and prospects. *Journal of Contemporary African Studies*, *28*(4), 459–477. doi:10.1080/02589001.2010.512741

Suberu, R. T. (2015). Lessons in Fiscal Federalism for Africa's New Oil Exporters. In A. C. LeVan, J. O. Fashagba, & E. R. McMahon (Eds.), *African State Governance*. Palgrave Macmillan. doi:10.1057/9781137523341_2

United Nations Conference on Trade and Development. (2019). Commodity-dependent countries urged to diversify exports. *UNCTAD News.* Retrieved from https://unctad.org/news/commodity-dependent-countries-urged-diversify-exports

Watts, R. (1996). *Comparing Federal Systems in the 1990s*. Institute of Intergovernmental Relations, Queens University.

Weingast, B. (1995). The economic role of political institutions: Market-preserving federalism and economic development. *Journal of Law Economics and Organization*, *11*(1), 1–31. https://www.jstor.org/stable/765068

Wheare, K. C. (1946). *Federal Government*. Oxford University Press.

World Bank. (2020). Nigeria: Overview. *Where We Work.* https://www.worldbank.org/en/country/nigeria/overview

World Bank. (2021). Ethiopia: Overview. *Where We Work* https://www.worldbank.org/en/country/ethiopia/overview

ENDNOTES

1 In 2017–2018, Amazon launched a highly-publicized site selection bid process for its proposed $5 billion investment project, dubbed HQ2.

2 South Africa adopts quasi-federalism, with increasing features of centralism and declining autonomy for constituent units.

Chapter 7
Structural Shifts and the Race to Net Zero:
A Policy Diffusion Analysis

ABSTRACT

Transitioning towards sustainable energy systems often involves optimizing multiple pathways. As the digital revolution shifts the composition of trade globally, not only is diversification required to help reduce dependence on natural resources, but it is also needed to create an innovation ecosystem that enables digital innovations to create exportable high-value business services – beyond traditional resources and manufacturing. This chapter recognizes this. As the energy landscape continues to shift around the world, it is argued that policy incentives and pathways that may help strengthen Africa's adaptive capacity need to be considered. Since differing economic structures and policy thrusts influence energy use and production patterns, the debate on energy system transformation will remain on the front burner of the global energy investment and policy agenda for years to come. Optimal outcomes will depend on how structural, efficiency, and jurisdictional nuances are balanced.

DOI: 10.4018/978-1-7998-7383-9.ch007

One day soon poor countries may actually benefit from their natural resources.

— The Economist

NATURAL RESOURCES REMAIN A KEY INPUT in the production process – either through direct economic use in satisfying human needs or indirectly by undergoing transformation into other goods and services that can serve the economy and society. To translate natural capital endowments into growth and development in a manner that protects communities, reduces carbon emissions, and provides opportunities for a broad segment of society, the right policies are a necessity. For a very long time, natural resources were considered beneficial to economic growth. The resource-growth nexus attracted a lot of attention after Sachs and Warner (1995) showed that an increase of one standard deviation in natural resource intensity (on average 16 percent of GNP) leads to a reduction of about 1 percent per year in economic growth. This has come to be known as the "resource curse".

The controversy generated by Sachs and Warner's results is understandable on a major premise: economic theory predicts that capital (of which natural resources constitute a part) has a positive effect on growth. However, the central question in the modern resource curse literature has gone beyond whether or not natural resources negatively impact economic growth as earlier argued; instead, it is now largely about the conditionality of the curse on some other factors.

The resource curse has two common explanations in the literature: (i) economic and (ii) political-institutional. The pioneering research of Corden and Neary (1982) forms the basis of the Dutch disease theory, a situation that leads to a diminished importance of the manufacturing sector due to the crowding out effect of natural resources – a major economic explanation of the curse. Corden and Neary use a two-factor, two-good model to explain what can cause a decrease in the competitiveness of the trade-exposed manufacturing sector. They assume a small open economy with three sectors – a non-tradable sector (service sector), an import-competing manufacturing sector, and a resource sector – and conclude that the resource boom will affect the rest of the economy through the movement of manufacturing resources and expenditures. This leads to a lagging export sector which suffers through the so-called deindustrialization.

Starting with the famous work of Sachs and Warner, which formally established the resource curse, their results support a dynamic version of the Dutch disease model by showing that on average, resource-abundant countries lag countries with less resources. Using the ratio of natural resource exports to GDP as a proxy for natural resource endowment, and 1971 as the base year, they control for other determinants of economic growth such as initial per capita income, trade policy, government efficiency, and investment rates.

Auty and Mikesell (1998) examine the problems faced by mineral-rich countries in achieving sustainable development, compared to their mineral-deficient neighbors. Focusing on nine countries – Botswana, Chile, Colombia, Indonesia, Jamaica, Namibia, Papua New Guinea, Peru, and Trinidad and Tobago – Auty and Mikesell offer a compelling argument on why nurturing the economic and social conditions that sustain economic growth is more important than the sustainability of mineral production itself.

The second popular explanation of the curse is the political-institutional dimension. This model blames the existence of the curse on rent-seeking behaviour. Robinson et al. (2006) present a formal political-economy framework of the resource curse by arguing that to understand whether or not natural resources are a blessing or a curse, it is imperative to analyze the political incentives that resource endowments generate, through a careful analysis of the interaction between institutions and resources. To fully analyze the effects of temporary and permanent resource booms, they use a two-period probabilistic model to consider some stock of natural resources with an intertemporal path of prices subject to exogenous price variation. This analytical setting captures the operating environment of small developing economies, subject to international commodity price variations. Their analysis reveals a complex relationship between resource extraction and the political environment. Where there are weak political institutions, resource booms will lead, through the political process, to inefficient resource allocation.

The authors conclude that the extent to which the predictions in their model generate the curse is determined by the quality of institutions – since countries with strong institutions benefit from resource booms, while those without suffer from the curse. Isham et al. (2005) corroborate this from the perspective that resource rents may create a wealthy class of elites who may be opposed to welfare-improving economic and political reforms.

INSTITUTIONS AND INNOVATIONS IN THE EXTRACTIVES SECTOR

Mehlum et al. (2006) improve on the influential work of Sachs and Warner through their findings which show that institutions are decisive for the resource curse. Using the average growth rate of real GDP per capita from 1965 to 1990 as the dependent variable, and an unweighted average of five indexes which ranges from zero to unity (rule of law index, bureaucratic quality index, corruption in government index, risk of expropriation index, and government repudiation of contract index) as a proxy for institutional quality, they demonstrate that countries with good institutional quality will not experience any resource curse as natural resources only inhibit economic growth in countries with 'grabber friendly' institutions, and not in countries with 'producer friendly' institutions.

They go beyond the regressions of Sachs and Warner by providing an alternative explanation for the understanding of the resource curse through the inclusion of an interaction term that captures their prediction: resource abundance is harmful to growth only when institutions are weak. In addition to finding a positive coefficient for the interaction term, the empirical results equally show that countries with institutional quality index higher than the threshold value of 0.93 do not experience the resource curse. As such, 15 out of the 87 countries included in the regression have institutional quality strong enough to neutralize the resource curse – which is manifested through a negative growth impact of a marginal increase in resources.

The extractive industries support the economies of 63 countries in significant ways, but many of these countries are EMDEs faced with traditional, agelong challenges of transforming natural capital endowments into other assets that can help drive development in a sustainable manner (World Bank, 2021). As highlighted under the various theoretical strands in the earlier chapters, many EMDEs are characterized by the volatility associated with commodity cycles. Among other things, the dominant features of these economies include low per capita income, structural issues, constrained domestic resource mobilization ability, informality, fragmentation, and limited access to international capital markets. In this context, the development orthodoxy (e.g., traditional Harrod-Domar-type models, where capital productivity and the rate of investment, through domestic savings rate, determine growth rate) becomes grossly inadequate.

Again, policy innovation can play an important role in improving the scenario depicted above. Fueling growth through digital transformation in the interconnected global economy has become necessary for long-term success and prosperity. Nowhere is this more evident than in the extractives sector. Digitalization and automation continue to transform how goods and services are produced, delivered, and consumed. Traditional business models are being turned upside down, while new sources of wealth are created across the board.

As the digital revolution shifts the composition of trade globally, not only is diversification required to help reduce dependence on natural resources, but it is also needed to create an innovation ecosystem that enables digital innovations to create exportable high-value business services – beyond traditional resources and manufacturing. The digital renaissance offers a unique opportunity for policy leadership as nations transform their economies into dynamic and competitive powerhouses. To partake in future gains from the evolving global digital economy, policy innovation can play an important role vis-à-vis determining and delivering the speed of adjustment consistent with the dynamics of the new economy.

Regulations, competitiveness, trade, and productivity performance of energy economic systems are key issues in the sustainability debate. Tackling climate change to transition towards a global low-carbon economy remains an urgent and important policy priority for the international community. The Paris Agreement on Climate Change, adopted in December 2015, provides a framework for stakeholders to accelerate and intensify the actions and investments needed for a sustainable low-carbon future (United Nations, n.d.).

In the short term, economies comprised of energy-intensive, trade-exposed (EITE) industries face stiff global competition. The "competitiveness" channel remains the carbon leakage channel that poses the greatest concern for policymakers (Fischer, 2015), since in the absence of a harmonized climate policy among trading partners, competitiveness pressures may be exerted on less competitive partners because of a higher carbon price. In addition to subjecting EITE industrial sectors to a competitive disadvantage, high compliance costs may provide an incentive for the relocation of emissions-intensive operations, creating the risk of carbon leakage and a loss in economic activity, market share, and capital investments to lower-cost jurisdictions.

The Porter (1991) hypothesis argues that environmental policies may, through technological innovation, lead to productivity gains in polluting firms, thereby making them more competitive. Since global emissions will remain unchanged from a mere relocation of greenhouse gas (GHG) emissions across the border, this could further undermine global efforts at reducing carbon emissions. Policy innovations based on policy design possibilities that pay attention to how energy intensity changes across important economic sectors, over time, is key to addressing the competitiveness impacts of carbon pricing policies on trade.

Technology has a major impact on the environmental consequences of social and business activity. In turn, new constraints and incentives with the ability to alter the future trajectory of technological innovations are potential byproducts of environmental regulations (Jaffe et al., 2003). To the extent that the trade-environment-energy nexus remains an important component of the sustainable development agenda, a better understanding of the dynamics of competitiveness impacts, in addition to demographic and structural shifts, will be important in future policy designs targeted at decarbonizing these economies. As the global energy transition gathers steam, Africa faces unique challenges. The continent's quest for industrialization is resolute. And contemporary evidence corroborates the argument that Africa's industrialization path should not necessarily follow that of the West or China. In light of the ongoing digital transformation, efficient and innovative approaches and technologies that prioritize Africa's responsible and sustainable use of natural resources to meet its development priorities remain key to addressing poverty and inequality.

STRUCTURAL SHIFTS AND THE GLOBAL ENERGY TRANSITION

The United Nations Sustainable Development Goal 7 (SDG 7) aims to "Ensure access to affordable, reliable, sustainable, and modern energy for all" (United Nations, n.d.). Indeed, improving access to affordable and clean energy for all, while reducing GHG emissions and the carbon footprint of the energy sector, is a laudable objective. Historically, the interplay between policy and markets has been a major driver of the global energy transition, albeit differing circumstances shape specific outcomes. For instance, in much of Europe, the privatization of energy assets in the UK heralded the reliance on market-based incentives to drive the transition to renewable energy.

Dell'Aquila et al. (2020) compare and contrast the decarbonization pathways in the UK and China through renewable energy deployment, while recognizing the differing energy transition strategies in both countries. They show that while regulation was deployed to harness market forces to pave the way for the energy transition in the UK, the ability of the country to successfully transition away from direct government support was largely due to policy flexibility and the unfettered ability of market forces to drive the decarbonization process – compared to other European countries where direct state support was crucial. Moreso, the depletion of the North Sea oil and gas reserves in the UK made decarbonization in the UK more of an economic, than an environmental, argument.

Dell'Aquila et al. espouse how the shift from public to private ownership of energy assets in the 1980s and the 1990s heralded the decarbonization of Britain's economy through unprecedented private investments which aided the building of new power plants from coal-fired to natural gas generation:

While the need to transition to a low-carbon economy was increasingly reiterated at international summits throughout the 1990s, the country had already achieved significantly reduced levels of coal in the energy mix thanks to an increasing reliance on nuclear and gas. Overall, during this period, a substantial decarbonization of Britain's economy was mainly driven by a need to ensure energy security through the support for nuclear, and by economic factors that made gas-fired generation increasingly cost-competitive with coal (Dell'Aquila et al., 2020; p. 233)

On the contrary, while technological advances and innovation have contributed to the energy transition process in China, Dell'Aquila et al. argue that climate concerns and social issues, combined, have paved the way for the relatively successful state-led energy transition in the country. As they put it:

China, on the other hand, began its journey towards decarbonization later, its motivation was driven partly by the availability of natural renewable resources—such as wind and sun—which in turn would reduce the country's need to import primary energy and secondly, abate emissions which were becoming particularly significant in urban areas risking a public backlash. China epitomizes a very large and topographically diverse country in which the role of the state has been instrumental not only in policymaking aspects of the energy transition, but crucially also in funding, building, owning and operating renewable energy power plants (Dell'Aquila et al., 2020; p.228).

In the same vein, Pistelli (2020) underscores why it is important to contextualize the notion of the energy transition in sub-Saharan Africa since the concept of "transition" itself connotes moving from one socioeconomic and technological arrangement to another. The author argues that in a way, this implies there is an existing arrangement; but the reality is that 600 million people lack access to electricity. Pistelli therefore cautions that if in fact the majority of the population cannot access energy, then, there is nothing to transit away from:

The 'transition' to cleaner forms of energy is thus only a complementary concern, second to that of providing access to energy. In other words, if the majority of the population does not have access to energy, it does not have anything to transit away from (Pistelli, 2020; p. 153)

Transitioning towards sustainable energy systems often involves optimizing multiple pathways. The "energy trilemma"[1] remains a central challenge for energy governance. The great oil crash of 2014, global economic rebalancing, environmental concerns, and improvements in energy efficiency due to technological innovations – all combined – continue to drive the gradual decarbonization of the global fuel mix. The case for the transition towards sustainable energy systems has never been stronger. As a result, economic diversification has moved to the front burner of the policy agenda in many countries, especially resource-rich ones.

ENERGY TRANSITION AND TOUGH CHOICES: A POLICY DIFFUSION IMPERATIVE

The idea of promoting economic diversification for sustainable development is not entirely new. We laid the theoretical foundation earlier on. Collier and Venables (2007), among others, opine that economic diversification is a potent long-term strategy that can help resource-dependent jurisdictions escape the resource curse. Resource-rich jurisdictions remain constrained regarding the extent of diversification that is attainable. The Dutch disease theory sheds light on the perils of mismanaging commodity booms; this supports, in a way, the notion that a concentrated resource base makes economic diversification difficult. At the other end of the spectrum are arguments that natural resource windfalls can help provide the much-needed funding for innovation, infrastructure, and other critical elements of an ecosystem that supports a vibrant and diversified economy. The debate rages on, and Africa's energy economic future needs to be situated, in the context of these ramifications, for optimal outcomes.

There are ample lessons from resource-rich developed economies (e.g., Canada, U.S., Australia), and a few countries in the Gulf region that have transitioned to become highly diversified, over time. Of course, this often requires tough policy choices, and sometimes, serendipity. We examine this further by analyzing the energy economies of Africa, Canada, and the Gulf region – three energy-intensive jurisdictions with varying low-carbon transition plans. Useful lessons for policy innovation are drawn afterwards.

Canadian Energy Innovation

Only a few countries in the world compare to Canada in terms of the quantity and diversity of natural resources and energy endowments. Canada is the world's sixth largest energy producer, the fifth largest net exporter, and the eighth largest consumer (Government of Canada, 2020). With diverse and abundant renewable and non-renewable energy sources, the country boasts a unique economic structure, compared to other countries in the industrialized world. Due to its climate, vast geography, and heavy reliance on resource-based industries, the Canadian economy is highly energy-intensive. Though the world's 10th largest GHG emitter, through a wide variety of federal and provincial climate policy initiatives, Canada's transition to a modern, low-carbon energy future is well underway (Gabbatiss, 2019).

The Pan-Canadian Framework on Clean Growth and Climate Change (PCF), introduced on December 9, 2016, is Canada's first ever plan "to include joint and individual commitments by federal, provincial, and territorial levels of government" (Government of Canada, 2021, p. 2). The PCF is also the first to have been developed "with input from Indigenous Peoples, businesses, non-governmental organizations, and Canadians from across the country" (p. 2). Anchored on four pillars – pricing carbon pollution; complementary actions to reduce emissions across the economy; adaptation and climate resilience; and clean technology, innovation, and jobs – the PCF is aimed at mobilizing stakeholders to "take ambitious action to fight climate change, build resilience to a changing climate, and drive clean economic growth" (p. 2).

While Canada's carbon pricing mandate is beginning to lead to reduced emissions from the electricity generation sector, the country remains the only G7 nation with rising GHG emissions since the Paris Agreement (Austen & Favelle, 2021). Given that most cleantech companies in the country are early-stage startups and SMEs, there are practical implications for policy diffusion, to the extent that incentive frameworks for firms drive the economic retooling process. While Canada's transition to a low carbon future – given the highly energy intensive nature of its economy –involves complex trade-offs, the nuances of its history, social makeup, and institutional design explain its recognition as one of the world's most decentralized federations (Simeon, 2002). In a way, this makes Canada a perfect model for countries and regions pondering how to navigate the complex waters of diversification and energy sustainability (Box 1).

Box 1. Canada's Energy and Political Economy Dynamics

Despite Canada's many achievements on the energy sustainability front, challenges remain. In particular, federal climate policy proposals often reverberate throughout the energy landscape, with huge implications for the labyrinth of federal-provincial relations. However, as it is often said, sustainability is a journey, not a destination. The country has made remarkable progress in its march towards sustainability, driven largely by its global leadership in technological and regulatory innovations.

For instance, the province of Saskatchewan is a world leader in the advancement of emissions-reducing technologies, through its carbon capture, utilization, and storage (CCUS) facility. As well, Saskatchewan's neighbour, Alberta, the epicenter of the Canadian energy industry, continues to prioritize energy innovation and investments in the green economy. A November 2016 Globe and Mail article notes the shift in the epicenter of green power development to Western Canada, calling Alberta and Saskatchewan "the new frontier for Canada's renewable energy industry".

From clean hydrogen and carbon-negative concrete to carbon sinks and the use of X-ray sensors on the industrial scoops in mining operations, the Canadian cleantech ecosystem has witnessed high-impact and scalable innovations in recent years. In 2022, Canada ranked second (with 13 firms) after the US on the annual Global Cleantech 100 list – a prestigious list of startups deploying innovative technologies to address the climate crisis (Cleantech Group, 2022).

As a global cleantech industry leader, Canada's exports to other regions, in addition to its main European and US markets, continue to grow in importance. The Toronto Stock Exchange (TSX) and the TSX Venture Exchange put the total market capitalization of the 83 companies listed at $42.8 billion – with 72 of those headquartered in Canada, and accounting for $37.8 billion of the total market capitalization (as of April 30, 2019).

Canada also ranks competitively in terms of investment in new domestic clean energy generation projects, with a total of 168 clean technology projects valued at $92.1 billion in 2021 (Government of Canada, Energy Fact Book, 2021). Not just that, R&D spending of Canadian pure play cleantech companies has increased significantly over the years.

Due to the ongoing global economic shift in the production and consumption of energy, the private sector in much of Canada is leading the way in creating solutions aimed at supporting energy transition alternatives. Earlier in 2021, BMO Financial Group announced its plan of "establishing goals for emissions reduction in its own operations, a net zero financing pathway, and sustainable finance targets" (Segal, 2021).

Perhaps even more compelling is the need to ensure SMEs are not left behind in the process. SMEs account for 99.8% of all Canadian companies; over 60% of all private sector workers in the country are employed by SMEs. One of the critical lessons is that renewables are strategically positioned as the driver of future growth across the energy value chain.

The Pulse of the Gulf Region

Ample lessons abound from the Gulf Cooperation Council (GCC) countries, albeit significant costs and trade-offs are involved. The Gulf countries remain one of the most resource-endowed jurisdictions in the world. In fact, the GCC countries of Bahrain, Kuwait, Oman, Qatar, Saudi Arabia, and the United Arab Emirates (UAE) have the highest energy intensity in the world, with implications for diversification prospects, energy use, and efficiency patterns across industry sectors (United States Energy Information Administration, 2019).

As the energy transition journey gathers momentum, policymakers in the GCC have continued to ponder a few questions. What implications do structural and efficiency trade-offs have for industry-level productivity and international competitiveness? Considering current energy use and efficiency trends, how sustainable and compatible are current policy thrusts with the historically complicated structural barriers to diversification in the region? What policy pathways may help strengthen GCC countries' adaptive capacity? Of course, to the extent that differing economic structures and policy thrusts influence energy use and production patterns, in the wealth creation process, optimal outcomes will depend on how structural, efficiency and jurisdictional nuances are balanced (Box 2).

Diversifying away from natural resources is difficult; broad reforms and transparent, coherent, and supportive regulatory and institutional frameworks remain critical. While it is true that the GCC economies have witnessed significant structural shifts over the past two decades, nonetheless, deeper reforms are needed.

Box 2: Diversification and Economic Retooling in the Gulf Region

The GCC first identified economic diversification as a strategic thrust for its members after the 1986 collapse in oil prices (Gately, et al. 1986 & Hvdit, 2013). Ever since, countries in the region have crafted various strategies and policies to ensure sustainability of their hydrocarbon revenues.

As governments in the region continue to envision the future they want, recent economic retooling and development strategies are targeted at boosting skills acquisition to foster entrepreneurship and innovation, in addition to curtailing the rapid growth in government spending.

A 2015 United Nations Educational, Scientific and Cultural Organisation (UNESCO) Science Report notes that while Saudi Arabia, the UAE, and Qatar have made some progress in their diversification efforts – through the non-oil sectors – much work remains to be done in Bahrain and Kuwait. In the same vein, the Global Innovation Index shows that the Gulf region's innovation economy continues to advance, with the UAE leading the pack, while Kuwait and Bahrain are making major advances in the Arab world's digital technology space.

A few years ago, the Grandmaster of oil, Saudi Arabia, stepped-up its diversification campaign by visiting Washington D.C. and New York to pitch the Kingdom's new market-driven, post-oil audacious idea: *Saudi Arabia's National Transformation Plan.* A critical element of the Plan is incentivizing the private sector to play a more active role in advancing the region's diversification agenda.

What do the two case studies on Canada and the Gulf region mean for Africa? To the extent that entrepreneurship and innovation remain vital in the wealth creation process in the new digital economy, there are ample lessons – vis-à-vis policy diffusion – for the emerging venture capital ecosystem across the continent, particularly in the renewable energy sector. No doubt, policy innovation matters here. This is discussed further below from the lens of the leapfrog effect.

LEAPFROGGING, DECARBONIZATION, AND THE JOURNEY TO NET ZERO IN AFRICA

The debate on whether or not Africa can leapfrog its way into development is overflogged. The simple answer is yes. But with a caveat. Managing Director of the International Finance Corporation and former World Bank Vice President for Africa, Makhtar Diop, succinctly summarizes this: "Not all leapfrogging attempts will be successful. African countries, as well as the private sector or development partners, must be willing to take risks and learn from failures" (Diop, 2017; para. 7).

Africa's Energy Economy

Africa's energy deficit poses a substantial challenge for development. The case for building sustainable energy systems to create wealth and employment on the continent has never been stronger. Every year, Africa loses between 2-4 percent of GDP to energy-related bottlenecks and power shortages (Kende-Robb, 2016). Sub-Saharan Africa is home to three-quarters of the global population without access to electricity (International Energy Agency, 2020).

The African Development Bank (AfDB) (2015) suggests over 645 million Africans lack access to electricity. At about 181 kWh per annum, compared to 6,500 kWh in Europe and 13,000 kWh in the United States, sub-Saharan Africa's average per capita electricity consumption is abysmally low. Considering its enormous energy resource endowments, multiple pathways to energy transformation are required to ensure sustainable development on the continent.

As the energy landscape continues to shift around the world, policy incentives and pathways that may help strengthen Africa's adaptive capacity need to be considered. Since differing economic structures and policy thrusts influence energy use and production patterns, the debate on energy system transformation will remain on the front burner of the global energy investment and policy agenda for years to come. It goes without saying that optimal outcomes will depend on how structural, efficiency, and jurisdictional nuances are balanced.

Energy and Pandemic Shocks

COVID-19 is having differing impacts on energy systems across the world. While reduced traffic on the roads in the immediate aftermath of the pandemic triggered a concomitant emissions improvement in the transportation sector, the health crisis also hampered the expansion of clean energy technologies and investments. Amid the COVID-19 crisis, the compounding effect of rapid population growth and pandemic-induced economic difficulties puts millions of Africans in an increasingly precarious situation.

As well, the public health crisis is pushing countries farther away from achieving universal electricity access. As governments continue to shift resources away from other sectors, in a bid to contain the virus, recent gains in energy poverty alleviation are being eroded. According to the International Energy Agency (2020)'s Stated Policies Scenario[2], released in October 2020, "In 2030, 50% of the global population without access is concentrated in seven countries – Democratic Republic of the Congo, Nigeria, Uganda, Pakistan, Tanzania, Niger, and Sudan."

The pandemic has disproportionately affected micro-, small, and medium enterprises (MSMEs). Due to their largely informal nature in Africa, MSMEs are among the worst hit financially. Economic recovery in many jurisdictions often depend on the ability of MSMEs to survive and thrive. As countries strategically position clean energy as the driver of future growth across the energy value chain, it is important to ensure MSMEs are not left behind. The MSME sector is key to economic and industrial revival. African countries must ponder policy measures capable of tilting the incentive structure in favor of MSMEs, research institutions, investors, and other players in the entrepreneurial ecosystem. This will be important for localizing the SDGs; strategies targeted at moving the needle must be adapted to the specific contexts and needs of different cities, regions, and countries.

Africa's Energy Policy Paradigms

On September 17, 2015, the AfDB unveiled its landmark initiative to mobilize support and funding to fast-track universal access to power by 2025: the New Deal for Energy in Africa (NDEA). The NDEA unifies all the other initiatives geared towards achieving the Bank's universal energy access ambition; it is anchored on five key principles: (i) raising aspirations to solve Africa's energy challenges, (ii) establishing a Transformative Partnership on Energy for Africa, (iii) mobilizing domestic and international capital for innovative financing in Africa's energy sector, (iv) supporting African governments in strengthening energy policy, regulation, and sector governance, and (v) increasing the AfDB's investments in energy and climate financing (AfDB, 2017, p. 2).

The NDEA proposes four targets: (i) increase on-grid generation to add 160 GW of new capacity by 2025, (ii) increase on-grid transmission and grid connections that will create 130 million new connections by 2025, (iii) increase off-grid generation to add 75 million connections by 2025, and (iv) increase access to clean cooking energy for around 130 million households.

The potential for Africa's vast renewable energy resources to help its sustainable development prospects has been discussed earlier on. Moreso, the continent's ability to adopt innovative, clean, indigenous, and affordable renewable energy solutions through the notion of "leapfrogging to renewables" continues to dominate the clean energy transition debate. Much like in South Asia, Africa's ability to bypass the use of fixed telephone lines through massive adoption of cellular phones remains a compelling example of the benefits that come with leapfrogging expensive and often complicated investments in physical infrastructure – to advance from the margins to the mainstream of global commerce.

The political commitment of African leaders, through the Africa Clean Energy Corridor (ACEC), is helping to drive the strengthening of regional energy institutions and transmission infrastructure, forming large competitive markets, and lowering costs across production sectors (International Renewable Energy Agency (IRENA) n.d). Clean Energy Corridors across the east, southern, and west regions of the continent are aimed at accelerating the development of renewable energy potential and cross-border trade of renewable power.[3] The ACEC model is backed by more than 30 countries, regional agencies, development partners, and financial institutions along five pillars: (i) zoning and resource assessment to site renewable power plants in areas with high resource potential and suitable transmission routes; (ii) national and regional planning to identify the most cost-effective renewable power options; (iii) enabling frameworks for investment to open markets and reduce financing costs; (iv) capacity building to integrate higher shares of renewable electricity generation within power grids and markets; and (v) publicity campaigns to raise awareness of how large-scale renewables can provide secure, sustainable and affordable energy (IRENA, n.d; para. 4).

Initially designed as a regional initiative within the Eastern Africa Power Pool and Southern African Power Pool – to operate based on a $25 billion per year power generation investments until 2030, and an incremental $15 billion per year for grid infrastructure – the West African Power Pool and part of the Pan-Arab Clean Energy were later integrated into the model (IRENA, n.d.). The corridors are designed to leverage utility-scale renewable energy development, using cross-border trade possibilities as an incentive to minimize fragmentation and benefit from scale economies in the use of Africa's abundant energy resources (IRENA, 2020).

Policy Innovation for Africa's Energy Transition

Decarbonization is fundamental to resolving Africa's high hydrocarbon dependence, but the path to net zero emissions is narrow. In a recent study, Alova et al. (2021) warn that despite the perceived progress in Africa's decarbonization agenda, the share of non-hydro renewables in electricity generation will be less than 10 percent by 2030. With the aid of a machine-learning model that combined country-level characteristics with "the largest dataset on historic and planned power plants available for Africa", the study analyzed over 2,500 power plants across 54 African countries and found that non-hydro renewable sources like geothermal, solar, and wind energy account for only 3 percent of Africa's power supply.

These findings show that fossil fuels will make up two-thirds of all electricity generated on the continent by 2030, with close to 40 percent of solar energy generation coming from South Africa alone. Apart from the "high carbon lock-in risks" this portends in terms of derailing Africa's low-carbon transition, it also underscores the need for large scale private sector investment.

Foreign direct investment (FDI) remains a key driver of innovation. In addition to creating jobs and injecting capital into the local economy, its positive impacts on productivity gains – through supply chain linkages and technology transfers – remain desirable. At the macroeconomic level, FDI could provide a stable and predictable stream of financing to help offset fiscal deficits caused by reduced government spending necessitated by ongoing reforms. Africa is already leveraging policy to tilt incentive structure in favour of SMEs, research institutions, investors, and other players in the entrepreneurial ecosystem. The momentum must continue.

With most governments across the continent prioritizing resource mobilization to rebuild their healthcare and economic systems in the aftermath of the ruins inflicted by the COVID-19 pandemic, policy innovation is required to devise alternative financing channels and optimization pathways.

As well, significant capital mobilization is required for capital reallocation from high-carbon to low-carbon technologies. Perhaps even more compelling is the pivotal role played by the private sector in the digital revolution that swept through the continent in the last two decades, thereby enabling Africa to make some gains in terms of bridging existing gaps in development with the rest of the world. However, unlocking the continent's renewable potential still requires significant investments and drastic policy innovation.

As the name suggests, policy change underpins the energy transition debate. As argued in the preceding chapters – particularly under the eight theories of policy change – policy innovation is fundamental to understanding and achieving optimal outcomes in energy transitions given its ability to disentangle policy alternatives.

To the extent that sustainable decarbonization pathways involve policy mixes that prioritize accelerated deployment of renewable energy and energy efficiency technologies, while recognizing economic growth and industrialization imperatives, the policy innovation lens in the energy transition discourse is compelling.

The world of policy has many policy subsystems that make it compelling for political actors to advance their policy priorities through advocacy coalitions. In the context of the energy transition, the political economy of fossil fuels, particularly the politics of coal phase-out and fossil fuel subsidies, is complicated. This often hinders policy innovation efforts since advocacy coalitions may be required in the policy process if elected officials and the top echelons of the bureaucracy do not align on key aspects of the policy agenda.

More so, in a complicated policymaking environment where political short-termism is pervasive, top bureaucrats may not favor decision-making under ambiguity and high uncertainty. To avoid reversing some of the hard-fought gains along the energy transition journey, policy entrepreneurship – discussed in detail under the Kingdon MSF analysis – can help unlock innovative tools, resources, strategies, and partnerships capable of charting alternative policy pathways and the adoption of the necessary models to achieve the intended objectives.

Whether through policy entrepreneurship or policy diffusion, bold actions are needed to support innovation and behavioral changes that underpin a successful energy transition. Public-private policy partnerships – the focus of the next chapter – can go a long way in making this happen. Even so, there are no easy fixes. For optimal solutions, the promises and challenges of Africa's energy economy must be fully accounted for.

As the world sleepwalks to climate catastrophe, young people are ringing the alarm bells. They understand better than many in power that time is running out. My message as they fight for their right to a future remains: Never give up. Never retreat. Keep pushing forward.

— António Guterres

REFERENCES

African Development Bank. (2015). *Energy and climate change: Implications for inclusive and green growth in Africa.* Annual Report. https://www.afdb.org/fileadmin/uploads/afdb/Documents/Publications/AR2015/Annual_Report_2015_EN_-_Chapter_2.pdf

African Development Bank. (2017). *The new deal on energy for Africa: A transformative partnership to light up and power Africa by 2025. Update on Implementation.* https://www.afdb.org/fileadmin/uploads/afdb/Documents/Generic-Documents/Brochure_New_Deal_2_red.pdf

Alova, G., Trotter, P. A., & Money, A. (2021). A machine-learning approach to predicting Africa's electricity mix based on planned power plants and their chances of success. *Nature Energy*, *6*(2), 158–166. doi:10.103841560-020-00755-9

Austen, I., & Favelle, C. (2021). Trudeau was a global hero. Now Canada risks falling behind. *New York Times.* https://www.nytimes.com/2021/04/21/world/canada/trudeau-climate-oil-sands.html

Auty, R. M., & Mikesell, R. F. (1998). *Sustainable development in mineral economies.* Clarendon Press.

Blackwell, R. (2016). Alberta, Saskatchewan turn focus to renewable energy. *Globe and Mail.* https://www.theglobeandmail.com/report-on-business/industry-news/energy-and-resources/alberta-saskatchewan-turn-focus-to-renewable-energy/article32903173/

Cleantech Group. (2022). *Global Cleantech 100.* https://www.cleantech.com/the-global-cleantech-100/

Collier, P., & Venables, A. J. (2007). Rethinking trade preferences: How Africa can diversify its exports. *World Economy*, *30*(8), 1326–1345. doi:10.1111/j.1467-9701.2007.01042.x

Corden, W., & Neary, J. (1982). Booming sector and de-industrialisation in a small open economy. *Economic Journal (London)*, *92*(368), 825–848. doi:10.2307/2232670

Dell'Aquila, M., Atzori, D., & Stroe, O. R. (2020). The role of policy design and market forces to achieve an effective energy transition: A comparative analysis between the UK and Chinese models. In M. Hafner & S. Tagliapietra (Eds.), *The geopolitics of the global energy transition. Lecture notes in energy* (Vol. 73, pp. 227–255). Springer International Publishing AG. doi:10.1007/978-3-030-39066-2_10

Diop, M. (2017). *Africa can enjoy leapfrog development.* World Bank Group. https://www.worldbank.org/en/news/opinion/2017/10/11/africa-can-enjoy-leapfrog-development

Fischer, C. (2015). *Options for avoiding carbon leakage.* Geneva Reports on the World Economy. Centre for Economic Policy Research.

Gabbatiss, J. (2019). The carbon brief profile: Canada [Country Profiles]. *Carbon Brief.* https://www.carbonbrief.org/the-carbon-brief-profile-canada

Gately, D., Adelman, M. A., & Griffin, J. M. (1986). Lessons from the 1986 oil price collapse. *Brookings Papers on Economic Activity, 17*(2), 237–284. doi:10.2307/2534475

Government of Canada. (2020). *Canada and Sub-Saharan Africa.* https://www.international.gc.ca/world-monde/international_relations-relations_internationales/africa-afrique/index.aspx?lang=eng

Government of Canada. (2021). *Energy fact book.* Natural Resources Canada. https://www.nrcan.gc.ca/sites/nrcan/files/energy/energy_fact/2021-2022/PDF/2021_Energy-factbook_december23_EN_accessible.pdf

Government of Canada. (2021). National inventory report 1990–2019: Greenhouse gas sources and sinks in Canada: Canada's submission to the United Nations framework convention on climate change [Executive Summary]. *Environment and Climate Change Canada.* https://publications.gc.ca/collections/collection_2021/eccc/En81-4-1-2019-eng.pdf

Hvidt, M. (2013). *Economic diversification in the GCC countries-past record and future trends.* Research Paper No. 27: Kuwait Programme on Development, Governance and Globalisation in the Gulf States.

International Energy Agency. (2020). *SDG7: Data and projections.* International Energy Agency. https://www.iea.org/reports/sdg7-data-and-projections

International Renewable Energy Agency. (2020). *Scaling up renewable energy deployment in Africa: Detailed overview of IRENA's engagement and impact*. Author.

International Renewable Energy Agency. (n.d.). Africa Clean Energy Corridor. *IRENA*. https://irena.org/cleanenergycorridors/Africa-Clean-Energy-Corridor

Isham, J., Woolcock, M., Pritchett, L., & Busby, G. (2005). The varieties of resource experience: Natural resource export structures and the political economy of economic growth. *The World Bank Economic Review*, *19*(2), 141–174. doi:10.1093/wber/lhi010

Jaffe, A. B., Newell, R. G., & Stavins, R. N. (2003). Technological change and the environment. In K. G. Mäler & J. R. Vincent (Eds.), *Handbook of Environmental Economics* (Vol. 1, pp. 461–516). Elsevier Science Publishers.

Kende-Robb, C. (2016). *Africa's energy poverty is keeping its people poor.* World Economic Forum. https://www.weforum.org/agenda/2016/09/africa-s-energy-poverty-is-keeping-its-people-poor

Kingdom of Saudi Arabia. (2022). *Vision 2030: Saudi Arabia's National Transformation Plan*. https://www.vision2030.gov.sa/v2030/vrps/ntp/

Mehlum, H., Moene, K., & Torvik, R. (2006). Institutions and the resource curse. *Economic Journal (London)*, *116*(508), 1–20. doi:10.1111/j.1468-0297.2006.01045.x

Pistelli, L. (2020). Addressing Africa's Energy Dilemma. In M. Hafner & S. Tagliapietra (Eds.), *The Geopolitics of the Global Energy Transition. Lecture Notes in Energy* (Vol. 73, pp. 151–174). Springer International Publishing AG. doi:10.1007/978-3-030-39066-2_7

Porter, M. (1991). America's green strategy. *Scientific American*, *264*(4), 168. doi:10.1038cientificamerican0491-168

Robinson, J. A., Torvik, R., & Verdier, T. (2006). Political foundations of the resource curse. *Journal of Development Economics*, *79*(2), 447–468. doi:10.1016/j.jdeveco.2006.01.008

Sachs, J. D., & Warner, A. M. (1995). *Natural resource abundance and economic growth.* National Bureau of Economic Research [Working Paper]. https://www.nber.org/papers/w5398

Segal, M. (2021). BMO launches climate initiatives encompassing net zero ambitions, sustainable finance goals. *Environment, Social, and Governance (ESG) Today*. https://www.esgtoday.com/bmo-launches-climate-initiatives-encompassing-net-zero-ambitions-sustainable-finance-goals/

Simeon, R. (2002). Federalism and decentralization in Canada [Conference Paper]. *International Conference on Decentralization. Forum of Federations,* 398-426.

UNESCO. (2015). *UNESCO science report: Towards 2030.* http://uis.unesco.org/sites/default/files/documents/unesco-science-report-towards-2030-part1.pdf

United Nations. (n.d.). *Sustainable Development Goal 7: Ensure access to affordable, reliable, sustainable and modern energy for all.* Department of Economic and Social Affairs, United Nations. https://sdgs.un.org/goals/goal7

United Nations. (n.d.). *The Paris agreement: What is the Paris agreement.* United Nations Climate Change. Process and Meetings. https://unfccc.int/process-and-meetings/the-paris-agreement/the-paris-agreement

United States Energy Information Administration. (2019). The Middle East, Africa, and Asia now drive nearly all global energy consumption growth. *EIA. Today in Energy.* https://www.eia.gov/todayinenergy/detail.php?id=37932

World Bank. (2021). *Extractive industries: overview.* Understanding Poverty. https://www.worldbank.org/en/topic/extractiveindustries/overview

ENDNOTES

1. This is the conceptual framework for understanding the tensions inherent in balancing energy security, affordability, and environmental sustainability.
2. A scenario where today's current and announced policies continue.
3. Ibid.

Section 4

Public–Private Policy Partnerships

Chapter 8
Public-Private Policy Partnerships:
A Policy Innovation Paradigm

ABSTRACT

Optimizing the interactions in the policy-market-society nexus can spread socially beneficial innovations. While PPPs have for decades been a key tool in the delivery of critical public goods and other important interventions, this chapter makes a case for public-private policy partnership based on the notion that the public good construct in mainstream economic analysis has little or nothing to do with whether the public goods and services in question are in fact provided by the state or by private enterprises. PPPs as a policy approach combine the best of competitive market attributes and government operations in designs targeted at improving public policy. Given Africa's peculiar structural and institutional dynamics, interventionist policies must recognize the microeconomic realities of the continent's largely informal actors who constitute the backbone of the private sector.

DOI: 10.4018/978-1-7998-7383-9.ch008

But innovation comes from people meeting up in the hallways or calling each other at 10:30 at night with a new idea, or because they realized something that shoots holes in how we've been thinking about a problem.

— Steve Jobs

PPPs REMAIN A VITAL TOOL for policymakers in harnessing important aspects of the innovation economy. Over the last three decades, PPPs have evolved gradually as a policy framework in the delivery of public services and infrastructure.

The case for deploying PPPs as a policy tool for achieving societal goals is nuanced. At the core, the underlying questions and policies are either matters of political economy or public policy. Partly due to the stiff opposition meted out to the neoliberal policies of privatization, liberalization, and marketization in the 1990s, in favor of the prevailing Keynesian welfare-state institutional arrangements that emerged after World War II, in practice, contemporary policy is rarely applied as pure neoliberal underpinnings would suggest.

To put things into perspective, harnessing PPPs to address knotty public policy problems is borne out of the need to advance the culture of "an advocacy process where a strong challenge to an established policy — even a good policy — can result in a better policy" (Patton et al. 2012). This gives room for policy design, time, and space for experimentation in a bid to expand the problem definition, as well as consider multiple optimal solutions, in the policy development and innovation process. In essence, PPPs remain a veritable means of sourcing private sector expertise to enhance public service delivery.

In the last few decades, several governments across developed and developing nations have fulfilled their social contracts using PPPs as a bridge. Nonetheless, PPPs are not without controversy. Their effectiveness as a tool in the delivery of public services has been long questioned; till date, evidence on the efficacy of PPP is mixed (Romero, 2018). It is therefore prudent to clarify that the appropriateness, legitimacy, effectiveness, or efficiency of PPPs as a service delivery framework is not relevant for the purposes of the discussion in this book. Rather, the focus of this work, to the extent that PPP is employed, is to unpack how the involvement of private actors in traditional public sector operations can help push the policy envelope.

There is no universal definition of PPP; it is a concept in a constant state of flux. The PPP Knowledge Lab (n.d.) defines PPP as "a long-term contract between a private party and a government entity, for providing a public asset or service, in which the private party bears significant risk and management responsibility, and remuneration is linked to performance." Nonetheless, it is important to include that any definition of PPP is essentially caveated since the institutional, legal, investment, and public procurement settings of the jurisdiction and agreement in question define the overall meaning.

Also, while PPP has traditionally been leveraged to address challenges in physical and digital infrastructure – e.g., bridges, roads, subways, power generation, broadband, and other place-based facilities – several components of soft infrastructure like education, health, and other social services have also benefited from this arrangement.

The theoretical underpinning and political economy ramifications of PPPs as a policy paradigm are discussed in detail below.

PPPS AS A POLICY PARADIGM: THEORETICAL UNDERPINNINGS

From John Stuart Mill and Knut Wicksell to Paul Samuelson and Richard Musgrave, the theory of public goods in modern economics lays the foundation for the analysis of the varying roles of public and private sector actors in the use of PPPs as a vehicle for public goods provision. Due to the positive-normative ramifications in the public goods discourse –and the economic, political, and cultural importance of public goods to a well-functioning socioeconomic system – it is important to resolve the inherently contradictory elements of the philosophical foundations, ethics, value, and judgment, in the context of positivism and normativism. This is important for offering useful insights into how externalities, under-provision, free ridership, and other sources of market failure explain the economic and ethical dilemma in the discussion on the provision of public goods.

A good starting point in the public-private policy partnership analysis is to establish that the public good construct in mainstream economic analysis has little or nothing to do with whether the public goods and services in question are in fact provided by the state or by private enterprises. Rather, as with several other instances in orthodox economics – where elegant theorems and proofs based on restrictive assumptions in analytical paradigms pave the way for the oversimplification of complex systems – satisfying the non-rivalry vs. non-excludability criterion in public goods modeling is a more compelling rationale. This has implications for policy innovation through PPPs.

In economic theory, market failures due to the externalities created by public goods provide the basis for the provision of such goods. Following this logic, goods are defined as public goods if – and only if – they are both non-rivalrous and non-excludable. Examples of goods that satisfy this definition include infrastructure, security, national defence, education, healthcare, science, and environment. Given the non-excludability and non-rivalry properties, public goods generally tend to be insufficiently provided by the market, thereby making collective action important in ensuring adequate and sustained provision.

By implication, rivalrous and excludable goods are essentially private goods. While non-excludability infers that no one can be excluded from the consumption of the good, even without paying, non-rivalry establishes the fact that the consumption of the good by one individual does not diminish the amount available for consumption by another (Samuelson, 1954). While there are further extensions of this model – e.g., pure public good if both conditions are satisfied and impure public good if only one condition is satisfied – the key issue is that classifying goods as public and private based on a simplistic market-state dichotomy of neoclassicism is not only inadequate, but also constitutes a source of confusion vis-à-vis determining the appropriate policy devices and analytical tools to help achieve public policy goals.

Starr (1988) puts this into perspective: "Many things seem to be public and private at the same time in varying degrees or in different ways. As a result, we quarrel endlessly about whether some act or institution is really one or the other" (p.7).

Robertson et al. (2012) amplify the above sentiment:

To methodologically and analytically determine what constitutes a public or private good, Paul Samuelson's theory of public goods delineates those goods which are not adequately provided by the market, basing this distinction on the notions of non-rivalrousness and non-excludability. The normative implication in the field of economics is that that the public sector should only take on issues or services where there is market failure.........However, scholars in other disciplines take a less fixed view of private-public distinctions, seeing both the state and the market, and therefore the public and the private, as historical and cultural constructs. The distinction between the public vs. private is therefore understood as something that has evolved based on specific types of exchange relations in human society, and the development of different social and political orders. From this more culturalist viewpoint, the construction of public-private distinctions deserves careful interrogation (Robertson et al., 2012; p. 4)

THE POLITICAL ECONOMY OF NEOLIBERALISM

From a historical perspective, the Great Depression shaped much of the global political economy dynamics of the 20th century. Among other vestiges, the crisis expanded the role of the US federal government in the economy and society, and heralded the enactment of the Social Security Act of 1935 which offered benefits to the elderly, unemployed, handicapped, and dependent mothers and children. In the same vein, the Wagner Act of 1935 led to sweeping changes in labor negotiations by promoting unions and prioritizing fair labor contract negotiations.

In several ways, World War I constituted a major upset in the global political economy by triggering significant shocks that brought the global financial system to a halt. Among other factors, the temporary suspension of the gold standard – which had hitherto served as the anchor for the monetary systems of major advanced economies – meant that the resultant inflexibility in domestic and international financial markets reduced the resilience of economies to the shocks that arose afterwards. As the Great Depression – the worst economic downturn in the history of the industrialized world – dragged on from the stock market crash of 1929 to 1939, the US adopted a somewhat post-World War I-type isolationism.

While major economies around the world were significantly damaged in the aftermath of World War II, the US enjoyed unprecedented economic prosperity, and over time, this contributed to its emergence as the new global economic powerhouse of the 20th century and the leader of the free world. Unlike the isolationism that characterized much of its global politics in the aftermath of World War I, the US assumed a leading role on the global stage after World War II and spearheaded rebuilding efforts in war-torn European cities through the creation of the $13 billion European Recovery Plan, the Marshall Plan, dedicated to the rebuilding of Western Europe. The Marshall Plan received widespread support from Americans and triggered a resurgence of industrialization by reviving Western European economies through massive investments in ongoing industrial development (Hogan, 1987).

The Marshall Plan received wide support based on the economic premise that the preservation of global peace and order was a necessary precondition for a thriving global economy that would in turn protect markets for US goods and services. This logic is consistent with the fact that global trade integration tends to promote peace between countries. Moreso, the leading role of the US in the preservation of the global political order and peace was bolstered with the creation of the United Nations in 1945.

After World War II, reconstruction efforts triggered unprecedented growth in Europe and reversed the deleterious effects of the war and economic instability that devastated the region during much of the first half of the 20th century. For over three decades after World War II, Keynesianism remained the dominant global economic policy paradigm. However, because of the stagflation witnessed in many industrial capitalist economies, leading up to the 1970s, Keynesian economics came under scrutiny due to its explanatory impotence in the context of devising policy solutions to the pervasive inflation and slow growth that heralded the period. By the mid-1970s, after a series of events and intellectual contradictions that swept through the Keynesian school of thought, the trust in Keynesianism waned; neoliberalism and its appealing free markets ramifications ascended and became the mainstream economic approach.

Two central tenets of neoliberalism are the theoretical underpinnings of income distribution and employment determination. Income distribution under the neoliberal framework is based on the notion that labor and capital are rewarded according to what they are worth. For instance, the supply and demand for labor imply that the marginal revenue product of labor is equal to the wage rate. Wages and rents are driven by the relative scarcity (supply) and productivity (vis-à-vis demand) of factors of production. On the other hand, the neoliberal thesis on employment determination opposes wage determination through non-economic forces. Over time, neo-Keynesianism has become the preferred economic management and policy doctrine – largely because to the extent that the market is not self-regulating, achieving economic growth and stability is more prudent than full employment.

Africa and the Washington Consensus

The election of Margaret Thatcher as British Prime Minister in 1979 and Ronald Reagan as US President in 1980 heralded a new era of neoliberal economic policy dominance, and in many ways, signaled a resurgence of 19th-century-type free-market capitalism.

As discussed above, while the previous post-World War II 35-year period had witnessed bourgeoning neoliberalism in both the advanced and developing economies, the era of neoliberalism was characterized by slower economic growth and widening income gaps both within and between countries (Palley, 2021). This led to the adoption of neoliberal policies of privatization, liberalization, and marketization in much of the 1980s and 1990s, including the weakening of social safety institutions and macroeconomic austerity, under the "Washington Consensus."

The Washington Consensus, a term coined by economist John Williamson in 1989, refers to a list of policies targeted at addressing the macroeconomic imbalances and debt crisis of developing countries in Latin America from the early to mid-1980s. These policies, as prescribed, were focused on tax overhaul, fiscal discipline, openness to trade and investment, market-oriented reforms, and property rights. In the aftermath of the adoption of the Washington Consensus, the mixed evidence on results around policy reforms turned the term to a rather controversial phrase.

In the African context, the structural reforms of the 1980s and the adoption of market-oriented instruments for economic management across African nations led to dismal socioeconomic performance with adverse impacts on vulnerable populations. This has a major implication: given Africa's peculiar structural and institutional dynamics, interventionist policies must recognize the microeconomic realities of the continent's largely informal actors who constitute the backbone of the private sector. Irwin and Ward (2021) echo this sentiment based on their argument that in many instances, the policy prescriptions of the Washington Consensus are at variance with the reality on the ground in the concerned countries, since "these policies contradicted conventional wisdom in developing countries, many of which embraced state dominated systems in the 1950s."

Palley (2004) corroborates this:

The failure of the Washington Consensus to deliver faster growth in developing countries—it has actually delivered slower growth—has contributed to a backlash that has significantly discredited it. There is now widespread recognition that: international financial markets can be prone to instability, export-led growth is not sufficient for domestic development and can promote global deflation and a "race to the bottom," democracy and institutions promoting social inclusiveness are needed for development, and labor market protections are needed to prevent exploitation. However, though much progress has been made in countering the Washington Consensus, little progress has been made in combating the "U.S. model." This poses a danger, since the U.S. model is the source of neoliberal policy, including the Washington Consensus (Palley, 2004; para. 25)

The PPP-Innovation Nexus

Evidence on the exact nature of the relationship between PPPs and innovation is mixed. While some studies establish a positive association (e.g. Himmel & Siemiatycki, 2017), others show an inverse relationship (e.g. Barlow & Köberle-Gaiser, 2008). Using Belgian and Dutch data from 24 PPPs and based on the specific research question, "How do conditions related to 'procurement for innovation' logics and conditions related to 'collaborative innovation' logics stimulate the creation of innovation in PPPs and what is their combined effect on this innovation?", Callens, Verhoest, and Boon (2022) explore the nature of the relationship in the context of how procurement and collaboration serve as the transmission channels for the PPPs-innovation nexus. Their work leverages insights from both the "public procurement for innovation" literature (e.g. Edquist, Vonortas, & Zabala-Iturriagagoitia 2015) and the literature on "collaborative innovation" (e.g. Torfing 2019) to predict under what circumstances PPPs produce innovation – with the caveat that the 24 cases examined focused more on the presence of the conditions and the outcome; less so for the data generation process.

As an innovative public procurement approach, PPPs have become a popular, collaborative policy instrument in the delivery of complex public sector projects. At its core, the argument for PPPs is that they are uniquely positioned to create value because the private sector delivers on innovation in ways that the inherent nature of bureaucracies does not allow. As such, to the extent that PPPs have become popular models for delivering on infrastructure and public services globally, central to understanding the nuanced nature of the PPP procurement process is bundling. This is discussed further below.

The PPP literature identifies the pros and cons of bundling in project procurements, in the context of specific policy objectives implementation. For instance, while engaging a single entity on one contract fosters greater flexibility and transparency, unintended consequences such as incomplete contracting and asymmetric information may create inefficiencies later, due to renegotiations (see Sarmento & Renneboog 2016).

The World Bank (2017) corroborates such dilemma thus:

Governments should only develop PPP projects that are cost-benefit justified, provide better value for money than traditional public procurement, and are fiscally responsible. However, it is difficult to assess whether a project meets all these criteria until the project is fully designed, and the decision cannot be confirmed until bids are received. This creates a dilemma—government does not want to incur the considerable costs of developing a PPP unless it knows the project meets the criteria, but cannot tell if it meets the criteria until the project has been developed (World Bank, 2017; p. 113).

The PPP Reference Guide of the World Bank offers practical insights on navigating each stage of a PPP project development and implementation, with emphasis on screening projects more rigorously at each successive stage of development. Akin to public policy management, Marques (2017) underscores the importance of three key dimensions in PPP contract management: administrative management, operational management, and relationship management.
Dolla and Laishram (2019) ask:

For instance, how do relationship management issues such as communication, confidence, conflict management, and sharing affect the efficacy of the delivery mode, be it a single PPP contract or multiple and different delivery models? A similar question applies to the administrative management on matters concerning the financial situation, payments, change management, payments, reporting and penalties (p.1).

By applying organizational and economic models to contemporary PPP procurement thinking and research practice, Dolla and Laishram (2019) use a longitudinal case study methodology to analyze the sources of variations in the two dominant procurement models: bundling and unbundling. With the aid of 39 semi-structured interviews with key PPP actors, the authors investigate the municipal solid waste (MSW) management practices of six Indian cities, with a focus on partnership activities – with the MSW management infrastructure as the unit of analysis.

Given that multiple case studies often deliver more robust and compelling evidence in case study research, empirical evidence from the bundled and unbundled cases informs the subsequent inferences. As well, following Yin (2014), the use of multiple case studies in the research design ensures the four key criteria of construct validity, internal validity, external validity, and reliability are met. As discussed extensively under policy change theories in chapter 3, the following eight theoretical constructs – informed partly by the transaction cost thesis – provide the necessary grounding for the subsequent analysis and conclusions: life cycle innovation, maturity of markets, quality specifiability, economies of scope, tendering to subsidiaries, competition, information asymmetry, and transaction attributes (Dolla & Laishram, 2019).

Contrary to much of what obtains in the literature, the findings show that pro-bundling factors like lower transaction costs and life cycle innovation play relatively insignificant roles. The authors conclude that this is a radical departure; bundling is the "North Star" in the contemporary PPP procurement discourse. This has a major implication: mixed bundling or unbundling is necessary for efficiency gains.

According to Dolla and Laishram (2019):

When the public sector outsources work, they often become less mature in managing projects. If PPPs are the solution, the public sector needs to be trained on how to be a good "project owner" since they will lose their capability to manage projects (p.19).

While not definitive, the fact that their study did not account for specific variables like project size, cost, and prevailing socioeconomic conditions may have impacted the results. Since both public policies and project-specific technologies are likely to remain in a state of flux throughout a project life cycle, (Marques 2017) cautions on the need to strike a right balance between efficiency considerations for delivery model and contract management.

For instance, the various strands of neoclassical growth theories (e.g., Harrod-Domar and Solow models) predict long-run growth rates exogenously based on the savings rate or technical progress. However, the endogenous growth model is more relatable in the policy circle because it recognizes the importance of the spillover effects of innovation on economic development, since public-private collaborations can lead to greater levels of investments in human capital, which aided by the current digital revolution, can increase productivity. As such, the rise and popularity of industrial policy can be explained, to a large extent, by this trend. Due to market failure, government corrects private sector underinvestment in R & D by using a wide variety of tools.

THE POWER OF MARKETS FOR POLICY INNOVATION

Research remains the cornerstone of innovation. Theory and empirical evidence support the notion that in the absence of government interventions, the level of private sector investments in R & D will be lower than the socially optimal level (David et al., 2000). Among other factors, positive externalities arising from incomplete appropriability of research outcomes and the risks associated with success often produce sub-optimal private R&D expenditures, compared to the socially optimal levels (Arrow, 1962). The economic justification therefore is that central planners are better positioned to correct this market failure by subsidizing the capital costs of R&D activities (Cin et al., 2017).

Moving innovative technologies through the commercialization pipeline to industry requires striking a right balance among key players in the research community, industry, government, and the funding mechanisms. Clearly, innovation commercialization is both an art and a science.

Stiglitz and Wallsten (1999) provide a theoretical underpinning for public sector support for industrial R & D activities, as well as the implications for public-private partnerships in the technology sector. Their analysis covers the trend in public-private technology partnerships across a wide range of models covering direct public investments in R & D projects led by industry, as well as publicly funded private sector research collaborations and others involving scientists in the industry-government nexus.

Stiglitz and Wallsten explain public partnership policy in terms of its core mandate being the fulfillment of public objectives within the limits of public resource constraints that pay attention to the peculiarities of private incentives and public political processes. They argue that public policy, as a matter of necessity, must be sustainable since electoral support at some point in the cycle is key. And that PPPs produce the best policy outcomes when there are common shared objectives, albeit beneficial results are still possible even in the presence of disparate interests. They caution, however, that when actors in a PPP have separate interests, the incentive-accountability framework needs some level of scrutiny. These authors argue that the expected total returns on research is the sum of the expected private and social returns, with a wide range of possible outcomes for the government support component (Figure 1).

The diagrammatic framework in Figure 1 sheds light on the effectiveness of a public-private policy partnership under a social-private returns dichotomy. The model explains how government support can tilt the outcome of a project in several directions. For instance, projects under Area C in the chart are inframarginal projects that are deemed to be privately profitable without government subsidies. Any government support for such projects is considered a mere transfer payment, with no allocative effect beyond the distortionary impact of raising the revenue.

Figure 1. Projects targeted by an optimal government-industry R & D program
(Credit: Public-Private Policy Partnerships, edited by Rosenau; MIT Press, 2000)

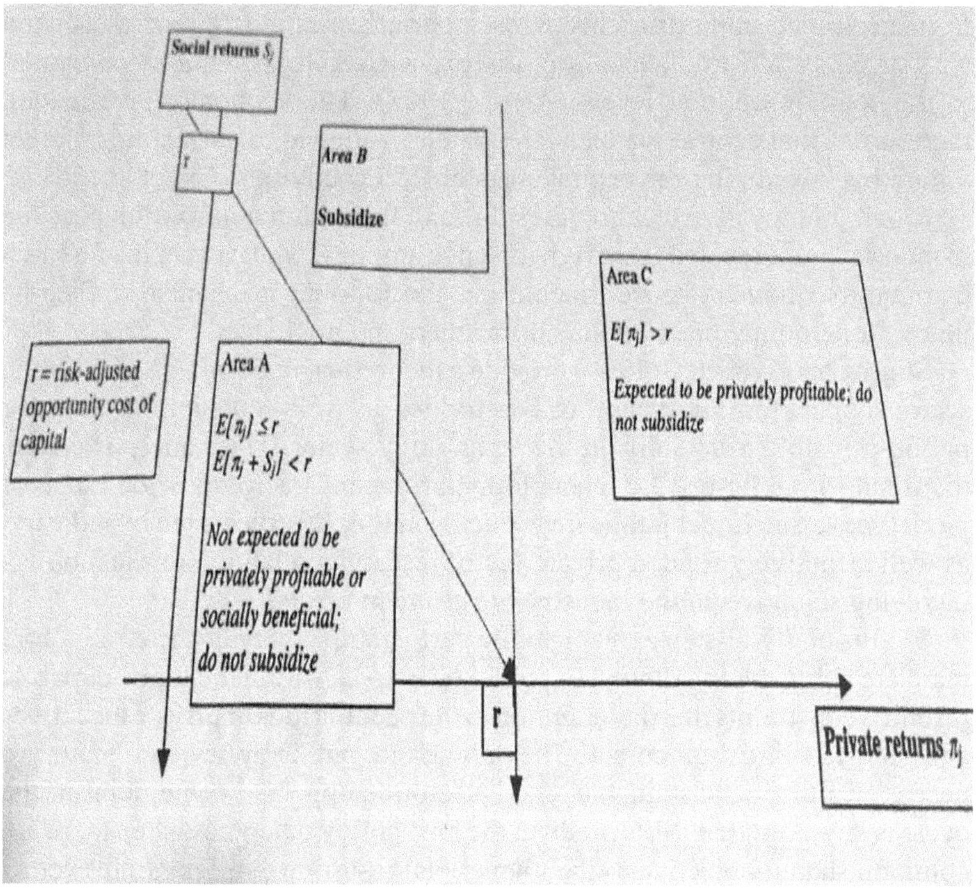

Projects in Areas A and B on the other hand are considered marginal projects, which implies without government grants, profit-seeking firms will not undertake such. In the absence of any spillovers that provide a basis for government intervention, any subsidies will incentivize firms to embark on unproductive projects at the margin (Area A of the diagram). Such subsidy regime will also lead to the execution of projects by firms at the margin in Area B, where the total returns exceed the opportunity cost of capital. In this case, without government support, the project would not proceed. Stiglitz and Wallsten explain that under this scenario, the net social benefit is ambiguous. They advocate further research and analysis of the incentives that drive the behavior of program managers, politicians, and private firms.

A major takeaway from this model is that policy entrepreneurship is largely about identifying projects with reasonable social returns that are not attractive to the private sector. Optimizing the desirable elements of the interactions in the policy-market-society nexus then becomes the basis for deploying the power of the markets to spread socially beneficial innovations. While it may be difficult to implement in practice, this framework does a good job in providing a basis for funding socially beneficial projects that may not see the light of day without subsidy, while declining inframarginal proposals that would be privately funded even without government support.

THE SOCIAL POLICY DIMENSION

The preceding sections underscore why making a distinction on public and private responsibility in the provision of public goods is key to understanding the policy dynamics in the PPP discourse. Resolving both the definitional and normative nuances on the involvement of public and private actors in the provision of social services is important for incremental policy innovation ability.

Before emerging as an alternative policy approach in the social services sectors like education and healthcare, PPPs have for decades been a key tool in the delivery of critical public goods and other important interventions, particularly in the infrastructure domain, such as power generation, sewage, water supply, transportation, urban renewal, etc. Moreso, from local and regional governments to state/provincial and national governments, PPPs have gained popularity as a project delivery vehicle that bridges policy capacity gaps by harnessing innovation capabilities of the private sector in a bid to mitigate the adverse impacts of perceived inefficiencies in direct state service provision.

The forces of globalization, digitization, and the rapidly evolving global political economy order of the past three decades have triggered significant changes in the governance dynamics of key domains in the social services sector. From education and healthcare to security and preparedness and emergency management efforts, the importance of social services in increasing socioeconomic mobility for the less well-off cannot be overemphasized.

Over the years, the policy debate on adopting more flexible and hybrid models that harness the capabilities of both state and non-state actors across the value chain has gained support among key stakeholders at the local, regional, national, and transnational levels (Robertson et al., 2012). In the education domain, for instance, "These newer forms of education governance often operate across scales, through interactions between local, regional and national governments and intergovernmental organizations, and between these and national and transnationally configured profit firms, philanthropists, NGOs and religious organizations (Robertson et al., 2012; p.1).

In *Public-Private Partnerships as an Education Policy Approach*, Verger and Moschetti (2017) contend that while PPPs can help advance a wide variety of policy options, their dual role both as an analytical category and as a policy generation tool puts them in an "ambiguous policy category", meaning their beneficial impact in the education policy debate is not definitive.

Compared to traditional infrastructure domains such as energy and transportation – or even social sectors like health services – the use of PPPs as a policy approach in public education is somewhat new, albeit it is increasingly becoming popular (Verger & Moschetti, 2017). Before PPPs as a policy innovation paradigm became increasingly mainstreamed in the social policy agenda in the 2000s, the first ever published reference to "PPPs for education" (ePPPs) was in a report jointly published by the World Bank and the Asian Development Bank in 2000 under the title: *The New Social Policy Agenda in Asia: Proceedings of the Manila Social Forum* (Marshall & Bauer, 2000).

One of the key reasons PPPs have become commonplace as a policy innovation tool in the education sector is their ability to expand access to educational opportunities by supplementing provision by the public sector's limited capacity. While this approach has many obvious advantages, beyond the demand and supply ramifications, its inherent ability to serve the needs of historically underserved populations, thereby addressing a fundamental equity concern, is novel. Apart from the efficiency gains made possible from the partnership between governments, education providers, donors, and other key stakeholders in the entire value chain, the expansion possibilities made possible by such collaborations are a major advance.

As corroborated in the theoretical underpinnings section, to the extent that PPPs are a mere arrangement made between actors in the public and private sectors for the delivery of public goods and services, the non-rivalry vs. non-excludability criterion in the public good construct in neoclassical economics should have little or nothing to do with how and the extent of cooperation between state and non-state actors in the provision of the public goods and services in question. The fundamental premise that PPPs as a policy approach combine the best of competitive market attributes and government operations should be a key factor in policy designs targeted at improving public policy.

This model recognizes the need to harness the desirable benefits of PPPs such as lower cost, improved quality, and risk-sharing.

To help unpack the social policy dynamics in the use of PPPs as policy innovation tools, Klijn (2010) identifies two broad categories of policy rationales: New Public Management (NPM) and Public Governance (PG). According to Verger and Moschetti (2017) and Klijn (2010), the central tenets of the NPM approach include:

- to increase the level of financial resources committed to public services such as basic education, and to provide better value for money
- to allow governments to focus on those functions where they have comparative advantage (planning, policy, quality assurance, and curriculum development), whereas the private sector is in charge of service delivery
- to allow for greater innovation by focusing on outputs and outcomes, rather than processes
- to allow governments to bypass operating restrictions (especially those related to unionization and regulations seen as 'unnecessarily restrictive employment laws and outdated government pay scales'
- to introduce competitive pressure on the provision of public services, and thus innovation and efficiency gains (Verger & Moschetti, 2017; p.3)

In the same vein, the arguments for the PG approach reinforce transparency, stakeholder engagement, and sustainability in public administration:

- to allow the public education sector to leverage private sector knowledge, skills, and innovation through network collaboration
- to reduce the politicization of schooling and the degree of corruption in the education sector
- to make costs more transparent through contracts, explicit costing schemes, and accountability measures
- to promote stakeholder participation –including civil society– in public services delivery and related decisions (Verger & Moschetti, 2017; p.3)

TAKEAWAYS

Based on the insights from this analysis, it is worth mentioning that achieving optimal policy outcomes needs not be an all-or-nothing proposition. In practice, public policy is a non-linear process that requires decent doses of both the NPM and PG public sector reform paradigms. As discussed under the section on the political economy of neoliberalism, the dominance of neoliberal economics in the 1980s has had a major influence on the provision of public goods and services in the last four decades. Not only that, the debate on the relative importance of the state and the market in resource allocation and functioning of economic systems and society has equally undergone a profound evolution. For instance, in the US, while the mainstream argument for PPPs has always been the need to overcome perceived inefficiencies in the direct provision of public goods and services by the state, progressive doctrines generally tend to favour PPPs as a policy approach on the basis that the involvement of state actors will dampen market-oriented tendencies (see Wettenhall, 2003).

Robertson and Verger (2012) characterize how PPPs have become a sort of compromise between the state and the market by serving as an intermediate policy approach between:

too much state (Keynesianism), on the one hand, and too little state, on the other (privatization). In acting as a bridge between each sector, partnerships were also presumed to act as a conduit enabling the values of each partner to be capitalized upon (Robertson & Verger, 2012; p. 26).

Drawing a line between the precise roles of state and non-state actors in education is not a straightforward exercise. Again, Verger and Moschetti (2017) amplify this:

Defining the type of private partners – i.e. religious or non-religious organizations, local or transnational school chains or single providers, for-profit or not-for-profit – is also crucial both for voucher and charter frameworks. Different types of partners – and their corresponding motives, ethos, incentives – have different political and educational implications in the context of ePPPs (Verger & Moschetti, 2017; p.6).

EDUCATION UNDER DISRUPTIVE TECHNOLOGIES

John Page with the Africa Growth Initiative at Brookings Institution unpacks how "industries without smokestacks" can aid a large-scale job creation strategy to help Africa harness its youth dividend (Page 2019; p. 46). The African Development Bank (2016) alludes to the highly entrepreneurial nature of Africa's youths, who continue to carry most of the unemployment burden. And in terms of policy, the Bank amplifies the implications of the heterogeneous nature of Africa's economies for youth development policies. That is, considering varying demographic paths and economic structures, youth policies need to be context-specific; a one-size-fits-all approach will not achieve timely and sustainable employment outcomes

By 2050, the number of young Africans entering the labor force will exceed that of the rest of the world combined (Page, 2019). Louise Fox, Chief Economist at the United States Agency for International Development, corroborates the important role of skills training in maximizing Africa's youth bulge:

Youth is widely recognized as an important skills-building period, with education being a crucial part. Africa's education systems could do a lot better at building the foundational skills for the future labor force. However, educational and skill-building institutions do not create jobs. Firms and people do. Wage employment is created when new firms are created and existing firms expand production, finding new markets. This takes time, probably decades before most employment will be in modern firms in the case of African countries. Indeed, it could be argued that owing to better education policy than economic policy, young Africans are over-skilled for their economies, which is one reason why unemployment is highest among the most educated youth. Lacking opportunities to use their skills, they are frustrated and vocal. (Fox, 2019, p. 58)

Before the pandemic, the digital revolution was already changing traditional higher education and the future of work dramatically, leading to concerns on the potential labor market polarization. For context, management consulting firm McKinsey predicted dramatic shifts in the labor market, driven by automation, leading to more pronounced gaps in urban-rural job growth. COVID-19 only accelerated job displacements, with disproportionate impacts on marginalized groups across income, gender, age, and racial lines (Lund et al., 2019). McKinsey's post-COVID-19 research concludes that 25 percent more workers may need to switch occupations than what was envisaged before the pandemic:

We find not only that a larger share of workers will likely need to transition out of the bottom two wage brackets but also that roughly half of them overall will need new, more advanced skills to move to occupations one or even two wage brackets higher. (Lund et al., 2021; section 2, para. 2)

McKinsey calls for policymakers to support the corporate sector to expand and enhance digital infrastructure, in addition to supporting workers migrating between occupations. A major bright spot and policy innovation opportunity that emerged from the pandemic is the realization that while traditional higher education will continue to be relevant, other digital pathways will be required for career advancement. And such pathways must necessarily integrate nontraditional alternative education providers. Nowhere is this more relevant than in Africa. The education system in Africa needs retooling to serve the needs of the digital economy.

The Managing Director of the International Finance Corporation, Makhtar Diop (2017), articulates this:

On a trip to Guangdong province, China, a couple of years ago, I toured one of the world's largest mobile phone assembly plants. I was stunned to find out that nearly all of the young workers I met there only had a high school degree but their level of technical literacy probably exceeded that of the average African college graduate. The truth is we cannot achieve innovation without a properly trained workforce and a robust education system. (Diop, 2017, para. 2)

As seen in the edtech venture capital space since the pandemic, funding appetite continues to rise for programs focused solely on helping students acquire job-specific skills (Wan, 2021). In the US, startups in the edtech domain raised the highest investment total in history for a single year, with over $2.2 billion across 130 deals in combined venture and private equity capital – about 30 percent increase from the $1.7 billion raised across 105 deals in 2019.

After COVID-19, the European Union launched the Pact for Skills (European Commission, 2020), a skills partnership in the automotive, microelectronics, and aerospace and defense industries, targeted at addressing mismatches and shortages in skills, while also preparing workers for the digital and green transitions to help meet Europe's skills needs. The Pact is a collaborative framework comprised of industry, vocational education and training providers, civic leaders, and national, regional, and local governments as stakeholders – with €7 billion of private and public funding dedicated to enhancing the skills of 700,000 automotive workers.

In Africa, like other regions of the world, the pandemic disrupted education and some form of remote learning was implemented across countries on the continent, albeit the lack and inadequacy of digital resources constituted major barriers. The demand-supply imbalance has given rise to various edtech companies providing a wide range of learning and development interventions across the continent. In the same vein, edtech firms serving the African continent continue to make giant strides in the venture capital scene (Boniface, 2021).

In its May 26, 2021 online edition, Digest Africa corroborates how the pandemic triggered a major shift in the edtech sector in Africa, with funding increasing by 89.5%, compared to the same period in 2020. In addition to many new entrants in the edtech ecosystem, these firms also recorded increases in newly registered students and aspiring teachers. For context, based on figures compiled since 2018, the top five countries receiving funding in the education sector are: South Africa ($50.6M), Nigeria ($11.9M), Kenya ($4,46M), Egypt ($2.17M), and Tunisia ($980K). In comparison, edtech startups receiving over $1 million in funding since the pandemic include: South Africa's SPARK Schools ($11.7M), Nigeria's uLesson ($7,5M), South Africa's Valenture Institute ($7M), South Africa's Student Hub ($2.9M), South Africa's iXperience ($2.5M), Kenya's Kidato ($1.525M), and Egypt's Zedny ($1.2M) (Digest Africa, 2021).

The discussion above underscores the policy innovation imperative. In addition to exacerbating existing inequalities across a wide range of sectors, the pandemic has changed the reality of what a workplace means for the future. As COVID-19 and the digital transformation converge to drive change, now is the time for policy innovation to help create a decent mix of intervention that balances career and economic mobility pathways. This brings talent financing to the forefront. This is discussed further in the next section.

TALENT FINANCING

As extensively discussed under the sections on policy diffusion and the helix models of innovation, forging a more dynamic economy across Africa requires solutions based not only on research, but on testing, piloting, prototyping, and experimentation with innovative approaches. This is critical for fostering an entrepreneurial environment in the public policy development process by harnessing opportunities in the policy-market nexus to transform policy innovation on the continent. In the context of human capital development, the private sector has a key role. Beyond private ownership of educational institutions, policy designs targeted at incentivizing companies to support the development of a vibrant, resilient, and digitally compliant workforce will go a long way.

In his 1955 seminal paper, *The Role of Government in Education*, Milton Friedman floated the initial thesis that later formed the central tenet of the notion of financing higher education through equity rather than debt – the so-called "skin in the game" proposition. Over time, the debate has crystalized into what is now termed Income Share Agreements (ISAs), an approach that allows learners to raise the money needed for their education in exchange for a share of their post-graduation income. The model also incorporates provisions that allow students participating in the ISA to only pay back if their earnings surpass a certain threshold, while also ensuring successful learners never pay back more than a pre-determined capped limit (see Box 3). For those who do not find employment or end up with low-paying jobs, the lending institution absorbs a disproportionally higher share of the risk in the form of a low return on investment or no return at all.

Box 3: Income Share Agreements

Innovative financing mechanisms in the education sector is another important domain where policy innovation is critical. Apart from pioneering new approaches to education, training, and credentialing – to unlock economic opportunity for underprivileged students – ISAs have become a popular model of talent financing innovations that support more choices and affordable pathways for low-income and underprivileged populations, while also fostering diversity, equity, and inclusion.

Given Africa's peculiar challenges, with the right data, tech infrastructure, public-private framework, and the appropriate risk-sharing model among the beneficiaries of the investment – i.e., employers, workers, and government – ISAs could become a game changer by transforming the education financing and policy innovation landscapes.

Friedman (1955) summarizes the constraints in the initial ISA proposition thus:

This underinvestment in human capital presumably reflects an imperfection in the capital market: investment in human beings cannot be financed on the same terms or with the same ease as investment in physical capital. It is easy to see why there would be such a difference. If a fixed money loan is made to finance investment in physical capital, the lender can get some security for his loan in the form of a mortgage or residual claim to the physical asset itself, and he can count on realizing at least part of his investment in case of necessity by selling the physical asset. If he makes a comparable loan to increase the earning power of a human being, he clearly cannot get any comparable security; in a non-slave state, the individual embodying the investment cannot be bought and sold. But even if he could, the security would not be comparable. The productivity of the physical capital does not--or at least generally does not--depend on the cooperativeness of the original borrower. The productivity of the human capital quite obviously does--which is, of course, why, all ethical considerations aside, slavery is economically inefficient. A loan to finance the training of an individual who has no security to offer other than his future earnings is therefore a much less attractive proposition than a loan to finance, say, the erection of a building: the security is less, and the cost of subsequent collection of interest and principal is very much greater (Friedman, 1955; p.9).

For context, Friedman ascribed much of the underinvestment in higher education on a fundamental market failure in the underlying financing model. He argued that since lenders must assume a higher level of risk, interest rates on education loans are high despite high returns to schooling. Unlike mortgages or auto loans, education loans are not backed by collateral in the form of physical assets. Friedman explained this in terms of factors including varying fortunes of individual students.

The education system in Africa needs retooling to serve the needs of the digital economy. The need for a tech-powered, affordable, innovative, and solutions-oriented industry- and policy-focused higher education approach on the continent has never been more compelling. The time is indeed ripe for policymakers to devise novel solutions and take full advantage of technology and emerging opportunities to reimagine and redefine policy education in Africa. ISAs can radically change the face of higher education on the continent.

At its core, ISA is an equity financing model anchored on the notion that a private investor could purchase a "share" in the future earnings of a learner. In return for the upfront financing, learners would earmark a portion of their future earnings over a fixed period. While the model has undergone various iterations over the years, its central tenet remains the same: the transfer of risk from the learner to the investor. In the face of dwindling government revenue and philanthropic interventions in Africa, innovations in talent finance are key.

The ongoing transformation in the higher education sector will be difficult to reverse. To the extent that workers need training or retraining to help them transition to better jobs, increased interventions to help traditionally disadvantaged and financially vulnerable groups through innovative solutions can go a long way in incentivizing participation – since this can provide a pathway by reducing the up-front costs and/or long-term debt associated with retraining.

The Berlin Wall wasn't the only barrier to fall after the collapse of the Soviet Union and the end of the Cold War. Traditional barriers to the flow of money, trade, people and ideas also fell.

— Fareed Zakaria

REFERENCES

African Development Bank. (2016). Africa's youth in the labour market. In *African Development Report 2015 Growth, Poverty and Inequality Nexus: Overcoming Barriers to Sustainable Development.* https://www.afdb.org/en/documents/document/african-development-report-2015-growth-poverty-and-inequality-nexus-overcoming-barriers-to-sustainable-development-89715

Arrow, K. (1962). *Economic Welfare and the Allocation of Resources for Invention.* National Bureau of Economic Research. doi:10.1515/9781400879762-024

Barlow, J., & Köberle-Gaiser, M. (2008). The private finance initiative, project form and design innovation: The UK's hospitals programme. *Research Policy, 37*(8), 1392–1402. doi:10.1016/j.respol.2008.04.027

Boniface, E. (2021). Nexford University raises $10.8 million series A to scale its flexible remote learning platform. *Ed Tech and Digital Literacy News.* http://edugist.org/nexford-nexford-university-raises-10-8-million-series-a-to-scale-its-flexible-remote-learning-platform/

Callens, C., Verhoest, K., & Boon, J. (2022). Combined effects of procurement and collaboration on innovation in public-private-partnerships: A qualitative comparative analysis of 24 infrastructure projects. *Public Management Review, 24*(6), 860–881. doi:10.1080/14719037.2020.1867228

Cin, B. C., Kim, Y. J., & Vonortas, N. S. (2017). The impact of public R&D subsidy on small firm productivity: Evidence from Korean SMEs. *Small Business Economics, 48*(2), 345–360. doi:10.100711187-016-9786-x

David, P. A., Hall, B. H., & Toole, A. A. (2000). Is public R&D a complement or substitute for private R&D? A review of the econometric evidence. *Research Policy, 29*(4), 497–529. doi:10.1016/S0048-7333(99)00087-6

Digest Africa (2021). *Most Funded EdTech Companies in Africa*: https://digestafrica.com/most-funded-edtech-companies-in-africa

Diop, M. (2017). *Africa can enjoy leapfrog development.* World Bank Group. https://www.worldbank.org/en/news/opinion/2017/10/11/africa-can-enjoy-leapfrog-development

Dolla, T., & Laishram, B. S. (2019). Governance issues in public utility public–private partnerships: a theoretical perspective. *Journal of The Institution of Engineers (India): Series A, 100*(3), 509-514.

Edquist, C., Vonortas, N. S., Zabala-Iturriagagoitia, J. M., & Edler, J. (Eds.). (2015). *Public Procurement for Innovation.* Edward Elgar Publishing.

European Commission. (2020). *The Pact for Skills: Mobilising all partners to invest in skills.* Press Release. https://ec.europa.eu/commission/presscorner/detail/en/ip_20_2059

Fox, L. (2019) Three myths about youth employment in Africa and strategies to realize the demographic dividend. *Foresight Africa – Brookings Institution:* https://www.brookings.edu/wp-content/uploads/2019/01/BLS18234_BRO_book_007_WEB.pdf

Friedman, M. (1955). The role of government in education. In R. A. Solo (Ed.), *Economics and the public interest.* Rutgers University Press.

Himmel, M., & Siemiatycki, M. (2017). Infrastructure public–private partnerships as drivers of innovation? Lessons from Ontario, Canada. *Environment and Planning C. Politics and Space, 35*(5), 746–764. doi:10.1177/2399654417701430

Hogan, M. J. (1987). The Marshall Plan: America, Britain, and the Reconstruction of Western Europe, 1947-1952. Cambridge University Press.

Irwin, D. A., & Ward, O. (2021). *What is the "Washington Consensus?"* Peterson Institute for International Economics. https://www.piie.com/blogs/realtime-economic-issues-watch/what-washington-consensus

Klijn, E. H. (2010). Public-Private Partnerships: deciphering meaning, message and phenomenon. In G. A. Hodge, C. Greve, & A. E. Boardman (Eds.), *International Handbook on Public-Private Partnerships* (pp. 68–80). Edward Elgar Publishing. doi:10.4337/9781849804691.00011

Lund, S., Madgavkar, A., Manyika, J., Smit, S., Ellingrud, K., & Robinson, O. (2021). *The future of work after COVID-19.* McKinsey Global Institute. https://www.mckinsey.com/featured-insights/future-of-work/the-future-of-work-after-covid-19

Lund, S., Manyika, J., Segel, L. H., Dua, A., Hancock, B., Rutherford, S., & Macon, B. (2019). *The future of work in America: People and places, today and tomorrow.* McKinsey Global Institute. https://www.mckinsey.com/featured-insights/future-of-work/the-future-of-work-in-america-people-and-places-today-and-tomorrow

Marques, R. C. (2017). Why not regulate PPPs? *Utilities Policy*, *48*, 141–146. doi:10.1016/j.jup.2017.04.003

Marshall, K., & Bauer, A. (2000). *The new social policy agenda in Asia: Proceedings of the Manila Social Forum.* Asian Development Bank; The World Bank.

Miranda-Sarmento, J., & Renneboog, L. (2016). Anatomy of Public–Private Partnerships: Creation, Financing, and Renegotiations. *International Journal of Managing Projects in Business*, *19*(1), 94–122. doi:10.1108/IJMPB-03-2015-0023

Page, J. (2019). How industries without smokestacks can address Africa's youth unemployment crisis. In *Harnessing Africa's Youth Dividend: A new approach for large-scale job creation.* Brooking Institute. https://www.brookings.edu/wp-content/uploads/2019/01/BLS18234_BRO_book_007_CH3.pdf

Palley, T. I. (2004). From Keynesianism to neoliberalism: shifting paradigms in economics. *Public understandings of the economy also matter. Foreign Policy in Focus.* https://fpif.org/from_keynesianism_to_neoliberalism_shifting_paradigms_in_economics/

Palley, T. I. (2021). *Neoliberalism and the Road to Inequality and Stagnation: A Chronicle Foretold.* Edward Elgar Publishing. doi:10.4337/9781802200089

Patton, C., Sawicki, D., & Clark, J. (2012). *Basic methods of policy analysis and planning*. Prentice Hall.

PPP Knowledge Lab. (n.d.). What is a PPP: Defining "Public-Private Partnership". *PPP Basics: What and Why.* https://pppknowledgelab.org/guide/sections/3-what-is-a-ppp-defining-public-private-partnership

Robertson, S. L., Mundy, K., Verger, A., & Menashy, F. (2012). An introduction to public private partnerships and education governance. In S. L. Robertson, K. Mundy, A. Verger, & F. Menashy (Eds.), *Public private partnerships in education: New actors and modes of governance in a globalizing world* (pp. 1–17). Edward Elgar Publishing. doi:10.4337/9780857930699.00007

Robertson, S. L., & Verger, A. (2012). Governing education through public private partnerships. In S. L. Robertson, K. Mundy, A. Verger, & F. Menashy (Eds.), *Public private partnerships in education: New actors and modes of governance in a globalizing world* (pp. 21–42). Edward Elgar Publishing.

Romero, M. J. (2018). Opinion: Public-private partnerships don't work. It's time for the World Bank to take action. *Devex.* https://www.devex.com/news/opinion-public-private-partnerships-don-t-work-it-s-time-for-the-world-bank-to-take-action-92585

Samuelson, P. A. (1954). The pure theory of public expenditure. *The Review of Economics and Statistics*, *36*(4), 387–389. doi:10.2307/1925895

Starr, P. (1988). The meaning of privatization. *Yale Law & Policy Review*, *6*(1), 6–41.

Stiglitz, J. E., & Wallsten, S. J. (1999). Public-Private technology partnerships: Promises and pitfalls. *The American Behavioral Scientist*, *43*(1), 52–73. doi:10.1177/00027649921955155

The Pure Theory of Public Expenditure. (1954, November). Paul A. Samuelson. *The Review of Economics and Statistics*, 387–389.

Torfing, J. (2019). Collaborative innovation in the public sector: The argument. *Public Management Review. Taylor & Francis Journals*, *21*(1), 1–11.

Verger, A., & Moschetti, M. (2017). Public-private partnerships as an education policy approach: Multiple meanings, risks and challenges. *UNESCO Education Research and Foresight: Working Paper.*

Wan, T. (2021). A Record Year Amid a Pandemic: US Edtech Raises $2.2 Billion in 2020. *EdSurge.* https://www.edsurge.com/news/2021-01-13-a-record-year-amid-a-pandemic-us-edtech-raises-2-2-billion-in-2020

Wettenhall, R. (2003). The rhetoric and reality of public-private partnerships. *Public Organization Review: A Global Journal, 3*(1), 77-107.

World Bank. (2017). *PPP Reference Guide: Module 3.* https://ppp.worldbank.org/public-private-partnership/sites/ppp.worldbank.org/files/2021-08/PPP%20Reference%20Guide%20Version%203%20-%20PPP%20Cycle.pdf

Yin, R. K. (2014). *Case study research: Design and methods* (5th ed.). Sage.

Chapter 9
Development Finance and Venture Capital:
A Policy Diffusion Model

ABSTRACT

The need for substantial investment to close Africa's huge infrastructure gap has attracted considerable attention in the international finance and development circle in the last two decades. Closing this gap is important for the continent's ability to achieve the SDGs. While much progress has been made—due partly to improving economics and policy reforms—in attracting international private capital for the development of the continent's transport, ICT, energy, water, and sanitation sectors, achieving financial close remains an issue. If properly harnessed, with the right policy mix and financing architecture, the digital revolution can transition Africa from the margins to the mainstream of global commerce. From a development finance perspective, the unprecedented influx of international private capital in Africa in recent years has major implications. This chapter makes a case for Startup Acts as a policy innovation tool for the continent's burgeoning venture capital ecosystem.

DOI: 10.4018/978-1-7998-7383-9.ch009

African growth transcends mere economics. African growth depends on politics; it depends on the social contract between the government and the governed; and it depends on a host of other factors.

— Makhtar Diop

The 2015 ADDIS ABABA ACTION AGENDA (AAAA) of the Third International Conference on Financing for Development (United Nation, 2015) provides a framework for financing the SDGs, with Science, Technology, and Innovation (STI) recognized as a critical pillar for the realization of the 2030 Agenda. Action item 33 under Annex 1 of the AAAA focuses on financing the SDGs with emphasis on the importance of national and regional development finance institutions, financial inclusion, and financing of MSMEs (p. 10/37).

In addition to triggering the most severe recession in nearly a century, COVID-19 has disrupted global value chains, causing unprecedented damage to heath care systems, economies, and well-being. With both domestic and external financing drying up in the face of the pandemic, the continent's existing unmet infrastructure financing needs are being further exacerbated. As international investors rebalance their portfolios, many important questions linger.

The need for substantial investment to close Africa's huge infrastructure gap has attracted considerable attention in the international finance and development circle in the last two decades. Estimates from the AfDB indicate that while about \$130-\$170 billion per annum is needed to close this gap, unmet financing needs are in the \$68 -\$108 billion range every year (Jesse & Madden, 2019). Closing this gap is important for the continent's ability to achieve the SDGs.

While much progress has been made in the past two decades – due partly to improving economics and policy reforms – in attracting international private capital for the development of the continent's transport, ICT, energy, water, and sanitation sectors, achieving financial close remains an issue. A March 2020 McKinsey article concludes that in Africa, "80 percent of infrastructure projects fail at the feasibility and business-plan stage" (Lakmeeharan et al. 2020, para. 2). The report calls this "Africa's infrastructure paradox," stating "there is need and availability of funding, together with a large pipeline of potential projects, but not enough money is being spent" (para. 2). Clearly, this underscores the need for increased dialogue and PPPs to mobilize investments into priority projects.

In the immediate aftermath of the COVID-19 pandemic, business leaders, policymakers, and key players from global financial institutions and multilateral development banks emphasized the need to prioritize infrastructure investment in a bid to drive the post-pandemic economic recovery. However, in the last five years, most EMDEs have witnessed low commodity prices, sluggish GDP growth, low levels of domestic savings, and weak private capital inflows. As a result of the concomitant high debt levels and limited fiscal space, many of these countries and sovereign entities face credit downgrade risks in the current environment.

While the notion of an infrastructure-led recovery remains popular in many developed countries, clearly, traditional sources of infrastructure financing will likely not thrive in many post-pandemic EMDEs, particularly in Africa. Innovative financing mechanisms that can help finance the continent's vast ambitious development goals will be in order. Among other things, this brings the debate on the role of China in infrastructure financing in Africa – a traditional turf for the US and Western Europe – to the front burner of the debate.

China has become a major player in Africa's infrastructure space in contemporary times. For instance, Sino-Africa relations have recorded tremendous success since the end of the Cold War. China's model of economic engagement remains its principal source of soft power on the continent, and Chinese-led infrastructure projects – which remain visible in Africa's major urban landscapes – are fast becoming one of the indexes of this relationship. While many Western countries still rely on traditional humanitarian aid and development assistance, China continues to invest massively in infrastructure, in addition to rapidly expanding trade with the continent.

Regardless, as the Chinese economy continues its structural shift from an export-dependent manufacturer to a consumption-driven one, the country's relationship with Africa is evolving. Moreso, since the interplay between politics and economics is key in the emerging international order, in many ways, the war between Russia and Ukraine has renewed geopolitical rivalries and the clash of interests of superpowers. This has major implications in the medium- to long-term, particularly in the context of economic rebalancing and strategic geopolitical realignment.

AFRICA'S VENTURE CAPITAL ECOSYSTEM

The venture capital and entrepreneurial ecosystem in Africa is thriving. With multiple large fundraises and exits in the last few years (Kene-Okafor, 2021), the upward trends recorded across talent, capital, markets, and exits continue to generate interests in the policy arena – regarding potential interventions that would not only help to sustain the momentum, but also break new ground.

Digital technology platforms are disrupting traditional industries by reshaping the way they operate. One of the major implications of the world-shrinking impact of technology is that startups can now go global upon launch. While many such firms gain traction, organically, this model is no substitute for finding a competitive strategy that offers a sustainable advantage. As Africa's venture capital ecosystem matures, the AfCFTA must make this a priority.

Why innovation? Companies in the innovation economy create quality jobs with a huge global export growth potential. The benefits of agglomeration were discussed in the earlier chapters. Firms in the innovation economy are particularly well-positioned to benefit from the clustering advantages and the industry diversification that dense urban centers offer. Across Africa, tech entrepreneurship is bourgeoning. Compared to global venture capital epicenters like Silicon Valley, New York, London, Berlin, and Hong Kong – where the intersection of talent and funding unlocks wealth – venture capital investment in Africa is still negligible. However, as the youngest and fastest-urbanizing region in the world, the continent is ranked as one of the most entrepreneurial regions in the world (Duffy, 2021).

In its inaugural African Tech Ecosystems of the Future rankings, fDIintelligence ranked Nigeria as the country with the highest number of startups in Africa. The report notes that many of these firms are in the fintech sector and are taking advantage of the advances in the digital economy to serve the underbanked in the country. According to fDIintelligence, the potential of the startup ecosystem of Lagos – Nigeria's commercial capital and most vibrant regional economy – is huge but, as the report puts it, "there is a significant disconnect between the city's tech ecosystem, its surroundings and the wider country, which suffers from chronically poor infrastructure and education, and recurring political instability and security issues" (para, 10).

Clearly, in the context of policy diffusion, ample economic development and innovation lessons abound from these established venture capital hubs. Lagos can incorporate a few lessons from some of the established metropolitan and digital innovation economies in the world. New York is an exemplar here. For instance, after the demise of Lehman Brothers and Bear Sterns in the aftermath of the 2008 GFC, policymakers and stakeholders in the New York region realized the need for an economic development strategy radically different from those in the past, driven largely by traditional tax incentives and subsidies to attract companies (Box 4).

Box 4: Policy Diffusion: Lagos-New York Regional Innovation Ecosystems

Apart from being among the world's top megacities, New York and Lagos share many structural, economic, and demographic similarities. In addition to being the global capital of finance, New York has the second largest startup ecosystem in the world. From public schools to job training to new workspaces for tech firms and smart digital engagement, New York is a global leader in many areas. Like New York, Lagos boasts a bourgeoning venture capital ecosystem that supports startups and a robust pipeline of talent that produces innovative new companies well into the future. Both cities have a rapidly growing tech ecosystem where the public, private, civic, and academic sectors are constantly collaborating.

To put things into context, throughout history, New York has always reinvented itself. From its founding as New Amsterdam, a Dutch settlement in the 17th century, it has undergone various political, demographic, cultural, and industrial shocks that shaped its emergence as a global leader in finance and innovation. New York began as a trading outpost, grew into a commercial and maritime power, evolved into an industrial and manufacturing hub, and flourished to become the world's financial, real estate, and media capital.

Such innovation and transformation capacity explains how, in the aftermath of the 2008 financial crisis, policymakers recognized the need to diversify the economy of the city away from the financial services sector to enable it become more resistant and resilient to future exogenous shocks. Such policy innovation process understood that attracting and retaining talent would be crucial for keeping companies within the city.

The status of Lagos as a regional leader in technology-led innovation and early-stage entrepreneurship can help catalyze the reinvention of its industrial structure to achieve a more resilient and diversified economy.

Gutiérrez and Olayele (2021) corroborate how human capital and the innovation economy formed the basis upon which the New York metropolitan economy was rejuvenated and diversified away from financial services in the post-Great Recession era:

When New York set out to build its tech economy from the ground up, it aspired to become a capital for founders and entrepreneurial talent by launching a series of initiatives that would create the foundations for a well-functioning innovation ecosystem (Gutiérrez & Olayele, 2021; p.38).

Strategic investments in education and training pathways for increased access to industries better positioned to thrive in the "new normal" cannot be overemphasized. And so is accelerated investment in broadband, digital infrastructure, clean energy, public health, resilience, and neighborhoods for more adaptable spaces.
Again, Gutiérrez and Olayele (2021) echo this:

The innovation economy cuts across all segments of the economy, in both mature and emerging industries, such as life sciences, advanced manufacturing, design, software, financial services, and health care, and shares a number of common traits across different industries. It derives its primary value from intellectual capital and creativity and places a premium on top talent. It invests heavily in research and development (R&D) to develop new business models, harness new technologies, and leverage old technologies in new ways. And it disrupts the status quo to create new markets, often by collaborating across disciplines or with public or academic partners. Companies in the innovation economy create the good-paying jobs with growth potential that NYC sought and continues to seek — and are all particularly well-positioned to benefit from the cluster advantages that being located in the city offers. By supporting the innovation economy, instead of picking winners and losers in specific industries, New York has been able to support emerging sectors, bolster existing ones, create significantly more employment opportunities as new businesses sprout, and generate new tax revenue for its coffers (Gutiérrez & Olayele, 2021; p.37).

THE STARTUP ACT IMPERATIVE

The influx of international private capital in Africa, which has hit unprecedented levels in recent years, has major implications for Startup Acts as a policy innovation tool for the continent's burgeoning venture capital ecosystem. This has become necessary for second order effects – e.g., secondary sales to growth and private equity investors, deepening of commercial and technology linkages with established international tech companies and local and global unicorns, as well as seamless exit options for successful startups.

For context, the Startup Act became popular in the US in 2012 when Startup Act 2.0 (Congress.gov, 2012; Moran, 2012), a bipartisan legislation, was passed "to help jump-start the economy through the creation and growth of new businesses" (Rubio et al. 2012, para. 2). While the notion that existing firms of all sizes create and destroy jobs on an ongoing basis is true, thereby implying a positive annual net job gain, findings from Kauffman Foundation research (Kane, 2010) refute this by showing that net job growth in the US economy occurs only through startups, and that these firms were behind nearly all net new jobs in the US in the preceding three decades. This research provided the empirical evidence for Startup Act 2.0.

The US remains the global leader in startup and venture capital activity. However, rapid urbanization and advances in technology, combined, are breeding other metropolitan economies with burgeoning and significant innovation ecosystems. For context, despite being home to just one percent of the global population, the top six cities for venture capital and startup activity (i.e., San Francisco, Beijing, New York, San Jose, Boston, and Shanghai) attract more than half of all global venture capital investment (Florida & Hathaway, 2018).

From Ghana and Rwanda to Ethiopia and Uganda and Tunisia, Kenya, Mali, and Senegal, Startup Acts are becoming commonplace (Wolken, 2020) in the African venture capital and innovation landscape and are a much-needed policy innovation tool (Digital Africa, 2020). As a legislative tool, these Acts provide a framework to ensure innovative startups receive the necessary support and guidance to enable them receive funding and attract talent and ideas for success.

As discussed in the earlier chapters, the public-private policy partnership paradigm has nothing to do with whether or not public goods are provided by private firms or the government. My focus on public-private policy partnerships is to the extent that private actors participate in traditional public sector operations in specific policy domains. In many ways, establishing a clear distinction between the precise roles of state and private sector actors in the provision of social services is not an easy task; the reality is a lot more nuanced than what is depicted in economic models and other theoretical representations.

The theoretical underpinning, in public sector economics, is based on the notion that public goods – such as education, healthcare, infrastructure, security, environment, and national defence – create externalities that result in market failures. As such, the non-excludability and non-rivalry properties of such goods and services lead to under-provision, which then necessitates collective action in ensuring adequate and sustained provision. This has implications for policy entrepreneurship in Africa's development finance landscape, in so far as it is essentially about unlocking private capital to maximize aggregate welfare. Among other criteria, this will involve identifying projects with reasonable social returns that profit-maximizing firms will not consider, without government subsidies.

Akin to Stiglitz and Wallsten's (1999) diagrammatic framework, in the preceding chapter, on the role of the state in creating positive externalities that can help spread social innovations, when institutional arrangements foster synergistic interactions in the policy-market-society nexus, development financing has a major role in incentivizing private firms to consider unprofitable projects at the margin. In many ways, this resurrects the institutional dimension.

The role of good governance and strong institutions, as key drivers of prosperity and sustainable development, has been established earlier. However, it is important to add that the institutional dimensions of governance are more nuanced than what conventional political economy paradigms present. Patton et al. (2012) explain the public-private policy partnership imperative in the context of the need for "an advocacy process where a strong challenge to an established policy — even a good policy — can result in a better policy." Simply put, this is policy innovation; it is about leveraging private sector expertise to enhance public service delivery.

In the African context, demographic, political, and market nuances drive the interactions between economic and social structures that reflect jurisdictional investment competitiveness. To reiterate, the governance infrastructure of a country is a derivative of its political, institutional, and legal environment. While development finance can tilt the risk-reward framework and incentivize private actors to take on certain projects, in the final analysis, political stability and the business environment (e.g., market size, security, talent and skills, infrastructure, the regulatory environment etc.) are two key determinants of foreign capital inflows.

The less risky the overall business and political environment is, the higher is the likelihood of maximizing the outcomes of the interactions between market forces and state actors, as corroborated below:

Reducing the risks of private investment at the project level does not compensate for failing to de-risk regulations and institutions at the country level. Investment incentives or investment guarantees are frequently used to bolster locational competitiveness or investment viability for specific projects or sectors, but investment climate weaknesses must be addressed first. If fundamental elements at the country level are lacking, investors are unlikely to respond to even the most generous incentive packages or such incentives may only attract unviable investments. Governments can reduce risks to private investors through a policy and institutional framework that supports an enabling business climate and ensures good governance (World Bank, 2018; pp. 7-8).

AFRICA AND POST-COVID SUSTAINABLE DEVELOPMENT FINANCING

Research abounds on Africa's quest for development financing to fix agelong structural barriers. As countries on the continent seek economic growth and diversification opportunities to help them finance their national development priorities in line with the SDGs, the pandemic and recent geopolitical tensions have changed the conventional nature of the debate. Just as the post-pandemic recovery began to gain steam, the fallout from Russia's war in Ukraine has resulted in elevated uncertainty, rising interest rates, higher food and energy prices, and looming stagflation.

The substantial foreign currency reserves accumulated over the years risk depletion in many African countries due to currency depreciation and a slowdown in global trade, among other factors. While debt vulnerabilities were persistent across the continent before the pandemic, the prospects of debt overhang will further tighten global financing conditions and hamper resource mobilization prospects from the private sector.

Mobilizing sustainable investments in the aftermath of the pandemic requires a strategic framework which prioritizes leveraging debt to unlock growth in the face of a magnified slowdown in the global economy. Transitioning to a sustainable future requires innovative paradigms, huge investments, and a reconfiguration of existing financial instruments, models, and tools to harness public and private capital at a scale large enough to produce the desired impact. While there is a wide array of sustainability-oriented financing options, political economy ramifications across countries on the continent imply there is no one-size-fits-all scenario. A few case studies are discussed below.

Sustainable Ocean Finance in Seychelles: A Policy Success Story

The blue economy remains key to the realization of the SDGs in Africa. With a diverse and productive array of marine areas, covering 38 coastal and island states and a coastline of over 47,000 km, these assets cover everything from food to shelter for communities. However, climate change poses long-term sustainability risks with a plethora of threats, including marine pollution and overexploited fish stocks. Seychelles is the richest nation in Africa in GDP per capita terms (World Bank, 2021). The Indian Ocean archipelago of 115 islands is home to about 100,000 people, with tourism and fishing as major economic drivers.

In the aftermath of the sovereign debt default due to the 2008 financial crisis, Seychelles implemented a reform program aimed at addressing structural imbalances in its economy. Thereafter, the Seychelles economy

Box 6: Seychelles: Policy Innovation Lessons from Sovereign Blue Bond

Seychelles launched the world's first sovereign blue bond in 2018. A pioneering financial instrument designed to support sustainable marine and fisheries projects, proceeds from the $15 million bond raised from international investors would support the expansion of marine protected areas, improved governance of priority fisheries, and the development of the Seychelles' blue economy.

As a precursor to the blue bond launch, in January 2018, Seychelles unveiled its Blue Economy Strategic Framework and Roadmap, an integrated approach to ocean-based sustainable development which brings together economy, environment, and society, consistent with Sustainable Development Agenda 2030.

The Roadmap is dedicated to harnessing the blue economy potential of Seychelles driven by its comparative advantage based on sustainability credentials. It also aims to build on the country's national and international legal and policy frameworks and successful flagship initiatives such as marine spatial planning and innovative finance – all in alignment with the SDGs and a prioritized agenda for action and investment to 2030.

Despite the relatively low volume of the blue bond in market terms, a robust ecosystem of policy entrepreneurs and innovation agents worked with the World Bank, which supported the issuance, to facilitate a private placement for the 10-year bond with three US-based impact investing firms - Calvert Impact Capital, Nuveen, and Prudential –through Standard Chartered.

The success story here reinforces the important role policy innovation has in spreading socially beneficial public-private policy partnerships.

became more resilient[1], with a marked increase in economic stability and fiscal sustainability. By 2015, Seychelles had achieved high income country status, with high quality of life for Seychellois in the form of comprehensive social services like free health and education, housing support, water, and waste management services. In the decade after the crisis, the economy grew at an annual average rate of 4.2 percent (World Bank, 2021).

Despite its high-income status and high ranking on major global socioeconomic development indices, structural and institutional challenges in the form of productivity lags, limited data analytics, inefficient public sector management, and limited private sector participation in the economy remain.

Clearly, marine ecosystems face enormous challenges and new ways of thinking – both in terms of innovative preservation and financing tools – have become necessary to deliver a resilient and sustainable future for the health and economic well-being of Africa's ocean economy. With global leadership and a successful track record in blue economy financing, lessons abound from Africa's ocean finance success story, Seychelles (Box 6).

Seychelles boasts excellent global ocean leadership credentials. While climate change adaptation – particularly strengthened disaster preparedness systems and enhanced coastal management – remains on the front burner of its sustainable development policy agenda, the archipelago nation is a global exemplar in natural assets preservation.

Not only is the country deploying global best practices in its transition towards a blue economy, with environmentally sustainable and equitable models as it harnesses its vast ocean resources for economic growth, but it is also at the forefront of devising innovative financing mechanisms to execute its development priorities without compromising the quality of life for future generations of Seychellois.

As African states increasingly integrate within the international financial system, state bonds and other financial instruments for raising capital and stabilizing budgets will become more important. This highlights the critical role of PPPs in bridging existing gaps, and in this case, harnessing international private capital to deploy innovative financing to advance sustainability in Africa's ocean economy. Ample lessons abound for other nations with an ambitious agenda in capturing sustainable value from their natural endowments, while remaining on a blue growth trajectory with resilient economies and healthy communities.

Human-Wildlife Conflict in Gabon and Policy Innovation

The need to address the problematic issue of deforestation in Africa has been in the news for a long time. While various incentives-based models aimed at deterring developing countries from tree-cutting haven't achieved much success, Gabon recently made international headlines as the first African country to be paid for reducing carbon emissions by protecting its rainforests.

Rainforests are critical to tackling the climate crisis because of their ability to absorb global climate-heating emissions. Located in Central Africa, Gabon is a resource-endowed country located on the Atlantic Ocean, with a population of 2 million and 85 percent of its territory covered by forests, thereby capturing more carbon emissions than the country emits. Forests in Gabon absorb 140 million tons of CO2 per annum and emit about 30 million tons. In addition, they are home to pristine wildlife and megafauna, with 50,000 emblematic forest elephants (60 percent of their remaining population) in Central Africa endangered (Central African Forest Initiative (CAFI), n.d.).

The country is one of the most forested countries in the world, with forests covering 23.6 million hectares and accounting for about 18 percent of the entire Congo Basin forest (CAFI, n.d.). Despite this, Gabon boasts one of the highest urbanization rates in Africa, with over 80 percent of its citizens living in cities. Gabon's political and commercial capitals – Libreville and Port Gentil – account for almost 60 percent of the national population (World Bank, 2021).

Gabon's lackluster business climate constitutes a major barrier to the successful diversification of its economy, and to address this, a recent World Bank analysis concludes that recent interventions aimed at bolstering the business environment include "a one-stop shop for investors, a public-private partnership (PPP) framework, a domestic arbitration court, and codes for hydrocarbons and mining" (World Bank, 2021, para. 12)

On the social policy front, Gabon established integrated social programs for its most vulnerable population groups, created income-generating activities for the poorest Gabonese, and reduced inequalities in access to basic public services (World Bank, 2021).

Apart from its adverse impact on the sustainability of community livelihoods in Africa, human-wildlife conflict (HWC) poses a serious threat to the survival of endangered species. As countries face competitive pressures to exploit natural resources for economic growth, harnessing forested landscapes could lead to habitat loss and fragmentation, posing major threats to wildlife.

In 2017, the Government of Gabon and the World Bank explored strategic policy innovations aimed at examining the root causes and drivers of HWC, as well as ways to incentivize communities to promote a regime with thriving human-wildlife coexistence.

Policy innovations, through new tools and best practices, targeted at addressing the inherent trade-offs in wildlife's importance and land use options can support integrated landscape management, while addressing HWC. As governments chart economic growth paths, options that guide against harming the vast forests in their regions are vital to addressing the climate crisis, in the same way that conserving forest elephants is key to boosting the rural economy (Box 7).

Box 7: Gabon and Decarbonization in the Congo Basin Forest

An upper-middle-income country and the fifth-largest oil producer in Africa, Gabon is highly dependent on manganese and the petroleum economy. However, in the face of declining oil reserves, falling prices of commodities, the diversification imperative, and the sustainable development agenda, Gabon has moved decarbonization to the front burner of its economic development agenda, with ambitious targets on the preservation of ecosystems and biodiversity.

With its fiscal position deteriorating in 2015, having recorded a fiscal deficit for the first time since 1998, the government prioritized FDI attraction in the non-oil sectors through specific incentives to foreign investors, in addition to a renewed effort towards domestic revenue mobilization.

Targeted at Central African countries, the United Nations-backed CAFI is a $150 million, results-based 10-year deal aimed at reducing deforestation and forest degradation. Cameroon, the Central African Republic, the Democratic Republic of the Congo, Equatorial Guinea, and the Republic of Congo are the other countries on the continent that are part of CAFI. In June 2021, Gabon received the first payment of $17 million, with a total of $150 million expected over a 10-year period (BBC, 2021).

While the initial payment represents a meagre 0.1 percent of Gabon's economic output, the significance is more in the context of providing further incentives for the Gabonese authorities to deploy policy innovation to create further opportunities around deforestation and carbon emissions monitoring. In addition to other measures aimed at maintaining its carbon stocks through sustainable forestry over the years, Gabon initiated several conservation schemes, including the creation of 13 national parks (covering 10 percent of the country) in 2002 (CAFI, n.d.).

Gabon is expected to reduce GHG emissions from forests by 50 percent by 2025, compared to a 2005 baseline level in its Intended Nationally Determined Contributions "under the Paris Agreement and subsequently in its first Letter of Intent signed with CAFI in 2017, in which Gabon committed to the non-conversion of high value forest and limited and carbon neutral conversion of non-high-value forests." (CAFI, n.d.; para. 5).

CONCLUDING REMARKS

As encapsulated in the various cases examined in this chapter, the digital revolution has become a key driver of productivity in Africa. If properly harnessed, with the right policy mix and financing architecture, it can transition Africa from the margins to the mainstream of global commerce. The rapid pace of digitization, increased private sector participation in the economy, favorable demographic dynamics, and policy reforms in the innovation economy – under the appropriate public-private policy partnership framework – can drive knowledge and skills acquisition, scale innovations, and generate efficient multi-stakeholder collaborative arrangements that blur the differences between regions and sectors, thereby charting a sustainable path to prosperity for the vast majority of Africans.

Poverty is not intrinsically a trap, otherwise we would all still be poor.
— Paul Collier

REFERENCES

BBC. (2021). Gabon is first African country paid to protect its rainforest. *BBC News Africa.* https://www.bbc.com/news/world-africa-57567829

Central African Forest Initiative. (n.d.). *Partner Countries – Gabon.* https://www.cafi.org/countries/gabon

Congress.gov. (2012). *S.3217 - 112th Congress (2011-2012): Startup Act 2.0.* https://www.congress.gov/bill/112th-congress/senate-bill/3217

Digital Africa. (2020). Startups Acts – A lever for innovation in Africa. *Resilient Digital Africa.* https://resilient.digital-africa.co/en/blog/2020/09/14/startup-acts-a-lever-for-innovation-in-africa/

Duffy, A. (2021). African tech ecosystems of the future — the dawn of a new era: South Africa has come out on top of the inaugural African tech ecosystems of the future ranking. *FDI Intelligence.* https://www.fdiintelligence.com/article/79638?saveConsentPreferences=success

Florida, R., & Hathaway, I. (2018). *Rise of the global startup city: The new map of entrepreneurship and venture capital*. https://startupsusa.org/global-startup-cities/report.pdf

Gutiérrez, A. A., & Olayele, F. (2021). Urban innovation and reinvention: The case of New York. *ICE. Revista De Economía*, (920), 29–48. doi:10.32796/ice.2021.920.7211

Jerry Mohan. (2012). *Startup Act 2.0 Senate sponsors statement on house introduction: Now is the time to act - not after the election, not next year.* News Release. https://www.moran.senate.gov/public/index.cfm/news-releases?ID=5B8088DA-4D29-4A79-9062-B9BDA522E8B7

Jesse, G., & Madden, P. (2019). Figures of the week: Africa's infrastructure needs are an investment opportunity. *Africa in Focus - Brookings Institute.* https://www.brookings.edu/blog/africa-in-focus/2019/06/27/figures-of-the-week-africas-infrastructure-needs-are-an-investment-opportunity/#:~:text=To%20close%20this%20gap%2C%20the,and%20%24108%20billion%20per%20year

Kane, T. (2010). The importance of startups in job creation and job destruction. *Kauffman Foundation Research Series: Firm Formation and Economic Growth.* https://www.kauffman.org/wp-content/uploads/2019/12/firm_formation_importance_of_startups.pdf

Kene-Okafor, T. (2021). Venture capital investment in Africa predicted to reach a record high this year. *TechCrunch.* https://techcrunch.com/2021/05/25/venture-capital-investment-in-africa-predicted-to-reach-a-record-high-this-year/?guccounter=1

Lakmeeharan, K., Manji, Q., Nyairo, R., & Poeltner, H. (2020). *Solving Africa's infrastructure paradox.* McKinsey Global Institute. https://www.mckinsey.com/business-functions/operations/our-insights/solving-africas-infrastructure-paradox#

Patton, C., Sawicki, D., & Clark, J. (2012). *Basic methods of policy analysis and planning*. Prentice Hall.

Republic of Seychelles. (2018). *Seychelles blue economy: Strategic policy framework and roadmap charting the future (2018-2030).* http://www.seychellesconsulate.org.hk/download/Blue_Economy_Road_Map.pdf

Rubio, M., Moran, J., Warner, M., & Coons, C. (2012). Startup Act's economic benefits. *Politico.* https://www.politico.com/story/2012/05/startup-acts-economic-benefits-076579

Stiglitz, J. E., & Wallsten, S. J. (1999). Public-Private technology partnerships: Promises and pitfalls. *The American Behavioral Scientist, 43*(1), 52–73. doi:10.1177/00027649921955155

United Nations. (2015). Addis Ababa action agenda of the third international conference on financing for development (Addis Ababa Action Agenda). *United Nations General Assembly: Sixty-ninth session.*

Wolken, J. (2020). *Startup Acts are the next form of policy innovation in Africa.* Atlantic Council [Africa Source]. https://www.atlanticcouncil.org/blogs/africasource/startup-acts-are-the-next-form-of-policy-innovation-in-africa/

World Bank. (2021). Gabon: Overview. *Where We Work* https://www.worldbank.org/en/country/gabon/overview

World Bank. (2021). Seychelles: Overview. *Where We Work* https://www.worldbank.org/en/country/seychelles/overview

ENDNOTE

1 Martin (2012) explains economic resilience as the ability of an economic system to adapt and return to a pre-existing state, or to a new, better path of growth and development, after undergoing certain shocks.

Chapter 10
Tax Policy Innovation and Financial Inclusion

ABSTRACT

The core argument in this chapter is that efficiency gains from the increased adoption of digital technologies have reshaped fiscal policy through innovations in how information on public revenue is collected, processed, shared, and acted upon. However, while these innovations have drastically transformed fiscal policy formulation and implementation, existing institutional and capacity constraints mean there is more work to be done. Multilateralism and shared responsibility are needed to address the issue of revenue losses to tax havens and secrecy-based jurisdictions. To enable Africa to reap more proportionate benefits from cross-border trade and investment transactions, policy innovation in the tax domain is in order. In the final analysis, this turn of events has implications for countries with a competitive advantage in tax havenry.

Where there is an income tax, the just man will pay more and the unjust less on the same amount of income.

— Plato

DOI: 10.4018/978-1-7998-7383-9.ch010

DIGITIZATION HAS HAD A PROFOUND IMPACT on resource mobilization and fiscal policy. Much has been said about the beneficial effect of increased fiscal space on the ability to finance services like health, education, security, social protection systems, infrastructure, and other vital public goods with positive externalities. However, for a wide variety of reasons, especially the presence of a large informal sector, the inefficiencies associated with domestic resource mobilization in developing economies remain a challenge.

Akitoby (2018) estimates that compared with the 40 percent of GDP collected in taxes by a typical advanced economy, the average developing economy collects only 15 percent. And when typical manifestations in the African context – like fragmentation, poor infrastructure, weak public financial management systems, low skills level, and high-level of illiteracy – are accounted for, a more disappointing outcome emerges. Considering the paradoxical reality that overseas development assistance to Africa is declining, while debt levels are rising (United Nations, 2019), critical reforms in domestic tax collection are needed to enable the continent to finance its development priorities in a sustainable manner.

Akintoby examines successful reforms in Cambodia, Georgia, Guyana, Liberia, and Ukraine –five diverse low-income and emerging market economies "which achieved some of the largest revenue gains after tax reform"— and concludes that structural and institutional constraints notwithstanding, country-specific tax policy innovations and reforms can enhance their domestic resource mobilization capacity.

That Liberia is included in the five-country case study here is profound because it controls for many Africa-specific qualifications that may otherwise affect the generalizability of the findings. The author highlights Liberia's success in terms of its ability to use a simple tax legislation to achieve a profound outcome in revenue mobilization, post-civil war, while also cautioning other low-income and emerging economies on the potential for revenue loss when tax exemptions are ill-designed.

Efficiency gains from the increased adoption of digital technologies have reshaped fiscal policy through innovations in how information on public revenue is collected, processed, shared, and acted upon. However, while these innovations have drastically transformed fiscal policy formulation and implementation, existing institutional and capacity constraints imply that country-specific incremental steps are needed, either to digitalize, or to leapfrog to more advanced policies and implementation regimes (Gupta et al., 2017).

THE LAFFER CURVE

Supply-side economics uses the Laffer curve[1] construct to argue in favor of tax cuts based on the notion that lowering the corporate tax rate would raise revenue because of the behavioral responses of entrepreneurs and owners of capital. The aggregate effect of all labor supply curves in the economy – through constructs such as backward-bending labor supply curve and conflicting income and substitution effects – explain the Laffer curve model. The Laffer curve explains how rising tax rates force taxpayers to reduce taxable income by working less, retiring earlier, scaling back plans to start or expand businesses, moving activities to the underground economy, restructuring companies, and spending more time and money on accountants to minimize taxes.

Based on conventional wisdom, corporate taxes support a more progressive society because the burden falls on capital income and thus on higher income individuals. However, evidence also supports the view that in open economies, the burden is shared by both capital and labor income (Gravelle & Hungerford, 2007). In the final analysis, outcomes vary based on jurisdictional differences in the supply elasticities of capital.

To the extent that jurisdictions compete over tax rates to attract business investment, which helps increase economic activity and expand employment opportunities, tax policies in neighboring jurisdictions also have implications for resource mobilization, especially under a relatively free capital mobility regime. As such, changes in tax rates in one jurisdiction can affect the amount of tax revenue in another, thereby creating horizontal tax externalities (Dahlby & Ferede, 2008). In other words, changes in marginal income tax rates have a major influence on individual and corporate behavior.

Identifying the impacts of different tax rates on overall tax revenues is very necessary for any meaningful tax reforms. Lower taxes could increase business and employment activity. However, adequate tax revenue is also important in providing the quality infrastructure and services expected by businesses and residents. Businesses operating in multi-jurisdiction environments also tend to shift income across jurisdictions in response to differences in tax rates and incentives.

To the extent that reductions in distortions can expand the tax base and help grow the economy, policy innovations that account for the largely informal nature of many African economies would go a long way in mobilizing additional resources to enhance public service delivery. Digitization has a major role here, as espoused by the Managing Director of the International Finance Corporation:

There is no doubt that technology and innovation are transforming Africa. Across sub-Saharan Africa, phones now act as banks for millions of Africans who cannot even dream of opening a traditional bank account. With the touch of a button, small farmers can find out how much they should be charging for their crops. People can buy solar energy using a phone, get their hearts examined in rural Cameroon using a medical tablet, or get blood delivered by drones in Rwanda. But these achievements mask a tougher reality. For Africa to leapfrog further into the future, a number of conditions must be met, including investment in infrastructure, having the right regulatory environment for new business models to be tested, and paying deliberate attention to research and development, science and technology (Diop, 2017; para. 1-2)

DIGITIZATION AND FINANCIAL INCLUSION

Digital Finance fosters productivity gains and financial inclusion in a cost-effective, fast, and convenient manner due to its inherent ability to leverage technology for financial services delivery. An economic impact study by Manyika et al. (2016) finds that by 2025, emerging economies could record an incremental value of $3.7 trillion in economic activity because of digital finance. Findings from the study further reveal that while digital finance has a larger economic impact on lower-income countries like Ethiopia, India, and Nigeria (adding between 10 to 12 percent to GDP), middle-income countries like China and Brazil benefit, sizably, too (4 to 5 percent to GDP).

To corroborate the findings above, we discuss below findings from Voorhies and Lamb's (2013) study on financial inclusion, based on a review of the payment systems in six countries: Nigeria, Kenya, India, China, the United States, and the Netherlands. In addition, more than 100 industry experts across these countries were interviewed. Figures 1 and 2 below summarize the results of Kenya and Nigeria's payment system and financial inclusion.

Based on a survey with about 6,500 respondents (adults 18 years or older), 40 percent of adults in Kenya have formal access, with higher financial inclusion in urban areas, among men, and those with at least primary education. The report concludes that overall, financial inclusion in Kenya is in the low-medium performance range; only 19 percent of women have formal financial accounts. A similar picture emerges for Nigeria: only 30 percent of adults are

Figure 1. Kenya's financial inclusion overview
(Credit: Voorhies and Lamb, 2013)

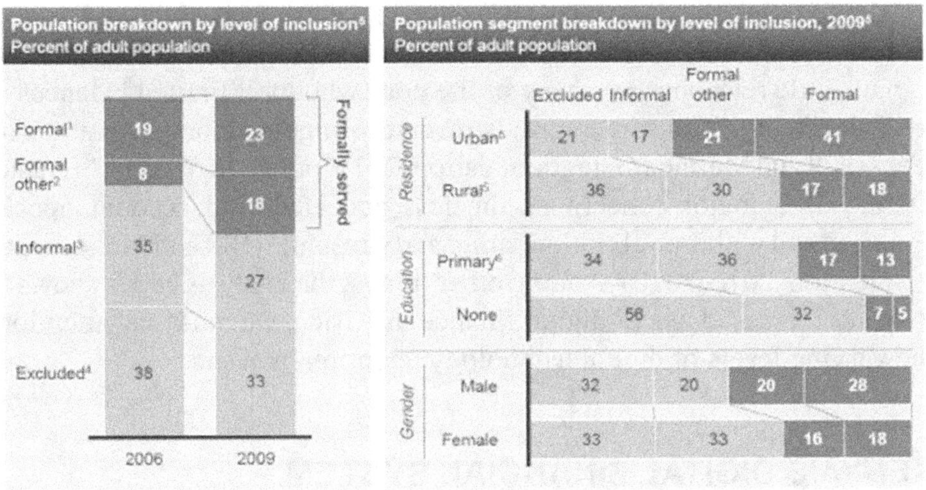

1 Formal: use a bank, PostBank or insurance product; 2 Formal other: use services from non-bank financial institutions such as SACCOs (Savings and Credit Cooperative Societies) and MFIs; 3 Informal: use informal service providers (e.g., ASCAs, RoSCAs) 4 Excluded: use none of the above; 5 Based on a survey of adults 18 years or older, with ~6,500 survey respondents; 6 Respondent with higher than primary education have yet higher access levels (34.7% and 70.3% formal inclusion for those with secondary and tertiary education, respectively)

SOURCE: FinAccess National Survey 2009; Dynamics of Kenya's changing financial landscape

Figure 2. Nigeria's financial inclusion overview
(Credit: Voorhies and Lamb, 2013)

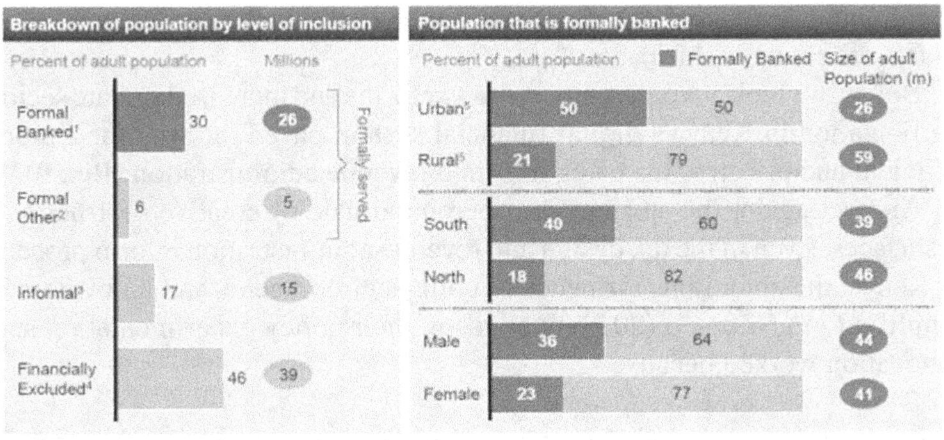

1 Banked: All adults who have access to or use a deposit money bank; 2 Formal other: All adults who use other formal institutions and financial products not supplied by deposit money bank, including insurance companies, microfinance banks, remittances; 3 Informal only: All adults who have access to or use only informal services and products. This includes Savings clubs/pools, informal remittances (via a transport service or recharge card); 4 Financially excluded: Adults not in the formal (banked), formal other or informal only categories; 5 EFInA data based on survey differs in its assessment of overall urban-rural split (~30/70) vs. other sources which give the urban-rural split to be ~50/50

SOURCE: EFInA Access to Financial Services in Nigeria 2010

banked, with greater inclusion in urban areas, in the South and among men. Again, only 23 percent of Nigerian women have formal financial accounts.

The report with country-specific data on payments systems and financial inclusion concludes that in Kenya, "Formal banking products are perceived to have little relevance for many of the poor who have limited balances and irregular income. Consumers are also averse to ongoing monthly maintenance fees" (Bill and Melinda Gates Foundation, 2016, p. 10). In Nigeria, "Financial literacy is a major concern as the less educated find account opening, deposits, and withdrawals intimidating and stressful" (Bill and Melinda Gates Foundation, 2016, p. 10). Among other things, the analysis above shows that to foster increased use of digital finance in Africa, we must pay attention to the varying levels of digital technology adoption by users.

KENYA'S DIGITAL FINANCIAL SYSTEM

Digitizing tax design and collection would minimize taxpayer–tax officer interactions and the concomitant opportunities for tax collusion and evasion. Recognizing Africa's highly heterogeneous economic, political, social, and technological dynamics, Kenya's relative success in tax design and revenue administration deserves an acknowledgement. Obviously, the role of M-Pesa in the transformation of the financial technology space and other innovation success stories in Kenya cannot be discounted, but the point to be made here is that the secondary effects of the digital transformation have also permeated fiscal policy with a beneficial impact on the traditionally challenging issue of tax collection in Africa.

Below, we look at a case study on how reforms and increased private sector participation in Kenya's digital financial system paved the way for a more efficient and effective tax categories and revenue administration (Box 9).

And yet again, the story of the "perennial gale of creative destruction" resurfaces. Even in the tax design and revenue administration reform process in Kenya, the ubiquitous influence of policy entrepreneurs and innovators is amplified. As Ndung'u (2018) explains it, their policy experimentation and innovation worked because:

Kenya's combination of a supporting policy environment with a sound regulatory and supervisory framework allowed space for innovators and entrepreneurs to introduce financial innovations and a diversification of products into the market. Regulators agreed with the innovators on prudent risk management, and the policy environment ensured a stable macroeconomic environment. These combined factors ensured Kenya's success. These are major outcomes that form a strong base for lessons for 2017 in the African continent as well as for Kenya to sustain the frontier and move to the next level (Ndung'u, 2017; p. 48).

Data from the Kenya Revenue Authority and Ndung'u's analysis unpack the beneficial impact of the innovation through an expanded tax base, overall

Box 9: Tax Design and Revenue Administration in Kenya

Kenya's role is pivotal to the regional economy in East Africa. With a growing youthful population that is leveraging the digital revolution to transform the country's agrifood sector, its dynamic private sector is contributing to beneficial structural changes in the overall economy. However, much work remains in terms of reducing poverty, inequality, governance, and low productivity to achieve a more sustained and inclusive economic growth.

Policy innovation and digitalization have played a key role in the design and execution of a more efficient and effective tax and revenue administration regime in Kenya. The former Governor of the Central Bank of Kenya, Njuguna Ndung'u, explains four critical ways in which digitization is transforming economies across Africa: retail payments systems, financial inclusion, sustainable business models, and revenue administration (Ndung'u, 2018). Ndung'u argues that given Kenya's relative success in the pursuit and utilization of digitization, there are useful lessons for policy innovation for countries on the continent.

The Kenya Revenue Authority leveraged digital innovations to implement a system which enabled a single view of the taxpayer's records, while also improving reconciliations and real-time monitoring of revenue collection and administration.

Ndung'u traces the development of the M-Pesa in four stages: (1) its use as a platform for transfers, payments, and settlement (2) the introduction of savings accounts and virtual banking services (3) a progression of supply and short-term credit disbursement via M-Pesa, and (4) expansion to enable cross-border and international remittances. He explains the policy innovation around tax design and revenue administration in Kenya as the outcome of six interrelated processes: customs reform and modernization, domestic tax reform and modernization, road transport reform and modernization, business automation, human resources revitalization, and infrastructure development.

The Internet access-economic growth nexus is not an absolute relationship (Melhem, 2016). What we have seen in the Kenya case is the ability to successfully harness the capabilities of both digital and analog infrastructure to innovate policy in a progressive manner that fosters greater revenue mobilization capability to unlock inclusive growth.

improvements in the design of new taxes and tax collection, and other secondary benefits (see Figures 3-6).

While digital innovation opened the door for the strengthening and revamping of the tax enforcement system by the Kenya Revenue Authority via third-party information sharing possibility, Gupta et al. (2017) conclude that the new platform would be integrated with national information systems in other segments of the economy and society in a bid to "facilitate identification of potential tax defaulters, unregistered businesses, and individuals, and increase active taxpayers and tax compliance." This is a big deal.

Figure 3. Cost of revenue collection including capital expenditure (percent)
Credit: Digital Revolutions in Public Finance; IMF (Gupta et al., 2017)

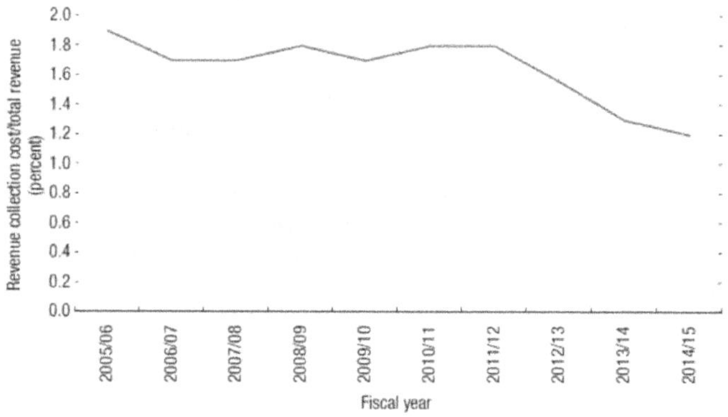

Figure 4. Kenya's tax effort (Tax to GDP in Percent)
Credit: Digital Revolutions in Public Finance; IMF (Gupta et al., 2017)

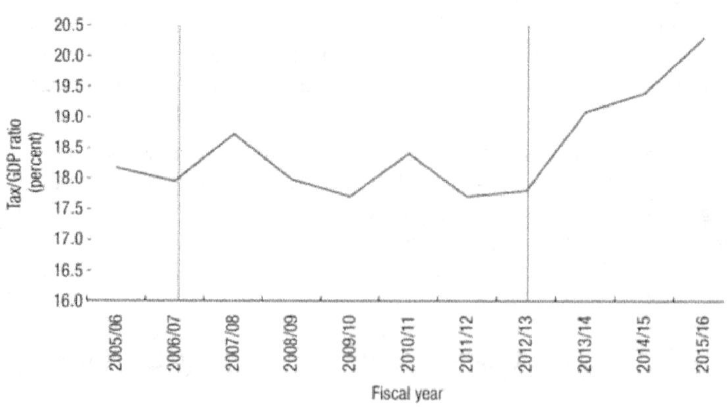

Figure 5. Annual performance of new tax categories (Tax to GDP in Percent)
Credit: Digital Revolutions in Public Finance; IMF (Gupta et al., 2017)

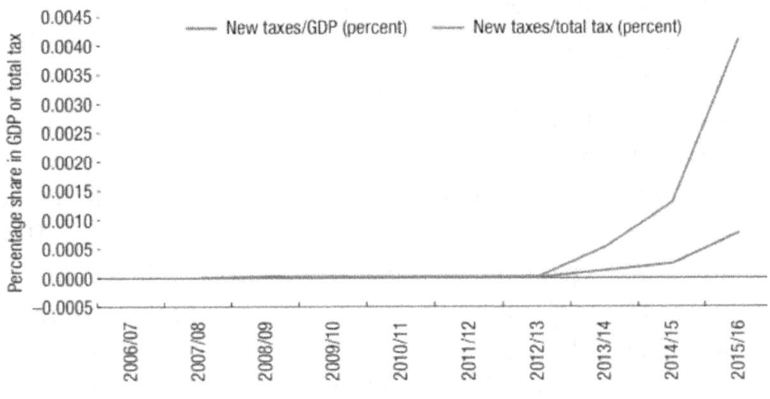

Figure 6. Contribution of new tax categories to total revenue
Credit: Digital Revolutions in Public Finance; IMF (Gupta et al., 2017)

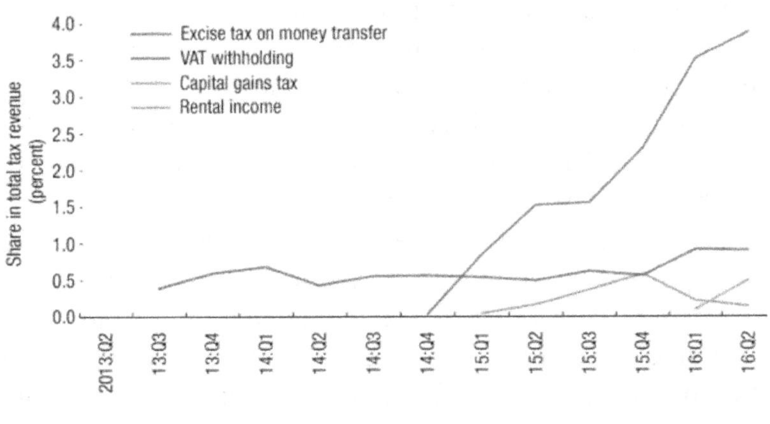

The Global Minimum Tax

Perhaps there is no better time to innovate tax policy in Africa than now. As the debate continues on discouraging multinational corporations from shifting profits and tax revenues to low-tax jurisdictions, regardless of where sales are made, the idea of a global minimum tax for corporations has moved to the front burner of the global policy debate.

A global minimum tax is one of the 14 recommendations that came out of the February 2021 United Nations High-Level Panel on International Financial Accountability, Transparency and Integrity – aimed at reforming, redesigning, and revitalizing the global architecture to effectively foster financial integrity for sustainable development. Among other things, this would signify a major reform in corporate taxation in recent times, with implications for the 'tax haven' business model in which multinational corporations shift incomes and divert profits to low- and no-tax jurisdictions.

Thomas Piketty in his 2017 book, *Capital in the Twenty-First Century*, argues that in the absence of a major intervention such as a globally coordinated tax on wealth, history may repeat itself with economic elitism resulting from wealth inheritance rather than work effort as witnessed in the 19th century. Taxing multinationals has become increasingly difficult in recent decades due to the combined forces of globalization and the rise of intangible capital. As such, the increased global cooperation aimed at reversing a race to the bottom on global corporate tax rates in recent times could become the much-needed game changer for a more effective revenue mobilization model that ensures multinational corporations using tax havens pay their fair share of income to both the home and host governments.

Finance leaders from the G7 countries during a June 2021 meeting agreed on a framework to overhaul global trade and investment in a bid to shore up public finances considering the budget shortfalls heralded by pandemic-related expenditures. In the US, as part of the ways to finance his $1.9 trillion infrastructure plan, President Biden proposed a minimum tax rate of 21 percent on the profits of US multinational companies.

While a global minimum tax is expected to establish a baseline level of revenue from profitable multinationals, such reform is only just the beginning. In the aftermath of the COVID-19 pandemic, a global minimum tax could become a source of additional revenue that can help pay for the significant investments needed to build a fairer, greener, and more equitable global economic system. This becomes particularly compelling when the increasingly dominant role of technology and superstar firms like Facebook, Amazon, and Google in the global economy is considered.

Moreso, the inherent business models of these firms reduce their incentive to shift profits to low-tax offshore havens since they can pay taxes regardless of whether they have a physical presence in a certain country or not. Given the huge wealth transfers recorded during the pandemic, reforming the global tax system to ensure it is more sensitive to the current digital economy will ensure existing gaps in socioeconomic inequalities are bridged. While the redesign would not fix the issues of income and profit shifting in its entirety, it will be a step in the right direction. This has major implications for Africa.

IMPLICATIONS FOR AFRICA

It has never been more important for tax administrators and policymakers in Africa to rethink their incentives framework to minimize revenue losses to other jurisdictions. Ocampo (2021) articulates the implications of the additional revenue from a global minimum tax for both the home countries of the multinational companies and their host jurisdictions, often in the Global South, where workforces and raw materials come from. Such equitable global revenue model will have impacts on the resource mobilization efforts of African nations.

UNECA estimates that Africa loses as much as $50 billion a year through illicit financial flows and leakages to developed countries (Tafirenyika, 2013). Such outflows obviously constitute a drag on the mobilization of resources to finance the continent's development priorities.

Compared to intra-regional economic exchanges, African countries' relationships with external partners rank relatively high, leading to the import of risks in illicit financial flows from outside the continent. The Tax Justice Network corroborates the adverse impacts of illicit financial flows on the economies, societies, public finances, and governance of African countries (Abugre et al., 2019). For context, UNECA defines illicit financial flows to:

constitute, among others, undocumented commercial transactions and criminal activities characterized by over pricing, tax evasion, false declarations, mispricing of trade exports and imports facilitated by some 60 international tax havens and secrecy jurisdictions that enable creating and operating of millions of disguised corporations, oil companies, anonymous trust accounts and fake charitable foundations. Other techniques used include money laundering, transfer pricing and corruption (UNECA, 2013, para. 14)

The varying nature of the risks associated with illicit financial flows across countries provides an opportunity for policy innovation to mitigate its adverse impacts:

These illicit financial flows undermine domestic resource mobilization, deepen poverty, distort the economy, let organized crime thrive, and enable grand corruption on the continent. The common denominator is that these illicit financial flows rely on secrecy in counterpart countries of cross-border economic transactions into and out of African countries (Abugre et al., 2019; p. 78)

While the risks in trade are concentrated with European and Asian jurisdictions, direct investment risks are more prevalent in Asia. On the other hand, risks around portfolio investments are majorly from the Americas, while the European Union accounts for a significant proportion of banking risks. The Tax Justice Network analysis shows that while there is a general trend on illicit financial flows on the continent, there are stark differences in key individual economic channels (Figure 7 and Table 1).

During a June 2013 High Level Panel on Illicit Financial Flows in Lusaka, Zambia, panel chair and former President of South Africa, Thabo Mbeki, highlighted the adverse impacts of illicit financial outflows on Africa's development. Mbeki called for greater cooperation by the G8 countries for greater transparency since these countries are a major destination for such flows.

Goldstein (2021) explains that compared to the worldwide average,

Figure 7. Vulnerability of stocks/flows, 2008-2018
(Credit: The Tax Justice Network, 2019)

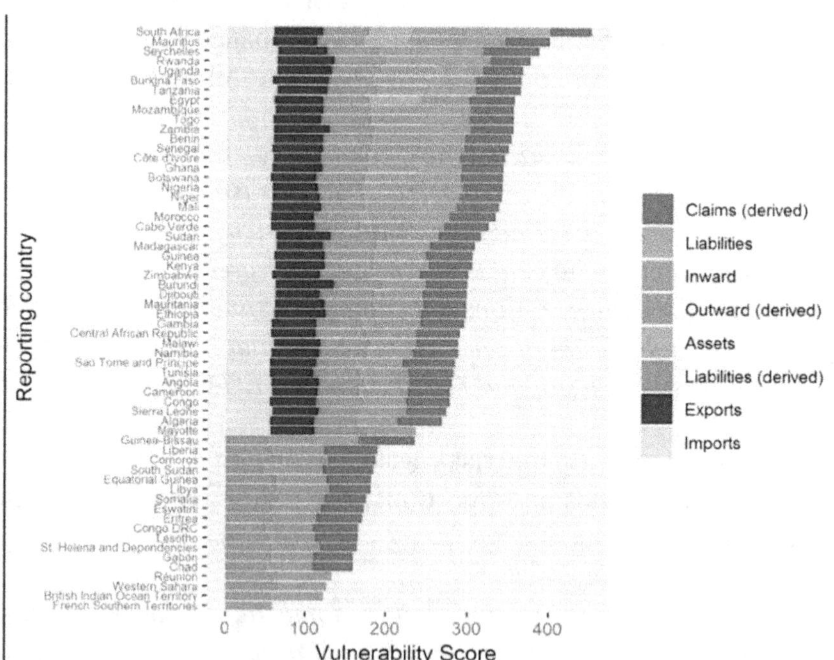

developing countries tend to have higher corporate income tax rates. According

Table 1. Illicit financial flows risk analysis, 2008-2018

IFF Channel / Dataset	Number of African reporter jurisdictions with data at least one observation 2008-2018 if secrecy scores of partner jurisdiction are also available	Coverage 2008 – 2018 (%, out of 60)	Number of African reporter jurisdictions with data at least one observation in 2016 if secrecy scores of partner jurisdiction are also available	Coverage 2016 (%, out of 60)[19]
Exports	42	70.0%	32	53.3%
Imports	42	70.0%	32	53.3%
FDI Inward	21	35.0%	17	28.3%
FDI Outward (derived)	60	100.0%	60	100.0%
Banking Claims (derived)	60	100%	60	100.0%
Banking Liabilities	1	1.7%	1	1.7%
Portfolio Assets	3	5.0%	3	5.0%
Portfolio Liabilities (derived)	59	98.3%	54	90.0%

(Credit: The Tax Justice Network, 2019)

to the Tax Foundation (Figure 8), nine of the 20 countries with the highest corporate income tax rates are in Africa. Europe has the lowest regional average corporate tax rate at 19.99 percent (24.61 percent when weighted by GDP), while Africa at 28.5 percent (28.16 percent weighted by GDP) boasts the highest rate. Of the 10 countries among 223 jurisdictions around the world that changed their statutory corporate tax rates in 2020, only Micronesia increased its rate, while Togo and Zimbabwe were among the nine countries that witnessed a decrease in corporate tax rates (Asen, 2020).

Etter-Phoya (2019) of the Tax Justice Network highlights the role of major OECD countries in the inefficient global corporate tax system and how this, in turn, perpetuates the current global corporate tax havenry. Etter-Phoya unpacks how former colonial powers maintain their stranglehold on their former African colonies thereby limiting their ability to effectively tax multinationals operating in their countries, in addition to the other risks posed by these corporate tax havens.

The G7 finance ministers recently agreed on the need for a minimum global corporate tax rate of at least 15 percent. Finance ministers from Indonesia, South Africa, and Mexico also threw their weight behind the call for an overhaul of the global corporate tax regime on the ground that the

Figure 8. Average tax revenue gains from Global Minimum Tax
(Credit: Tax Foundation)

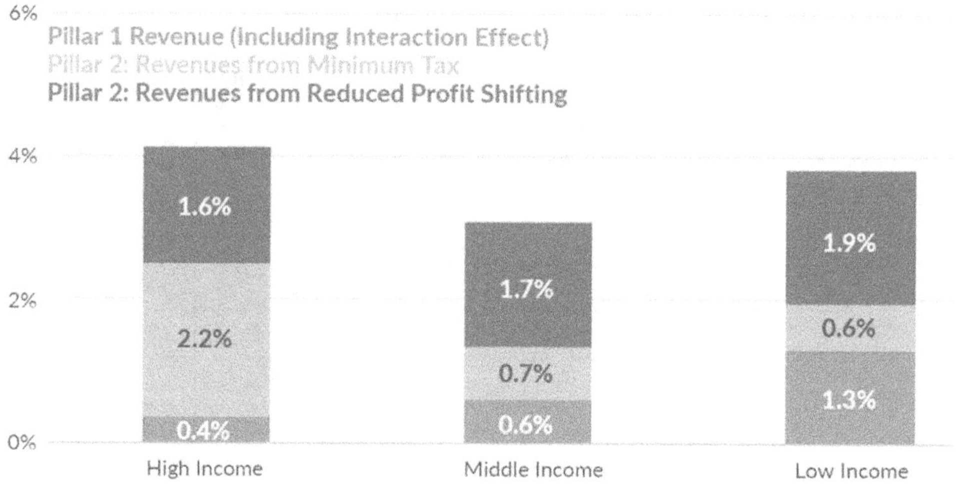

time is ripe for multinationals to pay their fair share in the new globalized and digitalized economic order (Reuters, 2021).

Multilateralism and shared responsibility are needed to address the issue of revenue losses to tax havens and secrecy-based jurisdictions. To enable Africa reap more proportionate benefits from crossborder trade and investment transactions, policy innovation in the tax domain is in order. In the final analysis, this turn of event has implications for countries with a competitive advantage in tax havenry. In the African context, Mauritius is the obvious candidate (Box 10).

While Mauritius started off as any other typical African economy – with usual characteristics like informality, ethnic fragmentation, high population growth rate, and being a world price taker – its stable democracy and strategic industrial policy around the transition from agriculture to an offshore financial hub for global corporations, among other factors, have seen it become a leader on almost all socioeconomic global development indexes.

As countries redesign their economic systems after emerging from pandemic-induced ruins, innovative resource mobilization is one issue that will linger on the front burner of the policy agenda. Governments obviously need resources to invest in healthcare and support small businesses and the marginalized and vulnerable segments of society. Mauritius – and other countries on the continent – must innovate to maintain its competitive edge.

Box 2: The Tax Innovation Imperative in Mauritius

In what has been dubbed the "the Mauritian Miracle" and the "success of Africa", since gaining independence in 1968, this tropical archipelago of 1.3 million people has progressively diversified its economy from a sugar-based monoculture to a prosperous economy powered by tourism, sugar, textiles, financial services, and increasingly, digital technologies.

From competitiveness and investment climate to ease of doing business and economic freedom, Mauritius enjoys a full-fledged free market economy and consistently ranks in the top 10, globally, often outperforming most OECD countries. However, the success of Mauritius has not been without controversy. Its attractiveness to global corporations and investors capitalizing on legal but opaque means of reducing their tax burdens has deprived other less well-off African countries the much-needed tax dollars to finance their budgets.

This becomes even more complicated when analyzed in the context of a zero-sum game in which one country's gain is essentially another's loss, thereby perpetuating the so-called race to the bottom. Policymakers face the risk of inaction due to the dilemma of losing these corporations to competing jurisdictions if taxes are raised.

If we choose to keep those tax breaks for millionaires and billionaires, if we choose to keep a tax break for corporate jet owners, if we choose to keep tax breaks for oil and gas companies that are making hundreds of billions of dollars, then that means we've got to cut some kids off from getting a college scholarship.

– Barack Obama

REFERENCES

Abugre, C., Cobham, A., Etter-Phoya, R., Lépissier, A., Meinzer, M., Monkam, N., & Mosioma, A. (2019). *Vulnerability and Exposure to Illicit Financial Flows risk in Africa.* Tax Justice Network. https://www.taxjustice.net/wp-content/uploads/2019/08/Vulnerability-and-Exposure-to-Illicit-Financial-Flows-risk-in-Africa_August-2019_Tax-Justice-Network.pdf

Akitoby, B. (2018). Raising Revenue: Five country cases illustrate how best to improve tax collection. IMF. *Finance & Development, 55*(1). https://www.imf.org/external/pubs/ft/fandd/2018/03/pdf/akitoby.pdf

Asen, E. (2020). *Corporate Tax Rates around the World, 2020* [Fiscal Fact, No. 735]. Tax Foundation. https://taxfoundation.org/publications/corporate-tax-rates-around-the-world/

Bill and Melinda Gates Foundation. (2016). Fighting poverty, profitably: Transforming the economics of payments to build sustainable, inclusive financial systems. Kenya. *Bill and Melinda Gates Foundation. Special Report Annex: Country-specific data on payments systems and financial inclusion.* https://docs.gatesfoundation.org/documents/fighting%20poverty%20 profitably%20full%20report.pdf

Bill and Melinda Gates Foundation. (2016). Fighting poverty, profitably: Transforming the economics of payments to build sustainable, inclusive financial systems. Nigeria. *Bill and Melinda Gates Foundation. Special Report Annex: Country-specific data on payments systems and financial inclusion.* https://docs.gatesfoundation.org/Documents/Fighting%20Poverty%20 Profitably%20Report%20Nigeria%20Appendix.pdf

Dahlby, B., & Ferede, E. (2008). *Assessing British Columbia's Incentive-based Tax Cuts. Studies in Economic Prosperity 5.* Fraser Institute.

Diop, M. (2017). *Africa can enjoy leapfrog development.* World Bank Group. https://www.worldbank.org/en/news/opinion/2017/10/11/africa-can-enjoy-leapfrog-development

Etter-Phoya, R. (2019). How can Africa take action against corporate tax havenry? Solutions from the Corporate Tax Haven Index 2019. *Tax Justice Network.* https://taxjustice.net/2019/06/18/%EF%BB%BFhow-can-africa-take-action-against-corporate-tax-havenry-solutions-from-the-corporate-tax-haven-index-2019/

Goldstein, J. (2021). The case for a global minimum corporate tax. *Atlantic Council.* https://www.atlanticcouncil.org/blogs/new-atlanticist/the-case-for-a-global-minimum-corporate-tax/

Gravelle, J. G., & Hungerford, T. L. (2007). *Corporate tax reform: Issues for Congress? CRS Report for Congress* [RL34229]. https://www.everycrsreport.com/files/20071031_RL34229_ a89f89777967b35330b0f334f0386f134b9d919b.pdf

Gupta, S., Keen, M., Shah, A., & Verdier, G. (Eds.). (2017). *Digital Revolutions in Public Finance*. International Monetary Fund. Retrieved from https://www.elibrary.imf.org/view/books/071/24304-9781484315224-en/24304-9781484315224-en-book.xml

Laffer, A. B. (2004). *"The Laffer Curve: Past, Present, and Future." Executive Summary Backgrounder No. 1765*. The Heritage Foundation.

Manyika, J., Lund, S., Singer, M., White, O., & Berry, C. (2016). *Digital finance for all: powering inclusive growth in emerging economies*. McKinsey Global Institute. https://www.findevgateway.org/sites/default/files/publications/files/mg-digital-finance-for-all-full-report-september-2016.pdf

Melhem, S. (2016). *Harnessing the Internet for Development*. World Bank. https://www.worldbank.org/en/news/feature/2016/01/13/connections-note-31

Ndung'u, N. (2017). Regulatory environment and technological innovation in Africa: Any tension? Foresight Africa 2017 Report. Brookings Institution.

Ndung'u, N. (2018). *New frontiers in Africa's digital potential. Foresight Africa 2018 Report*. Brookings Institution.

Ocampo, J. A. (2021). Taxing global rent-seeking to spur a just recovery. *Social Europe*. https://socialeurope.eu/taxing-global-rent-seeking-to-spur-a-just-recovery

Piketty, T. (2017). *Capital in the Twenty-First Century*. Harvard University Press. doi:10.4159/9780674982918

Reuters. (2021). Indonesia, South Africa, Mexico back G7 global tax reform proposal. *Reuters Business*. https://www.reuters.com/business/finance/indonesia-south-africa-mexico-back-g7-global-tax-reform-proposal-2021-06-10/

Tafirenyika, M. (2013). Africa loses $50 billion every year: Interview with Nigerian ambassador Segun Apata. *Africa Renewal*. https://www.un.org/africarenewal/magazine/december-2013/africa-loses-50-billion-every-year

United Nations. (2019). Declining aid, rising debt thwarting world's ability to fund sustainable development, speakers warn at general assembly high-level dialogue. *United Nations General Assembly: High-level dialogue on financing for development, am & pm meetings*. https://www.un.org/press/en/2019/ga12191.doc.htm

United Nations. (2021). *Secretary-General's message to launch the Final Report of the High-Level Panel on International Financial Accountability, Transparency and Integrity for Achieving the 2030 Agenda.* https://www.un.org/sg/en/content/sg/statement/2021-02-25/secretary-generals-message-launch-the-final-report-of-the-high-level-panel-international-financial-accountability-transparency-and-integrity-for-achieving-the-2030

Voorhies, J., & Lamb, M. O. (2013). Fighting poverty, profitably: Transforming the economics of payments to build sustainable, inclusive finance systems. *Bill and Melinda Gates Foundation. Special Report: Financial Services for the Poor.* https://docs.gatesfoundation.org/documents/fighting%20poverty%20profitably%20full%20report.pdf

ENDNOTE

1 The Laffer curve is a theoretical representation of the relationship between government revenue raised by taxation and all possible rates of taxation. The basic idea behind this relationship is that changes in tax rates have two effects on revenues: the arithmetic effect and the economic effect. The curve assumes the shape of an inverted *U*. Behavioral responses to changes in tax rates have important implications for the efficiency of the economy and the burden of the tax, as well as various policy decisions.

Chapter 11
Trade Policy Innovation and the AfCFTA Imperative

ABSTRACT

Orthodox economic prescriptions emphasize a reallocation of labor from low-productivity subsistence activities to high-productivity industrial activities as a precondition for structural economic transformation, but the global digital revolution has altered the economics of manufacturing. Africa's services economy remains a key wealth generator. While agriculture remains the mainstay of the heterogenous economies on the continent, Africa's young population and advances in technology are gradually reinventing its industrial structure to be less dependent on extractive industries. The implications of the AfCFTA for deep reforms capable of driving long-term structural changes across African economies are examined. To foster economic self-sufficiency, the analysis suggests the AfCFTA could help expand fragmented markets and provide access to foreign capital which, often, is highly sensitive to technological innovations and economies of scale and scope in global value chains.

DOI: 10.4018/978-1-7998-7383-9.ch011

The multilateral trading system is a global public good that we have collectively and carefully built up over 75 years. Though certainly not perfect, by historical standards it has delivered more prosperity to more people than every international economic order that came before it.

— Ngozi Okonjo-Iweala

ECONOMIC THEORY, through the Ricardian model and productivity gains, establishes the role of technology in fostering trade. In the same vein, productivity gains explain why EMDEs benefit disproportionately from the increased connectedness of countries to international markets, through mobile and digital technologies adoption.

Trade finance remains a huge challenge in Africa, and this underscores the importance of technology in fostering regional integration. Understanding the channels through which supply-side shocks hamper trade within Africa is key for trade policy innovation. Trade facilitation enhances competitiveness by lowering transaction costs. As a result of the consequences of positive externalities due to network effects, increased adoption of digital payments increases overall benefits to all users (Voorhies & Lamb, 2013).

Technology is revolutionizing Africa's trade in services, particularly financial services. Over the last decade, fintech has advanced to become one of the fastest-growing sectors in the continent's technology industry. The emergence of the African ICT ecosystem was bolstered by several high-profile visits and tours of tech hubs on the continent by the executives of global tech giants. This started with Airbnb's Brian Chesky and Microsoft's Satya Nadella in 2015, followed by Facebook's Mark Zuckerberg, Google's Sundar Pichai, Alphabet's Sergey Brin, Alibaba's Jack Ma, and Twitter's Jack Dorsey in subsequent years.

One of the vestiges of the rapidly growing digital economy is the high-profile venture capital deals and acquisitions that have dominated the continent's tech space in recent times, reaching an all-time high in 2019 with 234 startups raising over $2 billion in 250 equity rounds – a 74 percent increase over the $1.2 billion recorded in 2018 (World Economic Forum, 2021). With the right dose of policy innovation, staying course will have major implications for growth and job creation in the knowledge economy.

Nonetheless, while the ICT revolution has changed Africa's financial services landscape significantly, rural credit remains problematic. Among other things, delivering financial services to fragmented markets and dispersed farming communities in remote areas poses a major challenge to commerce

(Mullineux & Murinde, 2014). While many small, rural crossborder traders still depend almost exclusively on informal credit, based on networks of trust organized among trader-wholesalers, wholesaler-retailers, and retailers, financial sector reforms are changing the situation across a handful of African countries (Bouet et al., 2018).

AFRICA'S UNDERGROUND ECONOMY

The informal sector remains an important part of Africa's economy. The Economist (2017) puts the size of the continent's underground economy at 40 per cent of its GDP. Among other issues, Africa's informal markets produce efficiency losses, with significant impacts on resource mobilization capacity. On the latter point, Rizk et al. (2020) amplify the need for alternative metrics to better capture the significant innovations in the informal segments of the African economy and society. The Economist notes that compared to Latin America, Africa's underground economy is receding faster. This corroborates the narrative on the continent's much-anticipated emergence as the next pole of global growth.

In 1958, Albert Hirschman in *The Strategy of Economic Development* highlighted the critical role of government, public policy, and institutions in the economic development process. According to Hirschman, a chain of disequilibria is needed to keep the economy moving; development policy innovation must deliberately create imbalances in the economy in the absence of capital resources for a simultaneously integrated economy.

Against the backdrop of Hirschman's (1958) unbalanced growth theory, much has been said about how marginalization and economic exclusion foster participation in the informal economy. Hirschman famously argued that development "depends not so much on finding optimal combinations for given resources and factors of production as on calling forth and enlisting for development purposes resources and abilities that are hidden, scattered or badly utilized" (Hirschman, 1958; p.5).

Undoubtedly, digital and financial technologies remain critical in accelerating the transition of SMEs from the informal to the formal sector, and this has implications for the high representation of women, low-income wages, and poor working conditions that characterize Africa's informal economy (Verick, 2006). In addition to existing social safety nets, Guven and Karlen (2020) articulate policy innovations around social insurance programs and interventions capable of raising productivity across the income spectrum on the continent.

In many ways, their suggested approach (Figure 1) underscores the need for policy changes and reforms that can help reduce the deadweight loss associated with Africa's informal markets due to, among other factors, decreased tax revenue and unreliable statistics for development planning. In essence, Guven and Karlen's argument drives home the point that informality can constitute an entry point for the expansion of social protection programs in the urban informal economy.

Given the attention on the leapfrog effect, and its potential to positively alter

Figure 1. Social protection instruments across the income spectrum
Credit: Published on Africa Can End Poverty; World Bank (Guven & Karlen, 2020)

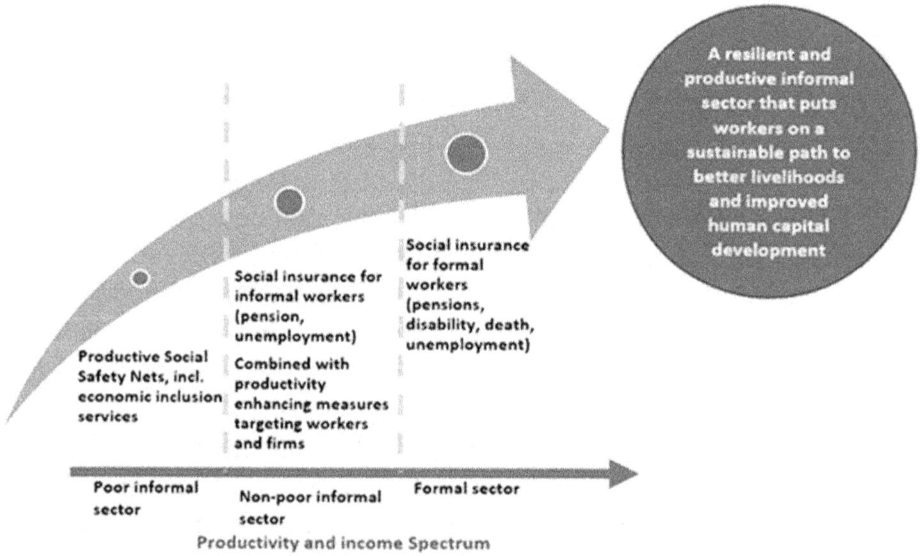

the trajectory of the continent's economic transformation journey, it makes sense to direct attention to the new jobs that will be part of the formal wage sector. African policymakers need new devices, frameworks, and paradigms to help harness the possibilities across the sector. The International Labour Organization (2018) corroborates how pivotal the urban informal economy is to poverty alleviation among African youth and women. About 96 percent of sub-Saharan African youth over ages 15-24 and 92 percent of women make a living in the underground economy.

As discussed in the earlier chapters, Africa's demographic trends have implications for resource mobilization and socioeconomic progress in the foreseeable future. According to Manyika et al. (2016), "Digital finance has the potential to provide access to financial services for 1.6 billion people in emerging economies, more than half of them women" (p. iv). Again, this underscores the importance of digital innovation in driving trade growth, through its impact on reducing transaction costs, and integrating less developed economies into global and regional trade and value chains. Considering the high revenue-generation potential of the underground economy, bringing the large number of unregistered taxpayers and incomes not captured in official statistics into the formal economy can enhance resource mobilization efforts.

THE SERVICES ECONOMY AND INCLUSIVE GROWTH

The clear lines demarcating the goods and services segments of the economy during the Industrial Revolution have been erased with the advent of the modern global digital economy. The transition of major economies from agriculture to manufacturing took centuries, but under the ongoing rapid digital transformation, the composition of the services sector in total output is witnessing a dramatic increase in most countries around the world.

Orthodox economic prescriptions emphasize a reallocation of labor from low-productivity subsistence activities to high-productivity industrial activities as a precondition for structural economic transformation. The Economist (2011) alludes to how India's services economy has turned its companies into global competitors, and its backwater cities into wealthy technology clusters. From India to Pakistan to Sri Lanka, the conventional wisdom in the development orthodoxy that modernization only occurs from agriculture through manufacturing and then services has been challenged.

The global digital revolution has altered the economics of manufacturing. Industry 4.0, the code name for the Fourth Industrial Revolution, is shifting globally integrated supply chains to more localized manufacturing. The interconnectivity, automation, machine learning, and real-time data attributes of Industry 4.0 are prompting many economies to leapfrog straight from agriculture to services without the need for a well-developed manufacturing sector (Sinha & Bhattacharya, 2017). And across the world, this economic shift began in the aftermath of the Great Trade Collapse which heralded the stagnation of merchandise trade after the Great Recession of 2008/09. As they become increasingly tradable and serve as key inputs in traded goods and services, services will play an increasingly more important role in the development process.

Africa's services economy remains a key wealth generator. While agriculture remains the mainstay of the heterogenous economies on the continent, Africa's young population and advances in technology are gradually reinventing its industrial structure to be less dependent on extractive industries. The global digital revolution and modern technologies adoption are transforming business operations and processes on the continent, pushing trade in services to the front burner of Africa's growth debate.

For instance, while a traditional, non-tradable service like a restaurant meal or a haircut is largely unable to benefit from specialization and economies of scale, this is not the case for modern services like digital solutions and outsourced business processes. This underscores the debate on the potential benefits of the global digital revolution; precisely, the notion that African economies can leapfrog manufacturing and go straight from agriculture to services. In the same vein, the services sector contributes about half of the continent's GDP and continues to grow twice as fast as the global average (Stephenson & Tumuhimbise, 2015). In small visitor economies like São Tomé and Príncipe, Djibouti, and Mauritius, services constitute close to 70 percent of economic output.

As digital technologies make tradable services easier to export crossborder, countries on the continent need to adopt technologies that are suitable to their specific services economies. Stephenson and Tumuhimbise examine five emerging regional services clusters in Africa: air transport services in Ethiopia, banking services in Nigeria, business process offshoring and ICT services in Senegal, cultural services in Burkina Faso, and education services in Uganda. Their findings reveal that while substantial services exports go to the regional market, a meaningful portion flows beyond the continent – meaning that despite the significant progress made on the services trade front, significant barriers remain (Stephenson & Tumuhimbise, 2015). This underscores the importance of this vital component in the continent's trade policy agenda.

ICT remains the backbone of the global digital economy, due to its impact on productivity growth in a knowledge-based economy. The forces of globalization are reinforcing the importance of crossborder trade in financial services in the international economy. Despite the globalization of finance and the plethora of innovations made possible by recent advances in technological capabilities, financial inclusion remains low and uneven in Africa.

The importance of, and need for, inclusive growth in Africa has received enormous attention in the literature (see United Nations Conference on Trade and Development, 2017; and Ancharaz et al., 2011). Improved financial inclusion remains a major prerequisite for inclusive growth; in addition to insulating economies against shocks during an economic downturn, by reducing borrowing constraints, financial development can also be a growth driver (Rewilak et al., 2017). Financial inclusion is key for wealth-building.

Wealth plays an important role in helping households to buffer economic shocks, in addition to making strategic investments capable of contributing to future economic well-being. The bourgeoning financial services industry in Nigeria, and the digital innovations that have changed Kenya's financial inclusion picture, are good examples of how crossborder banking can effectively foster inclusive growth. Crossborder banking drives growth and societal welfare due to competitiveness gains from efficiency, new investments, and skills (Claessens et al., 2001; Cull & Martínez Pería, 2010; and Dages et al., 2000).

DIGITAL CONNECTIVITY AND REGIONAL INTEGRATION

Digital connectivity remains essential for trade integration; inefficient regional payment systems impede crossborder trade, resulting in a deadweight loss. This is partly why economists model frictions that impede trade flows as trade costs. As technology continues to change the dynamics of international trade through its impact on, among other things, transportation and supply chain logistics, harmonization of standards on information exchanges, border cooperation, and related initiatives are, in turn, improving trade logistics.

ICT has contributed immensely to much of the recent decline in tariff barriers due to falling surface transportation costs because of technological advances like containerization, port modernization, and advanced logistics and trade facilitation (Hanna & Knight, 2012). For example, supply chains have become more connected, secure, and efficient due to technological innovations, with major impacts on logistics and supply chain.

From markets and trade expansion to scale economies and enhanced cooperation for risk mitigation, regional integration remains a powerful force that can help to harness the benefits of globalization for sustainable development in low-income countries with limited ability to compete for investments due to structural and institutional constraints (Africa Regional Integration Index Report (ARII) 2019).

Jointly developed by the African Union Commission, AfDB, and UNECA, the ARII provides a comprehensive assessment of the regional integration status and efforts of countries in Africa's eight regional economic communities. The ARII is a regional integration tool that provides benchmarking along five dimensions: trade integration, productive integration, macroeconomic integration, infrastructural integration, and the free movement of people. Ultimately, the Index is a socioeconomic development tool which offer insights on policy interventions aimed at driving growth and inclusive development by addressing issues around fragmentation and low competitiveness in global commerce.

In terms of overall performance, based on the 2019 ARII, South Africa is the most regionally integrated country in Africa, followed by Kenya, Rwanda, Morocco, and Mauritius in that order. South Africa is also the best overall performer on the infrastructure and productive dimensions. South Sudan performs poorly on the macroeconomic and infrastructure dimensions, ranking last on both metrics, while also emerging as the least integrated country on the continent. Eritrea, Burundi, Sierra Leone, and Sudan are the other least-performing countries in the order indicated (Figure 2).

Figure 2. Countries' scores and rankings on overall integration
Credit: ARII Report (2019)

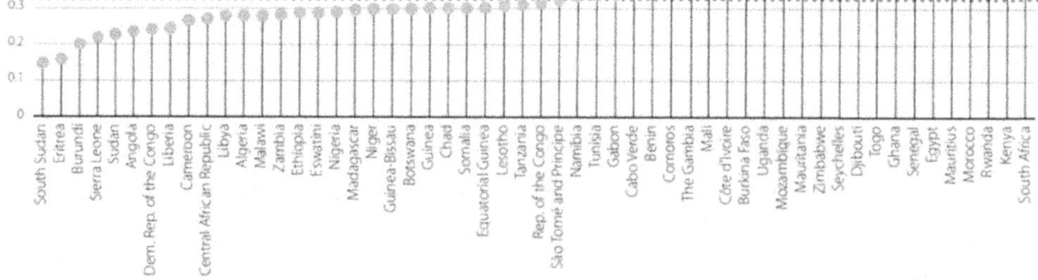

Clearly, much work remains to be done to fully harness the potential of increased interconnectedness to help mitigate the adverse impact of fragmented markets and efficiency losses that limit the contribution of intra- and extra-African trade to prosperity on the continent. And this explains why the AfCFTA is a major game changer. This is discussed in detail below.

Both classical and neoclassical economics argue, with good justification, that international trade brings overall benefits to society, but not without winners and losers. To a large extent, the distributional consequences of trade, combined with technological innovations, have had a profound impact on domestic and international politics in contemporary times.

Starting from Uruk in ancient Mesopotamia 6,000 years ago, trade contributed significantly to urbanization and wealth creation (New Scientist, n.d.). Despite the evolution of modern global trade from mercantilism in the 16th century to the classical political economy tradition that birthed Adam Smith's absolute advantage and Ricardian comparative advantage models of 1776 and 1817, respectively, before the neoclassical era ushered in Heckscher-Ohlin factor proportions theory (and its various strands), new trade theory, and the so-called "new-new" trade theory, the world has changed significantly, and so is how countries have historically traded with one another.

Even with the rise of firm-based theories like Linder's country similarity, Vernon's product cycle, Krugman-Lancaster's global strategic rivalry theory, and Porter's national competitive advantage, the basic argument remains the same: trade has net benefits for society, but unless the overall gains are redistributed, there will be welfare losses for some. And within the broader context of rising poverty and inequality in many countries, the importance of trade policy innovation cannot be overemphasized.

Branko Milanovic, in his 2016 book, *Global Inequality: A New Approach for the Age of Globalization*, explains the winners and losers from trade globalization, while proffering policy solutions to ensure economic justice. Milanovic explores the dynamics of globalization and inequality through the lens of the periodic rises and falls in inequalities to war and disease, education, technology, and redistribution, with the conclusion that inequality will not grow in perpetuity. He also sympathizes with traditional policymaking that relies on taxation and transfers as the remedy for inequality. His argument: both fiscal policy tools have reached their limit. As an alternative, he proposes the distribution of endowments by reducing disparities in both capital endowments and human capital.

POLICY INNOVATION AND THE AFCFTA

Launched on January 1, 2021, the AfCFTA is a unique opportunity for deep reforms capable of driving long-term structural changes across African economies. The largest free trade area in the world in terms of the number of countries participating, it connects 1.3 billion people across 55 countries with a combined output valued at $3.4 trillion.

The World Bank (2020) estimates the pact has the potential to lift 30 million Africans out of extreme poverty, boost the incomes of 68 million others who live on less than $5.50 a day, achieve an incremental, continent-wide gain in income of $450 billion (7 percent) by 2035, while adding $76 billion to the income of the rest of the world. Other economic impacts include an increase in exports by $560 billion (mostly in high-multiplier sectors like manufacturing), larger wage gains for women than for men (a major indicator of inclusivity), and relatively high wage increases for both skilled and unskilled workers, at 9.8 percent and 10.3 percent, respectively (showing no potential to exacerbate labor market polarization).

The distributional effects of the pact vary widely. Of note is the reduction in extreme poverty across the continent, with marked improvements in countries with currently high poverty rates, particularly in West Africa. The varying distribution of the $450 billion in income gains, attributable to stronger trade facilitation, is also profound. This corroborates the discussion earlier on the importance of lowering trade costs, streamlining border procedures, and addressing other frictions that create deadweight losses in crossborder transactions.

Achieving the pact's full potential will depend largely on policy innovation capacity. The most important consideration is to deploy a plethora of policies that can maximize potential gains and minimize risks, while addressing within-country effects, rather than cross-country impacts, on economic outcomes like prices, output, investment, and productivity. This will go a long way in stabilizing these economies considering the earlier discussion on the distributional implications of trade. As with most economic predictions, these estimates may be contradicted by real-world events. And that is okay, to the extent that the key takeaways help in the policy development process.

Given the varying degrees of growth opportunities and challenges across Africa's heterogeneous markets, the AfCFTA has become a compass for harnessing and maximizing the gains from trade. Africa's current 472 million urban population is expected to increase by 187 million by 2025, reaching

1 billion by 2040 (Lall et al., 2017). Under the right conditions, this rapid urbanization will transition many working poor into the middle class, thereby raising household consumption and business spending. The resulting efficiency and productivity gains can help accelerate the continent's development (Lall et al., 2017). This presents a tremendous opportunity.

We discussed earlier, existing complementarities in the regional innovation ecosystems of Africa and Canada. With strategic investments and collaborations with industry, academic, public-sector, and other relevant institutional partners, Africa is well-positioned – by virtue of its market size and growing technology needs – to explore technology diffusion opportunities that can help create a stronger innovation ecosystem which can help advance its ability to export is manufactured products and services.

As discussed under the resource curse chapter, not only is diversification required to help reduce dependence on natural resources, but it also helps create an innovation ecosystem that enables companies to leverage digital and technology platforms to create exportable high-value business services, beyond traditional resources. The era of rapidly proliferating supply chains in traditional sectors is gradually receding, with major implications for the future of trade in services. For instance, Manyika et al. (2013) believe with the right amount of infrastructure investments, the Internet could transform vital sectors and contribute as much as $300 billion per annum to Africa's GDP by 2025. To partake in future gains from global trade, the AfCFTA, which is already operational, must prioritize these dynamics.

Africa's SMEs and entrepreneurs need access to markets and digital infrastructure. To foster economic self-sufficiency on the continent, the AfCFTA could help expand fragmented markets and provide access to foreign capital which, often, is highly sensitive to technological innovations and economies of scale and scope in global value chains. With a market size of $3.3 trillion and a growing population projected to be over 3 billion by 2050, surpassing the entire population of both China and India, Africa's SMEs and entrepreneurs need enhanced access to markets and financing through improved digital infrastructure and policy innovations. Again, the AfCFTA and policy innovations around Startup Acts are moving the continent in the right direction.

We discussed the changing landscape in the education sector. Two-thirds of the African population are under the age of 35. Africa needs a long-term youth strategy: one that recognizes the potential of this youth bulge by focusing on digital finance solutions and training models that can help leapfrog the constraints of traditional, analog platforms while addressing the challenges of the future, as corroborated by the Global Partnership for Financial Inclusion (2017) in recognizing "financial inclusion as a global priority, capable of bolstering sustainable, balanced, inclusive economic growth at the macro level and promoting economic and social inclusion at the household and enterprise level (p. 6).

From a trade and development perspective, concise and flexible capacity building initiatives are needed to help broaden women's access to digital finance. The importance of trade for development has been discussed extensively. Unlike other regions of the world, Africa ranks very poorly on one of the biggest opportunities for growth: intra-regional trade. Without a support mechanism in place to help address supply-side constraints, including logistical bottlenecks to ease the free flow of goods, people, and factors across borders, the gains from trade will remain elusive. Manyika et al. support broadening access to digital finance as a sustainable way to help empower women.

The analysis above underscores that the size of Africa's informal economy is about half of the continent's GDP; a major feature of such underground economy is the significant representation of women, low wages, and lack of decent work, compared to the formal segment of the economy (Verick, 2006). Breaking out of the trap of informality requires a policy environment that organizes informal economy workers and promotes equality (The International Labour Organization, 2014). Africa needs capacity-building initiatives specifically targeted at addressing structural inequalities that limit women's full and effective participation in the digital economy.

As discussed under financial inclusion, since women own most SMEs, in addition to accounting for a relatively higher share of employment compared to men, prioritizing programs and policies targeted at helping them access digital finance will be in order. Among other factors, large informal sector, limited market size, trade-related infrastructure, fragmented economic space, and other demand- and supply-side constraints pose major impediments to regional economic integration on the continent. Compared to other regions, the relatively lower level of integration in Africa constitutes a major challenge for development, albeit albeit there is great optimism that the AfCFTA will help address this agelong issue over time.

As the continent transitions from the margins to the mainstream of global commerce, the global digital revolution is increasingly making it possible for African economies to leapfrog intensive manufacturing and move into the services phase in its development journey. Such high-value and digitally-enabled services trade could accelerate intra-regional trade and competitiveness to help bolster sustainable and inclusive growth. The changing composition of global trade underscores the need for trade policy innovation and redesign to address such structural shifts.

We hinge our fate on trade, that powerful tool that can be a source for good and bad. It was trade that led to the fragmentation of Africa; it was trade that took millions of Africans against their will to far-away lands. Today, we embrace the same trade as an instrument for progress; as a tool for reversing the damage it inflicted on Africa over many decades.

— Benedict Oramah

REFERENCES

Ancharaz, V., Mbekeani, K., & Brixiova, Z. (2011). Impediments to regional trade integration in Africa. *Africa Economic Brief: African Development Bank.* https://www.afdb.org/fileadmin/uploads/afdb/Documents/Publications/AEB%20VOL%202%20Issue%2011_AEB%20VOL%202%20Issue%2011.pdf

ARII Report. (2019). *African Union Commission (AUC), the African Development Bank (AfDB), and the United Nations Economic Commission for Africa (ECA).* https://www.integrate-africa.org/fileadmin/uploads/afdb/Documents/ARII-Report2019-FIN-R40-11jun20.pdf

Bouet, A., Pace, K., & Glauber, J. (2018). *Informal Cross-Border Trade in Africa: How Much? Why? And What Impact?* IFPRI Discussion Paper 1783.

Claessens, S., Demirgüç-Kunt, A., & Huizinga, H. (2001). How does foreign entry affect domestic banking markets? *Journal of Banking & Finance*, *25*(5), 891–911. doi:10.1016/S0378-4266(00)00102-3

Cull, R., Peria, M., & Soledad, M. (2010). *Foreign bank participation in developing countries: What do we know about the drivers and consequences of this phenomenon?* Policy Research working paper; no. WPS 5398. World Bank. https://openknowledge.worldbank.org/handle/10986/3882

Dages, B. D., Goldberg, L., & Kinney, D. (2000). Foreign and domestic bank participation in emerging markets: Lessons from Mexico and Argentina. *Economic Policy Review*, *6*(3), 17–36.

Global Partnership for Financial Inclusion. (2017). *The Global Partnership for Financial Inclusion*. https://www.gpfi.org/publications/gpfi-2017-work-plan

Guven, M., & Karlen, R. (2020). *Supporting Africa's urban informal sector: Coordinated policies with social protection at the core*. World Bank, Africa Can End Poverty blog. https://blogs.worldbank.org/africacan/supporting-africas-urban-informal-sector-coordinated-policies-social-protection-core

Hanna, N., & Knight, P. (2012). *National Strategies to Harness Information Technology, Innovation, Technology, and Knowledge Management*. Springer. doi:10.1007/978-1-4614-2086-6

Hirschman, A. (1958). The strategy of economic development. In A. N. Agarwal & S. P. Singh (Eds.), *Accelerating investment in developing economies. Oxford Press*.

International Labour Organization. (2014). Transitioning from the informal to the formal economy. *International Labour Conference*. https://www.ilo.org/wcmsp5/groups/public/---ed_norm/---relconf/documents/meetingdocument/wcms_218128.pdf

International Labour Organization. (2018). *Women and men in the informal economy: a statistical picture* (3rd ed.). ILO.

Lall, S. V., Henderson, J. V., & Venables, A. J. (2017). *Africa's cities: Opening doors to the world.* World Bank. https://openknowledge.worldbank.org/handle/10986/25896

Manyika, J., Cabral, A., Moodley, L., Yeboah-Amankwah, S., Moraje, S., Chui, M., Anthonyrajah, J., & Leke, A. (2013). *Lions go digital: The internet's transformative potential in Africa.* McKinsey Global Institute. https://www.mckinsey.com/~/media/McKinsey/Industries/Technology%20Media%20and%20Telecommunications/High%20Tech/Our%20Insights/Lions%20go%20digital%20The%20Internets%20transformative%20potential%20in%20Africa/MGI_Lions_go_digital_Full_report_Nov2013.pdf

Manyika, J., Lund, S., Singer, M., White, O., & Berry, C. (2016). *Digital finance for all: Powering inclusive growth in emerging economies.* McKinsey Global Institute. https://www.findevgateway.org/sites/default/files/publications/files/mg-digital-finance-for-all-full-report-september-2016.pdf

Milanovic, B. (2016). *Global Inequality: A New Approach for the Age of Globalization.* Harvard University Press. doi:10.4159/9780674969797

Mullineux, A., & Murinde, V. (2014). Financial sector policies for enterprise development in Africa. *Review of Development Finance, 4*(2), 66–72. doi:10.1016/j.rdf.2014.05.001

New Scientist. (n.d.). *Where was the first city in the world?* https://www.newscientist.com/question/first-cities-built/

Rewilak, J., Brighty, N., & Papadavid, P. R. (2017). *Financial barriers to economic growth in low-income countries.* Department for International Development.

Rizk, N., El Said, A., Weheba, N., & de Beer, J. (2020). *Towards an Alternative Assessment of Innovation in Africa.* Working Paper 10. https://openair.africa/wp-content/uploads/2020/05/WP-10-Towards-an-Alternative-Assessment-of-Innovation-in-Africa.pdf

Sinha, J., & Bhattacharya, A. (2017). Leapfrog beyond manufacturing: The path to becoming a middle-income country lies through digital services, not manufacturing exports. *The Times of India.* https://timesofindia.indiatimes.com/blogs/toi-edit-page/leapfrog-beyond-manufacturing-the-path-to-becoming-a-middle-income-country-lies-through-digital-services-not-manufacturing-exports/

Stephenson, S., & Tumuhimbise, C. (2015). Overview of services exports for growth and development: Case studies from Africa. In S. Stephenson & C. Tumuhimbise (Eds.), *Services exports for growth and development: Case studies from Africa* (pp. 1–14). African Union Commission.

The Economist. (2011). Another giant leap India's tech giants try to reinvent themselves. *Business and management: Schumpeter.* https://www.economist.com/schumpeter/2011/06/01/another-giant-leap

The Economist. (2017). *Africa's informal economy is receding faster than Latin America's.* Finance & Economics. https://www.economist.com/finance-and-economics/2017/05/13/africas-informal-economy-is-receding-faster-than-latin-americas

United Nations Conference on Trade and Development. (2017). *Beyond austerity: Towards a global new deal.* Trade and development Report 2017. https://unctad.org/system/files/official-document/tdr2017_en.pdf

Verick, S. (2006). *The Impact of Globalization on the Informal Sector in Africa.* Economic and Social Policy Division, United Nations Economic Commission for Africa (ECA) and Institute for the Study of Labor (IZA). Retrieved from https://conference.iza.org/conference_files/worldb2006/verick_s872.pdf

Voorhies, J., & Lamb, M. O. (2013). Fighting poverty, profitably: Transforming the economics of payments to build sustainable, inclusive finance systems. *Bill and Melinda Gates Foundation. Special Report: Financial Services for the Poor.* https://docs.gatesfoundation.org/documents/fighting%20poverty%20profitably%20full%20report.pdf

World Bank. (2020). *The African Continental Free Trade Area: Economic and Distributional Effects.* World Bank Group. https://openknowledge.worldbank.org/bitstream/handle/10986/34139/9781464815591.pdf

World Bank. (2022). *Services, value added (% of GDP) - Sub-Saharan Africa.* https://data.worldbank.org/indicator/NV.SRV.TOTL.ZS?locations=ZG

World Economic Forum. (2021). *Funding for Africa's startups is at a record high - this is where it's going.* https://www.weforum.org/agenda/2021/05/study-shows-virtual-capital-for-african-startups-is-steeply-increasing

Chapter 12
Regional Innovation Engines for Development

ABSTRACT

Through efficiency gains and productivity increases from the interactions between firms and people located near one another, agglomeration economies remain the basis for innovation ecosystems in cities and industrial clusters. This chapter draws on Michael Porter's thesis that nations and regions must compete to attract firms by offering the most productive environment. Porter, in essence, implies that to be competitive, regions must increase productivity in the use of human, capital, and natural resources. While the baseline for regional success is often available in many cases, policy innovations that can help sustain a robust innovation ecosystem would be important. Considering Africa's bourgeoning urbanization, manifest in the growth of its megacities and smaller towns and cities, innovation superclusters present a great opportunity. For success, it is imperative for policy paradigms, frameworks, and devices to be sensitive to Africa's unique but heterogenous socioeconomic dynamics. Harnessing the benefits of the innovation economy requires a strategic policy framework focused on unleashing the potential of the technology ecosystem, with the appropriate policy mix and doses of investments, talent, and risk sharing paradigm.

DOI: 10.4018/978-1-7998-7383-9.ch012

The AfCFTA is Africa's Marshall Plan; we must commit to regional and national value chain deepening. Imagine for a minute DRC Congo refining coltan; its share in the value chain will go from 3% to 28% of the revenue.

— Vera Songwe

AGGLOMERATION ECONOMIES remain the basis for innovation ecosystems in cities and industrial clusters, through efficiency gains and productivity increases from the interactions between firms and people located near one another. Innovation has become the key driver of the emerging, global knowledge-based economy. Moreso, most innovation occurs in large metropolitan areas due to agglomeration economies. Glaeser (2011) and Combes et al. (2010) argue, based on neoclassical theoretical framing, that despite the drastic fall in transportation and communication costs in recent times, industrial agglomeration remains key for innovation. The urban density-wages-total factor productivity nexus provides the empirical foundation for this thesis.

Larger regional economies tend to be more economically diversified. Economists believe that metropolitan cities succeed because agglomeration economies raise productivity and economic growth (see Porter, 1995; and Glaeser, 2011). Gutiérrez and Olayele (2021) explain the growth of New York's innovation economy in terms of an economic development strategy focused on talent as a growth engine, strategic urban investments, and an industrial policy anchored on the growth of New York's technology ecosystem. This framework provides a basis for understanding urban innovation and industrial diversification.

The rise of the knowledge economy continues to amplify interests in science-based growth in policy circles around the world. And PPPs are at the heart of this trend. Successful technology transfers are about navigating the path between academic research and commercialization. As discussed under the helix models of innovation, the evolving relationships among academic, industry, government, and community stakeholders are creating beneficial partnerships that make it much easier for several promising innovations to cross the "Valley of Death" and make it from research labs to commercial markets – while ultimately capturing the positive spillovers of government R&D investments. Through strategic interactions between SMEs and academic institutions in various communities, university-based growth has moved to the front burner of driving regional innovation ecosystems.

THE DIAMOND MODEL: A CANADA-AFRICA COMPARATIVE ANALYSIS

Michael Porter's (1990) diamond model identifies four drivers of regional productivity in the context of business environment dynamics: factor (input) conditions; firm strategy, structure, and rivalry; demand conditions; and related and supporting industries.

Porter argues to the extent that competitiveness is not a zero-sum game, nations and regions must compete to attract firms by offering the most productive environment. Porter, in essence, implies that to be competitive, regions must increase productivity in the use of human, capital, and natural resources. While the baseline for regional success is often available in many cases, policy innovations that can help sustain a robust innovation ecosystem would be important.

Contemporary regional innovation ecosystems draw inspiration from Porter's thesis. In the context of Africa's vast resource endowments, efficiency in the use of resources is key. Again, the Porter model posits microeconomic outcomes and the sophistication of local competition determine, to a large extent, productivity. By implication, if macroeconomic competitiveness is a necessary but insufficient condition for productivity, in the current digital economy, optimizing the interactions among key stakeholders under a business climate with a robust innovation ecosystem is critical for success.

To aid the discussion in this section, I draw a comparison between Canada and Africa vis-à-vis regional innovation dynamics. Despite the many political economy constraints faced by Canada, in the context of federalism, it has achieved modest success in its regional innovation policy and programming.

In many ways, Canada's energy and natural resource economy makes it a good comparator with many African countries, especially those organized African countries, especially those organized along federalist ground. Canada and several African countries also share many economic and political similarities. Despite Canada's many achievements on the energy, resource, and political fronts, many challenges remain, with practical implications.

Federal-provincial negotiations in Canada often generate tensions, based on expectations on the responsibilities in the constitutional authorities allocated to each level of government (Sweeting & Whitehead, 2020). In particular, health care financing and federal climate policy proposals often reverberate throughout the national landscape, with huge implications for the labyrinth of federal—provincial relations.

The ongoing acceleration in digital trends is contributing to the deepening of trade and the intensity of economic exchanges globally. Many important social and economic characteristics in Canada at the subnational level vary sharply from what is observed nationally. Given the pace of globalization and advances in technology in the global digital economy, the academic and policy literature recognizes the importance of paying attention to such heterogeneity and its distributional implications across regions (Olayele, 2019). This is also important for harnessing regional innovation capabilities through a laboratory that allows for the possibility of testing direct policy interventions that enable poorer jurisdictions to benefit from innovation-driven national economic systems. This is discussed in detail below.

CANADA'S INNOVATION SUPERCLUSTERS

The concept of an innovation supercluster is not new. Fraunhofer Institutes in Germany is a global innovation collaboration model which brings research experts and firms from around the world together to foster scientific progress and economic development. Fraunhofer's research activities are spread across 74 locations throughout Germany (Fraunhofer Institutes, n.d). Catapults, a network of world-leading technology and innovation centers in the UK, "supports businesses in transforming great ideas into valuable products and services" (Catapult Network, n.d. para. 1).

Perhaps there is no better template than Canada's innovation supercluster system to explain the uniqueness of PPPs as a policy innovation tool. Canada understood that it was lagging in terms of productivity and that it needed to catch up. It then made a deliberate choice to recalibrate and build its innovation economy from the ground up. In a simplistic term, Canada's Innovation Supercluster Initiative (ISI) is a policy design aimed at incentivizing SMEs and large companies to collaborate and boost high-growth sectors in the innovation economy. And the design of the ISI was a strategic policy decision.

According to then Canadian Minister of Innovation, Science, and Economic Development, Navdeep Bains, the ISI is a "made-in-Canada Silicon Valley that will produce tens of thousands of jobs" (Home-Douglas, 2019, para. 3). Canada recognized the fragmented nature of the collaborations between industry and technical and academic institutions, as well as the need for government to support scale economy and maximize output by harnessing the capabilities across the entire value stream (Kelly, 2018).

In 2018, the Canadian ISI was launched as a 10-year innovation system comprised of five superclusters spread across five regions of the country based on existing regional innovation ecosystems. The ISI was conceived as a policy innovation model that could address some of the pressing challenges facing the country, in addition to helping position Canada as a global leader in innovation.

The ISI harnesses capabilities in technology clusters across the country into industry-led consortia, with the overall goal of powering economic growth, attracting top talent, and advancing cutting-edge research and innovation. The uniqueness of the ISI model lies in the fact that the entity typically invites industry-led consortia comprised of industry leaders, academic and technical institutions, and SMEs to collaborate, lead, and invest in large-scale projects to leverage scale economies to supercharge regional innovation ecosystems (Box 10).

Much unlike the industrial clusters of the 1990s, where industries in the same region are grouped together, the ISI model is different in two ways. First, their links and reach outside their regions are much greater. Also, they

Box 10: Canadian Supercluster Model

In the Canadian ISI model, there are five regional innovation ecosystems: ocean sciences, protein industry, digital technology, artificial intelligence, and advanced manufacturing. In many ways, several elements of the quadruple helix model discussed earlier are reflected in the ISI. While each cluster has its regional innovation ecosystem at its core, the following elements are constant across the board: large and small companies, researchers and academics, not-for-profit organizations, and accelerators and incubators.

The clusters are expected to be supercharged with $950 million by March 2023 in federal government funding, through five non-repayable contributions, matched dollar-for-dollar by industry. Funding flows into the ISI through co-investment by government and industry, albeit industry investment has so far surpassed the initial target. In terms of the overall goal, the ISI is intended to create 50,000 jobs and $50 billion in GDP over a 10-year period.

Benchmarked against the 10-year target, and based on the 2018 launch year, the five superclusters have grown and evolved at varying speeds, with expectations far exceeded in some while others lag for a wide variety of reasons – ranging from structural and legal to intellectual property and data management issues.

As of October 2020, the ISI has supported 219 projects, involving 435 organizations, comprised of 53 percent SMEs, with 6,100 high-quality jobs, and over $800 million in public and private spending commitments.

are tech-anchored, and not sectors-based. Not only is the ISI expected to lead and invest in bold and ambitious proposals, but it is also mandated to support new partnerships between large firms, SMEs, and industry-relevant research institutions in a bid to generate globally competitive technology outcomes from Canada.

For instance, in a bid to build on Canada's global reputation as a leader in agricultural production, as part of the ISI, the Government of Canada announced, in 2018, a $153 million funding for the Protein Industries Canada Supercluster, with a mission to mobilize Canada's innovation and commercial cluster to collaborate in support of industry-driven market priorities and needs.

Headquartered in the Prairie province of Saskatchewan, the epicenter of agriculture in Canada, and covering the other two Prairie provinces of Alberta and Manitoba, the Protein Industries Canada Supercluster is an industry-led value chain consortium of small- to large-sized enterprises involved in food and food ingredient manufacturing, agriculture and food-related services, R & D, technology, economic development, finance and investment, education, and training.

The STIP Compass – an initiative of the European Commission and the OECD to collect in one place quantitative and qualitative data on national trends in science, technology, and innovation policy – succinctly corroborates the essential elements of the ISI model: "A small number of high-value, strategic investments will be made to build on shared private sector commitment, demonstrated through matched industry funding, to position firms for global leadership." (European Commission, 2020).

While the superclusters have achieved some impressive outcomes, they have also faced some challenges in terms of adequately capturing their impact on enhancing innovation capacity, as well as their overall social and environmental impacts, beyond economics (Beaudry & Solar-Pelletier, 2020). For instance, while spending commitments have surpassed 85 percent of the $950-million target, evidence is mixed on the job creation metric (Box 12).

To the extent that monitoring and evaluating the performance of the ISI remains key to providing insight on the progress and competitiveness of Canada's innovation economy, Box 11 provides a snapshot of the performance of each cluster in the hope of offering useful lessons for regional innovation ecosystems elsewhere. Through the interaction between traditional sectors and digital technologies, a new frontier of innovation is emerging and creating multiple pathways to wealth creation in a sustainable manner. More importantly, SMEs are fully participating in the entire value chain. This is a major advance in policy innovation. With the appropriate refinements, which

Box 12: Regional Clusters

Digital Technology Supercluster
- Core elements: Using virtual, mixed, and augmented reality, data, and quantum computing to solve productivity, health, and sustainability challenges.
- Economic impacts: $5 billion in GDP and13,500 jobs over 10 years
- Partners: Boeing, Deloitte, D-Wave Systems, Microsoft, and Telus Communications

Protein Industries Supercluster
- Core elements: Evolving agricultural production with plant genomics and novel processing.
- Economic impacts: $50 billion in GDP and 50,000 jobs over 10 years
- Partners: AGT Food and Ingredients, Maple Leaf
- DowDuPont, Dot Technology, and Roquette

Next Generation Manufacturing Supercluster
- Core elements: Designing next-generation manufacturing companies by adopting advanced processes and developing and deploying new technologies like robotics and 3D printing.
- Economic impacts: $13.5 billion in GDP and 13,500 jobs over 10 years
- Partners: AutoDesk, Clearpath, Linamar, Myant, University of Waterloo

AI-Powered Supply Chains Supercluster
- Core elements: Building the supply chains of the future using artificial intelligence and robotic technologies.
- Economic impacts: $16.5 billion in GDP and 16,000 jobs over 10 years
- Partners: Aldo, BCG, CGI, Cisco, Intel, PwC, Shopify

Ocean Supercluster
- Core elements: Solving global challenges like meeting energy demands through marine renewable energy, fisheries, aquaculture, oil and gas, defence, shipbuilding, and transportation.
- Economic impacts: $14 billion in GDP and 3,000 jobs over 10 years
- Partners: Cuna del Mar, Emera, Palaerospace, Smartice, Dalhousie University

recognize jurisdiction-specific nuances and political economy dynamics, it could be an exemplar for countries in the EMDEs – and Africa in particular – in the context of policy diffusion.

IMPLICATIONS IN THE AFRICAN CONTEXT

A major takeaway from the above analysis is that there is no one-size-fits-all model; every region must craft a strategy based on its unique assets and relative strengths. This is the core idea behind the innovation supercluster model.

Considering Africa's bourgeoning urbanization, manifest in the growth of its megacities and smaller towns and cities, innovation superclusters present a great opportunity. The African Energy Corridor discussed earlier is a good model. But there are many more incremental innovation opportunities in the context of demand-side stimulation. Stimulating demand in traditionally non-innovative companies can be achieved through policy innovations.

Importantly, channeling policy support and investments toward "practice-based" innovation is vital. Many vocational and technical training initiatives on the continent provide good examples. For the umpteenth time, policy paradigms, frameworks, and devices must be redefined to be sensitive to Africa's unique but heterogenous socioeconomic dynamics.

SECTOR SNAPSHOTS AND POLICY SUCCESS STORIES

Agriculture and Policy Innovation in Africa

Agriculture remains crucial to development in Africa; it is the dominant economic sector across the continent. However, untapped agricultural potential continues to undermine food security and development on the continent. At the AU Summit in Malabo, Equatorial Guinea in June 2014, Heads of State and Government adopted the Malabo Declaration on Accelerated Agricultural Growth and Transformation for Shared Prosperity and Improved Livelihoods. The Comprehensive Africa Agriculture Development Programme (CAADP) is the continent's policy framework for agricultural transformation, wealth creation, and food security.

About 200 million hectares – representing 50 percent of the world's uncultivated land – is on the continent, while agriculture continues to be plagued by low productivity, infrastructure deficit, and inadequate financing and access to markets (Food and Agriculture Organization of the United Nations & African Union Commission, 2018). Farming remains the major source of food and income, while also accounting for about 60 percent all jobs on the continent. This underscores the importance of smallholder agriculture for food security and nutrition in Africa.

The importance of maximizing Africa's shares of a rapidly growing and dynamic agricultural export market cannot be overemphasized. While the global population is expected to reach 9.7 billion by 2050 (United Nations, 2015), the demand for food is anticipated to increase between 59 percent and 98 percent by 2050 (Valin et al., 2014). This will have a profound impact on global agricultural markets in ways we have not seen before. To put things in perspective, Africa alone is expected to contribute more than half of the 2.4 billion increase in global population by 2050, while the continent's food and beverages subsector is expected to reach $1 trillion in value by 2030 (Diop, 2016).

Leke and Signe (2019) allude to the ongoing industrial revolution in Africa and estimate that industries on the continent stand to double production to $1 trillion within a decade, with the food processing sector, among others, accounting for three-quarters of the anticipated expansion. Therefore, the ability to grow and access nutritious and sustainable food will be critical in the coming years.

In its Feed Africa Strategy, the AfDB emphasizes the need to support smallholder farmers to achieve profitable agriculture and sustainable food security. As well, gender remains an important factor in land-use decision-making, and the entire agricultural value chain. The nuances of development interventions have major implications for participation and interaction by men and women in the value chains. This underscores the importance of ensuring such interventions are optimized to ensure sustainable poverty alleviation, social inclusion, food security, and gender-equitable results (Haverhals et al., 2016).

As discussed in the earlier chapters, policy entrepreneurs, in the Schumpeterian tradition, are agents of creative destruction as they champion the pursuit of policy change by seeking ideas and collaborative approaches to help reduce inefficiencies in the public policymaking process through faster adoption. Policy entrepreneurs remain important in the industrial transformation journey of Africa since they are interested in policy change and socially beneficial innovations.

Morocco and the Maritime Economy

Africa boasts diverse and productive marine areas, with 38 coastal and island states and a coastline of over 47,000 km (Waruhiu, 2018). The blue economy has been touted as the continent's new frontier of renaissance, given the potential for its enormous maritime resources to support its quest for realizing the SDGs.

The digital revolution is shifting the composition of global trade, and the rapidly proliferating supply chains in goods sectors like natural resources and manufacturing has implications for trade in services. Transitioning towards sustainable economic systems is not exactly a linear process. Multiple pathways are often involved, and the maritime industry is no exception. In addition to facilitating innovation for improved operational efficiency, 'triple helix' interactions could help Africa forge strategic collaborations that can result in scaling maritime innovations and technologies.

To the extent that trade increasingly follows investment, a good starting point is to map the capabilities of Africa's maritime powerhouses. This can serve as a model to help develop insights on existing complementarities among maritime hubs in Seychelles, South Africa, Kenya, Morocco, Nigeria, Ghana, Cote d'Ivoire, Djibouti, and Mauritius. This will be a good starting point in the quest for greater integration into regional and global value chains, particularly in the context of the AfCFTA, and broadly in terms of developing new solutions to drive seaborne trade for inclusive and sustainable growth. Morocco's ocean economy is a model in this context (Box 13)

Box 13: Tanger Med Port: Africa's Industrial Maritime Powerhouse

Located on the Strait of Gibraltar, about 40 km east of the Moroccan city of Tangier, the Port of Tanger Med is the largest port both in Africa and on the Mediterranean in terms of capacity. Built in 2007, Tanger Med is a transshipment hub and global logistics gateway connected to more than 180 ports worldwide. The port handles 9 million containers, exports million new vehicles, and transits 7 million passengers and 700,000 trucks annually.

Tanger Med leverages on Morocco's huge ocean economy and strategic location along the Strait of Gibraltar. And the country has done reasonably well in maximizing the opportunities provided by these possibilities to create value and wealth in the sector, with positive spillovers in the overall economy. With over 1,100 companies and more than $US5.9 billion in annual exports turnover in a wide range of sectors like automotive, aeronautics, logistics, textile, and trade, this industrial hub has become an economic engine for the North Morocco region.

Talking about innovation, and particularly in light of the COVID-19 pandemic, Tanger Med is deploying technological solutions to advance supply chains on the continent through port digitalization in a bid to foster increased connectivity and trade facilitation.

In light of the recent debate on innovations in port logistics, in the aftermath of the congestion that resulted from the obstruction of Egypt's Suez Canal – one of the busiest trade routes in the world – Tanger Med can serve as a model for efficient port management and operations through digitization in the region. No doubt, lessons abound for other maritime powerhouses on the continent, not just in maritime terms, but in terms of broader implications for free trade zones and foreign direct investment in Africa.

Ghana and Cultural Heritage and Tourism

The late President Jerry Rawlings of Ghana launched heritage tourism in the 1980s as an innovative economic development tool (The Conversation, 2021). While the resource economy – comprised mainly of cocoa, timber, and gold – was the major revenue earner for the country, there was no specific industrial policy around cultural heritage tourism. However, over time, innovations in this sector have turned it into a major resource mobilization opportunity. This is good for Ghana's ability to finance its development priorities.

From the National Museum and Museum of Science and Technology in Accra, Upper East Regional Museum in Bolgatanga, Volta Regional Museum, Cape Coast Castle Museum, St. George's Castle (Elmina Castle) Museum, and the Fort Apollonia Museum of Nzema Culture and History, museums play a huge part in Ghana's cultural heritage and tourism economy (Preko, 2020). Policy innovation, particularly through the influence of enterprise, in

Box 14: Policy Innovation in Ghana's Tourism Economy

Prior to the launch of the 2019 Year of Return initiative when Ghana welcomed an estimated one million foreign visitors, mostly Africans in the diaspora, to commemorate the 400 years of the first enslaved Africans arriving in the U.S., tourism receipts as a key source of foreign exchange grew in a linear fashion. However, in the aftermath of the 2019 event, Ghana's status as a regional leader in cultural heritage tourism ecosystem was established. Today, cultural heritage tourism has become a major driver of growth and prosperity in the country.

The Year of Return initiative was a year-long series of activities involving visits to heritage sites, healing ceremonies, theatre and musical performances, lectures, investment forums, and relocation conferences – all aimed at showcasing and harnessing Ghana's potential as a global tourist destination and investment opportunity. The multiplier effects are also key, considering this sector also stimulates growth in other industries.

In 2018, Ghana's need to crowd-in private sector investment as a necessary condition for transforming the tourism sector became a priority. This was so because of the need to channel scarce public resources towards priorities out of reach for the private sector. The World Bank supported Ghana's comprehensive "national marketing, promotion, and branding strategy and action plan that will include an innovative and cost-effective digital component, and clearly identified tactics for key segments and product packages—for example, weekend getaways, cultural tours, and safaris." (World Bank, 2018).

It was therefore not surprising that of the proposed $40 million five-year World Bank loan in 2018, $15 million was earmarked for developing tourism sites and destinations, while $4 million was for tourism branding and marketing.

Ghana's tourism and investment promotion ecosystem, has played a major role in the current upward trajectory in Ghana's visitor economy (Ghana Investment Promotion Center, 2021) (Box 14).

The interplay of policy, markets, digital sophistication, and marketing communication has contributed in no small measure to the tourism renaissance in Ghana. This is particularly profound in the context of Ghana becoming the primary market for African Americans with interest in exploring Africa's heritage tourism economy (Teye & Timothy, 2004).

THE POLITICAL ECONOMY OF RESOURCE EXTRACTION IN SOUTH AFRICA

Renowned as one of the most remarkable political transitions in contemporary times, the end of apartheid marked an important watershed in South Africa's history. After transitioning to democracy in the mid-1990s, South Africa has achieved significant economic and social progress, albeit progress has stagnated in the last decade (World Bank, 2021). With a Gini coefficient of 0.63 in 2015, inequality remains a pervasive challenge in South Africa.

According to a 2022 World Bank report titled *Inequality in Southern Africa: An Assessment of the Southern African Customs Union,* " South Africa, the largest country in SACU, is the most unequal country in the world, ranking first among 164 countries in the World Bank's global poverty database."

Marie Francoise Marie-Nelly, World Bank Country Director for South Africa, Botswana, Namibia, Lesotho, and Eswatini contextualizes the inequality in Africa's most sophisticated economy in terms of intergenerational dynamics thus:

We know from this report that inherited circumstances over which an individual has little or no control, drive overall inequality, and that despite SACU countries undertaking some of the most redistributive spending in the world, particularly on education and health, inequality remains extremely high (World Bank, 2022; para.3)

Mining remains one of South Africa's most important economic sectors, contributing close to 10 percent of total output. However, structural and institutional challenges constitute a major drag on growth. Given the country's history of exclusion, in the absence of policy innovations which recognize

South Africa's dual economy model and the increasingly digital nature of the global economy, these underlying structural economic issues may perpetuate widening inequality and its concomitant effect on aggregate demand. This has broader implications for the extractive industries and the political economy of post-apartheid South Africa.

Easterly (2001) discusses the harmful effects of resource rents on the vertical (between rich and poor) and horizontal (across regions) distributions of income in a country. High levels of vertical inequality may hamper development by reducing the potency of economic growth in poverty alleviation, while horizontal inequality can trigger violent conflicts. Clearly, having most of a nation's wealth in the hands of a small elite is a recipe for chaos.

We discussed earlier the political economy implications of resource-dependence. The capacity to innovate is a major contributor to economic

Box 15: Hydrogen and Mining Innovation in South Africa

As the energy transition debate intensifies across the world, attention is on hydrogen as a promising zero-carbon fuel. The global market for hydrogen is expanding rapidly, with a huge potential for the mining sector to reap significant rewards from it. With 80 million tons produced annually, with expectations that this will increase to 100 million tons by 2030, before ultimately hitting the 500 million tons mark by 2050, this could herald the start of a new global resource economy (Schnettler, 2020).

With a mineral reserve valued at $2.5 trillion and estimated as the world's fifth largest in terms of GDP, South Africa is a global leader in the mining sector. Over the years, mining has supported the country's economic growth and industrial diversification by attracting international investments and the concomitant employment, foreign exchange, productivity, and innovation.

A 2020 report by PwC titled *Unlocking South Africa's Hydrogen Potential*, highlights South Africa's potential to capitalize on the rapidly evolving global hydrogen economy to "revolutionize its own economy and supply green hydrogen to the world." (Metcalfe, Burger, & Mackay, 2020).

The authors allude to South Africa's comparative advantage given its renewable energy potential, and how this can be leveraged to position the country as a leading exporter of green hydrogen to other parts of the world. In addition, they opine that existing infrastructure could provide a basis for economies of scale:

> *The infrastructure needed to export hydrogen is similar to existing natural gas networks and is already being piloted in Australia and Japan. South Africa could leverage its existing port infrastructure to support this initiative and, in doing so, protect the jobs and infrastructure that are declining as a result of the drop in global demand for coal exports (Metcalfe, Burger & Mackay, 2020; p.32).*

stability, and in the South African case, a policy innovation agenda targeted at closing the wealth gap must include reforms in the resource economy, with increased roles for markets in spreading socially beneficial innovations.

In the context of decarbonization and the energy transition, the mining sector in Africa's most advanced economy stands to gain from the ongoing rapid pace of digitization. As the world embraces new energy and mining innovations, the potential of the hydrogen economy in South Africa's vast mining sector could be transformative (Box 15).

THE FUTURE OF AFRICA'S REGIONAL INNOVATION ECONOMY

Fragmentation is a key feature of Africa's economies; the low level of connectedness has major implications for productivity, capital inflows, wealth creation, and societal welfare. From arable land and water to oil, natural gas, minerals, forests and wildlife, the continent's huge land mass and vast natural resource endowments constitute the core of its economy.

With a population of 1.3 billion, Africa boasts 20 percent of the earth's surface, with 60 percent of the total arable lands in the world. Yet, the continent's dismal economic performance has attracted considerable attention in the development sphere and remains a source of concern to all stakeholders in the Africa project. To put things into perspective, most African economies – except for South Africa and countries in the Northern Africa region with relatively diversified economies – are characterized by informality, subsistence agriculture, poor infrastructure, and underdeveloped manufacturing sectors.

As discussed extensively in the preceding chapters, while the rise of the digital knowledge economy offers a glimmer of hope for Africa's economic future, leveraging the innovation economy to spark productivity gains and create decent jobs cannot be left to chance. Harnessing the benefits of the innovation economy requires a strategic policy framework focused on unleashing the potential of the technology ecosystem, with the appropriate policy mix and doses of investments, talent, and risk sharing paradigm. To achieve the Africa we want, foot-dragging is not an option. We explain why in the next (and final) chapter of this monograph.

Today's real borders are not between nations, but between powerful and powerless, free and fettered, privileged and humiliated. Today, no walls can separate humanitarian or human rights crises in one part of the world from national security crises in another.

— Kofi Annan

REFERENCES

African Development Bank. (2016). *Feed Africa: Strategy for Agricultural Transformation in Africa 2016–2025*. Available at: https://www.afdb.org/fileadmin/uploads/afdb/Documents/Generic-Documents/Feed_Africa-_Strategy_for_Agricultural_Transformation_in_Africa_2016-2025.pdf

Beaudry, C., & Solar-Pelletier, L. (2020). Ottawa's 'superclusters' can offer much more than just job creation. *Globe and Mail.* https://www.theglobeandmail.com/business/commentary/article-ottawas-superclusters-can-offer-much-more-than-just-job-creation/

Catapult Network. (n.d.). *Welcome to the catapult network.* Catapult Network Homepage. https://catapult.org.uk

Combes, P., Duranton, G., Gobillon, L., & Roux, S. (2010). estimating agglomeration economies with history, geology, and worker effects. *Agglomeration Economics,* 15-66. Retrieved from https://repository.upenn.edu/real-estate_papers/21

Diop, M. (2016). *Foresight Africa 2016: Banking on Agriculture for Africa's Future*. Brookings Institution.

Easterly, W. (2001). The middle-class consensus and economic development. *Journal of Economic Growth, 6*(4), 317–335. doi:10.1023/A:1012786330095

European Commission. (2020). *What is STIP Compass?* EURAXESS.

FAO & AUC. (2018). *Sustainable Agricultural Mechanization: A Framework for Africa.* Available at: https://www.fao.org/3/CA1136EN/ca1136en.pdf

Fraunhofer Institutes. (n.d.). *Fraunhofer Institutes and Research Units.* https://www.fraunhofer.de/en/institutes.html

Ghana Investment Promotion Center (GIPC). (2021). https://www.gipcghana.com/press-and-media/news-headlines.html?start=30

Glaeser, E. (2011). Triumph of the city [Excerpt]. *Scientific American.* https://www.scientificamerican.com/article/glaeser-triumph-of-the-city-excerpt/

Gutiérrez, A. A., & Olayele, F. (2021). Urban Innovation and Reinvention: The Case of New York. *ICE. Revista De Economía*, (920), 29–48. doi:10.32796/ice.2021.920.7211

Haverhals, M., Ingram, V., Elias, M., & Basnett, B. (2016). Gender and Forest, Tree and Agroforestry Value Chains – Evidence from Literature. In C. Colfer, B. Basnett, & M. Elias (Eds.), *Gender and Forests: Climate Change, Tenure, Value Chains, and Emerging Issues* (pp. 221–242). Earthscan/CIFOR.

Home-Douglas, P. (2019). Canada's new technology gambit: The government's innovation superclusters idea is a winner with universities. *PRISM.* http://www.asee-prism.org/canadas-new-technology-gambit/

Innovation, Science and Economic Development Canada (ISED). (n.d.). Innovation Superclusters Initiative. *STIP Compass: International Database on STI Policies.* https://stip.oecd.org/stip/policy-initiatives/2019%2Fdata%2FpolicyInitiatives%2F14949

Kelly, E. (2018). Canada's innovation superclusters ready to launch. *Science | Business.* https://sciencebusiness.net/news/canadas-innovation-superclusters-ready-launch

Leke, A., & Signe, L. (2019). *Africa's Untapped Business Potential: Countries, Sectors, and Strategies*. Brookings Institution Press.

Metcalfe, J., Burger, L., & Mackay, J. (2020). *Unlocking South Africa's hydrogen potential.* https://www.pwc.co.za/en/assets/pdf/unlocking-south-africas-hydrogen-potential.pdf

Olayele, B. F. (2019). Gravity, borders, and regionalism: A Canada–US sub-national analysis. *The International Trade Journal*, *33*(5), 416–443. doi:10.1080/08853908.2019.1628675

Porter, M. E. (1990). The competitive advantage of nations. *Harvard Business Review.* https://hbr.org/1990/03/the-competitive-advantage-of-nations

Porter, M. E. (1995). The competitive advantage of the inner city. *Harvard Business Review*. https://hbr.org/1995/05/the-competitive-advantage-of-the-inner-city

Preko, A. (2020). A good museum experience pays off for the tourism sector in Ghana. *The Conversation*. https://theconversation.com/a-good-museum-experience-pays-off-for-the-tourism-sector-in-ghana-146441

Schnettler, A. (2020). At the Dawn of the Hydrogen Economy. *Power*. https://www.powermag.com/at-the-dawn-of-the-hydrogen-economy/

Sweeting, T., & Whitehead, J. (2020). Understanding the tensions in Canada's federal-provincial relations. *Earnscliffe – Insights*. https://earnscliffe.ca/en/news-and-insight/understanding-the-tensions-in-canadas-federal-provincial-relations/

Teye, V. B., & Timothy, D. J. (2004). The varied colors of slave heritage in west Africa: White American stakeholders. *Space and Culture*, *7*(2), 145–155. doi:10.1177/1206331203256580

The Conversation. (2021). Ghana's Path to Heritage Tourism. *U.S. News & World Report*. https://www.usnews.com/news/best-countries/articles/2021-02-11/how-former-president-rawlings-pioneered-heritage-tourism-in-ghana

Valin, H., Sands, R. D., van der Mensbrugghe, D., Nelson, G. C., Ahammad, H., Blanc, E., Bodirsky, B., Fujimori, S., Hasegawa, T., Havlík, P., Heyhoe, E., Kyle, P., D'Croz, D. M., Paltsev, S., Rolinski, S., Tabeau, A., van Meijl, H., von Lampe, M., & Willenbockel, D. (2014). The Future of Food Demand: Understanding Differences in Global Economic Models. *Agricultural Economics*, *45*(1), 51–67. doi:10.1111/agec.12089

Waruhiu, R. (2018). Blue economy can be a lifeline for Africa: Sustainable exploitation of the oceans, lakes, rivers will increase countries' earnings. *Africa Renewal*. https://www.un.org/africarenewal/magazine/december-2018-march-2019/blue-economy-can-be-lifeline-africa

World Bank. (2018). *Ghana Tourism Development Project*. https://www.worldbank.org/en/news/loans-credits/2018/07/13/ghana-tourism-development-project

World Bank. (2021). South Africa: Overview. *Where We Work*. https://www.worldbank.org/en/country/southafrica/overview

World Bank. (2022). *Inequality in Southern Africa: An Assessment of the Southern African Customs Union*. https://www.worldbank.org/en/news/press-release/2022/03/09/new-world-bank-report-assesses-sources-of-inequality-in-five-countries-in-southern-africa

Section 5
Conclusion

Chapter 13
No Foot-Dragging:
Let's Transform Africa

ABSTRACT

The complex nature of society, contemporary policy problems, and the rapid advances in digitization significantly limit the ability of traditional policy devices and analytical paradigms to arrive at optimal policy solutions. This concluding chapter draws on lessons from several jurisdictions for Africa's development. To achieve the Africa of our dreams, policy reforms are needed to diversify the structure of production for long-term economic growth. In the same vein, the leapfrog effect has implications for fast-tracking the continent's development journey. Successful policy innovation requires nuanced policy paradigms, models, and devices under an empirical umbrella that optimizes the opportunities presented by regional economic integration under the AfCFTA. A one-size-fits-all model will not work.

GDP growth is not enough. Growth must be felt in the lives of people! Nobody eats GDP.

— Akinwumi Adesina

DOI: 10.4018/978-1-7998-7383-9.ch013

POLICY CAPACITY is a core fabric of public policymaking. The highly complex nature of society, contemporary policy problems, and the rapid advances in digitization significantly limit the ability of traditional policy devices and analytical paradigms to help in choosing the best policy among a set of alternatives. This has implications for the formulation and implementation of effective policies.

As discussed in much of this book, while public policy scholars and practitioners have varying opinions on the threshold of governance and institutional quality required as preconditions for policy capacity to aid the public policy innovation process, historical and structural issues in the African context – e.g., initial conditions, informality, extreme poverty, conflicts, colonial institutional vestiges, and highly fragmented economies – add an additional layer of importance which merits attention in the agenda-setting process.

Much like how cause-and-effect analysis is useful in understanding how different parts and sequences of a system interact with each other over time, the discussion in the preceding chapters has shown that policy capacity is important in the analysis of capacity deficit and how this, in turn, results in sub-optimal outcomes that ultimately trigger policy failures. I discuss extensively in this monograph that policy diffusion is the process by which a policy spreads once it is created. Another critical element of the policy innovation discourse is policy reinvention: the process by which a policy is changed by those who adopt it.

The theoretical underpinnings of institutionalism and the political economy dictates so far in this analysis establish one fact: public-private policy partnerships offer an institutional and alternative governance paradigm that balances the traditional state and market ramifications that often limit allocative efficiency and delivery of conventional social services. This is a new hybrid form of institutionalism that serves as an alternative governance model to central planning and markets in the delivery of public goods and services.

Transaction costs, property rights, governance, institutions, contracts, bounded rationality, and social capital are all fundamental to the new institutional economics paradigm. Chapter 3 of this book establishes the theoretical foundation of governance as the core of the PPP and public-private policy partnerships analysis. Since transaction costs are essentially about harnessing the best of the public and private sectors – through learning from the vantage point of others – the preferences of the individuals and actors involved in the policy diffusion process must be crystallized within the appropriate institutional structures.

Under the introductory chapter, I explain how group preferences in societies drive institutional outcomes based on allocative efficiency ramifications. In the policy arena, innovation reduces transaction costs by reducing risks and creating positive externalities among key stakeholders.

In the context of market dynamics, the capitalist mode of wealth creation has exacerbated income inequality and the climate crisis for decades now, resulting in populism and deep feelings of discontent. Clearly, capitalism is at a crossroads, and to avert a breakdown of the political and socioeconomic systems, fixing the status quo by addressing the huge and growing imbalances between the public and private sectors is long overdue. In the face of recent trends in the social justice movement, concerns on the climate crisis, the ongoing debate on ESG, the future of capitalism, and the governance dimension, these issues resonate.

The pitfalls of capitalism are many, but its unprecedented ability to create wealth through the invisible hand is incontrovertible. This implies there is a middle ground, and based on the discussion so far, a firm grasp of policy innovation is key to addressing some of the pitfalls of modern capitalism. In the absence of private property rights, allocative efficiency— efficiency in the distribution of factors of production across sectors— becomes difficult to achieve.

Again, transaction costs lie at the heart of the policy innovation discourse, and taken together, this discussion can be a useful interpretive lens – that guides reflection and action – from which African countries can identify specific policies in need of reform and the appropriate solutions that can help improve governance performance – since this permeates all other dimensions of public-private policy partnerships.

Both the content and scope of a policy have implications for adoption, and this explains, partly, why the higher the success rate of policies in other states, the higher is the likelihood of adoption. In this context, the policy learning-policy reinvention nexus is important in the overall context of policy capacity and policy innovation. While it is far from being a perfect model, post-genocide Rwanda offers some useful insights. This is discussed in detail below.

CRISIS AS A CATALYST FOR REINVENTION: POLICY LESSONS FROM RWANDA

During the Rwandan Civil War, an estimated 800,000 people in Rwanda – comprised mostly of the Tutsi minority ethnic group as well as some moderate Hutu and Twa – were killed by Hutu militiamen, soldiers, and ordinary citizens over a period of about 100 days between April 7th and July 15th in 1994.

Occurring through firearms, machetes, and a variety of garden implements, the speed and low-tech nature of the killings that decimated about 10 percent of the entire country's population at the time made international headlines. Samantha Power, former US ambassador to the United Nations and current Administrator of the US Agency for International Development, describes it as the fastest and most efficient killing spree of the 20th century (Power, 2001). Some commentators characterize the murder rate during the genocide to be three to five times faster than that of the Holocaust (see Kaufman, 2019).

Rwanda has made significant progress in economic and structural reforms since the end of the genocide, with impressive growth rates over time. Over the last decade before the COVID-19 pandemic, growth averaged over 7 percent, while per capita GDP grew at an average annual rate of 5 percent. The World Bank expects Rwanda to achieve Middle-Income Country status by 2035 and High-Income Country status by 2050, based on Rwanda's various strands of seven-year National Strategies for Transformation (NST) with detailed sectoral strategies aligned with the SDGs (Government of Rwanda, 2017; World Bank, 2021a). Rwanda's development model is primarily public-sector led, with economic growth heavily dependent on large scale public investments, which constituted over 12 percent of GDP in 2019.

In the aftermath of the genocide, the Government of Rwanda implemented a wide range of policy reforms across a wide range of sectors in the hope of rebuilding the economy and society. Jean-Eric Aubert (2018) explains the ultimate beneficial impacts in terms of Rwanda's ability to chart a knowledge-based development pathway which leverages technology diffusion to increase productivity and drive value creation in traditional and subsistence sectors (e.g., agriculture) which remain the mainstay of the economy. While the devil is in the detail, there are ample lessons for other countries on the continent vis-à-vis turning a crisis into an opportunity by devising new ways of seeing, thinking, and responding – especially via a multi-stakeholder approach that harnesses PPPs to optimize public service delivery.

Due to its peculiar model, Rwanda's development priorities are financed mainly through external borrowing like grants, concessional, and non-concessional borrowing. This has led to a relatively high increase in fiscal deficits (the debt-to-GDP ratio rose by close to 40 percentage points from 19.4% in 2010 to 56.7% in 2019) (World Bank, 2021a). Obviously, this trajectory is unsustainable; reforms and policy innovations for a more sustainable resource mobilization and development financing remain on the front burner.

The preceding analysis underscores the importance of partnering with the private sector to ensure incremental gains in policy innovations around resource mobilization align with market expectations. The World Bank corroborates this and notes the limitations in Rwanda's fiscal trajectory, in addition to the recommendation that "Stronger dynamism in the private sector will help to sustain high investment rate and accelerate the growth" (World Bank, 2021a, para. 9). In a sense, PPPs offer an optimal pathway to achieving this objective.

Rwanda's NST recognizes the key role of PPPs in the country's policy innovation process and expressly underscores that PPPs will be the conduit for major public investments and strategic policy innovations and interventions (Government of Rwanda, 2017). Not only that. Recognizing that the reforms and policy innovations needed to accelerate growth, sustain it, and make it inclusive are both complex and non-linear, Rwanda's long-term economic development strategy is anchored on four drivers of growth: innovation, integration, agglomeration, and competition. And the private sector is at the heart of everything given the emphasis on digital technologies, human capital, private sector development, regional integration and trade, infrastructure, agriculture, and urbanization (World Bank, 2019).

POLICY LESSONS FROM ELSEWHERE

While the notion of "African solutions to African problems"[1] is consistent with the African Union's Agenda 2063, policy capacity remains a major challenge. In the earlier chapters, I establish the important role of transaction costs in policy innovation, based on the NIE framework.

The capacity to innovate is a significant contributor to economic stability; the power of markets in this regard cannot be overemphasized. In a non-technical sense, transaction costs provide a lens to understand how PPPs are key to learning from the vantage point of others. Policy lessons abound from other jurisdictions; these are reviewed in the context of policy diffusion below.

New York and Reinvention

Throughout history, New York has always found new ways to reinvent itself. For context, the city began as a trading outpost, before growing into a commercial and maritime power, followed by its evolution into an industrial and manufacturing hub, before becoming the global capital of finance, innovation, entrepreneurship, and media. That capacity for transformation and ability to adapt, innovate, and recover, has always contributed to, and defined, New York's economic resilience.

In the aftermath of the fiscal crisis of the 1970s, the 9/11 terrorist attacks, the 2008 GFC, and Superstorm Sandy, New York persevered and bounced back. Despite being the global epicenter of the COVID-19 outbreak in spring 2020, the city leveraged its robust innovation ecosystem to turn the corner. The pandemic triggered unprecedented shocks and shuttered labor markets, with disproportionate impacts on marginalized communities and a wide array of small businesses. The large decline in employment and production further laid bare many flaws in existing social and economic structures.

Policy stakeholders in New York understood that because the crisis was triggered by a virus, understanding its impact on the economy and healthcare system would be critical for any meaningful policy action. In the aftermath of COVID-19, global personal protective equipment supply chains experienced significant disruptions, and hundreds of local manufacturers in the city stepped up to make medical goods like face shields, gowns, testing kits, and bridge ventilators for hospitals.

New York created a new lab for test processing and ran a rapid testing competition. Such innovation capabilities aided the use of advanced manufacturing technologies, with customization opportunities, rapid turn-around times, and supply chain stability, while simultaneously encouraging local job creation and reducing the carbon footprint of production.

And in terms of long-term economic redesign, climate action is at the heart of the city's recovery through impact investments to drive inclusive economic development by unlocking private capital to support the growth of strategic sectors.

Miracle in China

The economic rise of China has dominated the development literature for decades now. Clearly, there are useful lessons from China for Africa's development. The rapid development in China is one of the most important shifts in the global economy in contemporary times.

On October 1, 1949, in Tiananmen Square in Peking, Mao Zedong, the Chairman of the Communist Party of China, proclaimed the founding of the People's Republic of China. Following Mao's death in 1976, the new leader, Deng Xiaoping, instituted a series of economic reforms and liberalization in 1978 that opened the economy to international trade and allowed foreign direct investment.

Over the past four decades, the free market reforms have generated spectacular growth, averaging almost 10 percent per year – in what has been described by the World Bank as "the fastest sustained expansion by a major economy in history" (Congressional Research Service (CRS) Report, 2019, p. 1) Prior to that, China was "poor, stagnant, centrally controlled, vastly inefficient, and relatively isolated from the global economy" (CRS Report, 2019, summary page) The Chinese economy is now increasingly dependent on its growing middle class and domestic consumption as growth drivers.

Hsu, Wu, and Zhao (2012), in their book *In Search of China's Development Model*, shed light on why the China Miracle[2] defies or fits the development orthodoxy. Among other factors, large scale capital investment, rapid growth in manufacturing, increased domestic consumption, and international trade have contributed to China's economic surge. On a cautionary note, while moving over 800 million people out of poverty in 40 years is commendable, the rapid economic growth in China exceeded the pace of structural and institutional development, leaving important gaps that deserve China's attention. Moreso, China's peculiar model of economic internationalization and marketization under a socialist economic order produces certain complexities that make lessons from the country's success hard to replicate in other regions.

As the Chinese economy navigates the ongoing moderation in economic growth due to structural constraints – like declining labor force growth, diminishing returns to investment, and slowing productivity – finding new growth drivers, addressing social issues, and making tangible progress on the clean energy transition are some of the critical metrics that will ensure the country charts a new development path. Such path is key for consolidating its gains over the last four decades, without compromising the ability of future generations to meet their own needs.

In the context of policy diffusion, certain similarities in the economic structures of Africa and China are worth highlighting. First, both jurisdictions are endowed with vast natural resources which, under the neoclassical capital-output ratio construct, could help drive the growth process to derive sustainable economic benefit. Second, and perhaps more importantly, with roughly the same population of about 1.3 billion people, both jurisdictions are exemplars for the dictates of the dual-sector model of Arthur Lewis – based on the proposition that reallocation from low-productivity agriculture to high-productivity manufacturing can trigger growth.

Lewis (1954) argues that a developing economy can choose a new "capitalist sector" development path to employ the excess labor in its subsistence sector, thereby increasing productivity based on the prevailing low wages and poverty in the labor surplus economy. While the Chinese experience perfectly fits this, it may not be replicable in Africa in light of the "Africa leapfrogging" narrative. In the same vein, China appears to have now reached a turning point, due to rising wages in urban areas, among other factors. Nonetheless, ample lessons abound.

As the largest developing economy in the world, China's successful economic reforms have triggered interests globally to the extent that policy diffusion matters. Of course, the outcomes in China cannot be linked to a linear, deterministic mode. These are the result of the mutual interaction of many internal and external factors, with inherent randomness. The world's largest asset manager, BlackRock, highlights the changing business landscape in China: "China's changing economy is creating a new landscape of opportunity for potential portfolio growth, and it may continue to do so for the coming years." BlackRock further warns that, "If foreign investors exclude China from their portfolio, they may risk missing out on the explosive potential of the vast market."

Just like China, while the AfCFTA now presents an opportunity to harness the influences of internal factors to drive economic prosperity in Africa, much work remains on the external factors. As technological advances continue to drive services tradability, leading to greater prospects for developing countries to create additional economic opportunities, with productivity gains, the pact offers a generational opportunity to move millions out of poverty. The AfCFTA is poised to change the trajectory of Africa's trade and investment dynamics, and if well executed with a sustained momentum, the largest free trade in the history of multilateralism will, no doubt, move Africa from the margins to the mainstream of global commerce.

LET'S TRANSFORM AFRICA

As I conclude this monograph, there has never been a more important time to reimagine Africa's economic system. The scale of the economic challenge heralded by the COVID-19 pandemic presents a generational opportunity to redesign an economic future capable of fixing agelong structural weaknesses imposed by colonial intervention, while also addressing vulnerabilities from deliberate and ill-advised policy choices by both nationalist leaders and those guided by neoliberal technocracy. The longer-term direct and indirect health, economic, social, governance, and geopolitical implications of the pandemic will reverberate for a while, with intergenerational consequences.

Devising the paradigms, frameworks, and policy devices that recognize the nuanced nature of this puzzle is a fundamental reason this book is written. Governments and key actors in the policy cycle must provide inputs towards a detailed mapping exercise that recognizes the unique situation of each country. A one-size-fits-all model will not work. Successful policy innovation requires nuanced policy paradigms, models, and devices under an empirical umbrella that optimizes the opportunities presented by regional economic integration under the AfCFTA – and a supranational pan-African political economy governance such as the African Union.

Again, my core argument is that the current political economy framework in the context of reimagining policy innovation in Africa is broken, incompatible with mainstream policy devices and paradigms, and inconsistent with the continent's social and economic ideologies like Ujamaa, Ubuntu, and Harambee. To the extent that these paradigms are divergent from traditional African values like familyhood, interpersonal relationships, and togetherness, they have important microeconomic theoretical implications for resource allocation decisions.

In *Agenda 2063: The Africa We Want*, the Africa Union articulates the continent's new path for inclusive and sustainable development:

The need to envision a long-term 50 year development trajectory for Africa is important as Africa needs to revise and adapt its development agenda due to ongoing structural transformations; increased peace and reduction in the number of conflicts; renewed economic growth and social progress; the need for people centered development, gender equality and youth empowerment; changing global contexts such as increased globalization and the ICT revolution; the increased unity of Africa which makes it a global power to be reckoned with and capable of rallying support around its own common agenda; and emerging development and investment opportunities in areas such as agri-business, infrastructure development, health and education as well as the value addition in African commodities (African Union, 2015; para 3).

To achieve the Africa of our dreams, policy innovation is key. While there is no one-size-fits-all template to reduce inequality and poverty, policy reforms targeted at broadening the continent's economic base to diversify the structure of production will deliver long-term economic growth. There are many ways to get there. Given ongoing advances in technology and innovation on the continent, much has been said about the leapfrog effect and how it can help streamline the multiple pathways to fast-track Africa's development journey.

For instance, the case study on the role of digitization in the transformation of Kenya's tax design and collection through policy innovation in the digital financial system is presented earlier in the book. The impact of the second order effects of the policy changes in the context of changing the dynamics of fiscal policy is also well articulated.

Everywhere on the planet, COVID-19 has exerted significant pressures on the higher education industry. And the ongoing transformation in the sector will be difficult to reverse. While the pandemic is testing the limits of the traditional university system, a major bright spot and policy innovation opportunity is the realization that other digital pathways will be required for career advancement, while traditional higher education will continue to be relevant. And such pathways must necessarily integrate nontraditional alternative education providers. Nowhere is this more relevant than in Africa.

Much has been said about the informal sector and how it remains the backbone of Africa's economy, with its contribution surpassing 80 percent of employment on the continent (Guven & Karlen, 2020). In the same vein, fueled by burgeoning population and urbanization, the growth of megacities and smaller towns and cities makes the underground economy critical for absorbing most of the expanding labor force. Given that the urban formal wage sector is limited in its ability to accommodate new entrants and migrants from rural Africa, unofficial economic activity becomes pivotal in the context of mitigating economic vulnerabilities for the masses of unemployed people on the continent without social safety nets.

This pushes, again, policy innovation to the front burner. Significant innovations are needed in the policy sector to accelerate the transition of micro- and small enterprises from the informal to the formal sector. Again, from the case study on Kenya, the high revenue-generation potential of the underground economy, particularly in the context of increased participation of small businesses in the services economy, can bring the large number of unregistered taxpayers and incomes not captured in official statistics into the formal economy. Increased productivity and digitization can help informal players to transition incrementally to the formal sector, thereby bolstering revenue mobilization efforts for enhanced public service delivery. Clearly, policy entrepreneurship, in the context of Kingdon's MSF, has a major role.

The notion of a manufacturing renaissance and the conditions under which it is possible in Africa are robustly articulated under the chapter on the philosophical foundations of economic transformation. Is that even possible? Quite a rhetorical question, but valid all the same. In much of this book, the political economy ramifications of the development challenges in Africa and the way forward are succinctly discussed – with emphasis on the critical role of policy innovation through reforms and policy diffusion.

Paul Collier's 2007 book, *The Bottom Billion*, explains the causes of failure in 50 failed states home to the poorest people in the world. The central thesis of this work depicts much of the situation in several African countries. Collier argues that these countries are caught in at least one of four traps: the "conflict trap," "the natural resource trap," the trap of being "landlocked with bad neighbors" and the "bad governance in a small country" trap. These four transmission channels are discussed below vis-à-vis the central argument of this book.

On conflict trap, Collier explains that about three-quarters of the people in the bottom billion have recently been through – or are currently in the midst of – a civil war. As discussed extensively under the chapter on resource curse, resource endowments have an inherent tendency to promote rent-seeking behaviour – the antithesis of development and egalitarianism. To achieve the economic and political potential of Pan-Africanism, the current political economy under which rentierism and coercive political institutions thrive must be fixed.

In the context of Collier's thesis, not only is "being landlocked with bad neighbors" detrimental to increasing aggregate welfare, but it also underscores the whole notion of deadweight loss and inefficiencies from 54 separate markets, rules, laws, borders, cultures, and institutional dimensions that have plagued scale economies and regional integration on the continent for decades. The importance of trade, particularly for small open economies, remains compelling. The analysis under trade policy innovation corroborates the imperative of the AfCFTA in solving the age-long challenge of fragmentation.

On bad governance, the theories of policy change discussed earlier on – whether via incrementalism or the PET – shed light on the importance of reconciling the outcomes of centrally planned economic orientations in immediate post-independence Africa (informed largely by the resentments from colonialism) with the dictates of neoliberal economic doctrines culminating in the Washington Consensus. Policy reforms and socially beneficial innovations that recognize the role of markets in optimal resource allocation, à la policy innovation, are advanced as the feasible alternative for Africa.

Collier argues that given the relative ineffectiveness of aid dependency in fixing Africa's development challenges, innovations in policymaking are key. As he puts it, "aid is often ineffective, and globalization can actually make matters worse, driving development to more stable nations." In many ways, this thesis aligns with the popular debate that the aid dependency model has failed, and Africa needs to redefine its agenda and craft innovative ways to finance its development priorities (see Moyo, 2009).

Given that the AfCFTA has become the dominant paradigm in the trade policy and regional integration debate in Africa, it is important to look at other ramifications that may constrain a smooth and effective operationalization of the pact in the coming years. Again, Collier's work offers some insight. In his critique of *The Bottom Billion*, Ferguson (2007) characterizes the difficulty in achieving industrialization in Africa thus:

Trade, too, is not a sufficient answer. The problem is that Asia has eaten Africa's lunch when it comes to exploiting low wage costs. Now, to stand any chance of survival, African manufacturers need some temporary protection from Asian competition. So long as rich countries retain tariffs to shelter their own manufacturers from cut-price Asian imports, they should exempt products from bottom billion countries (Ferguson, 2007; para. 14).

Ferguson's critique above points to one thing: incremental policy innovation is key for success. Whether in trade policy, natural resource management, regional innovation, or the venture capital economy, the ability to innovate matters for economic reinvention and resilience.

In the introductory chapter, this book articulates how reallocation of workers from traditional, low-productivity to modern and high-productivity sectors has driven much of the sustained improvements in living standards recorded in modern history. Yes, the leapfrog paradigm has been discussed extensively in the African context, as is the pros and cons of premature deindustrialization. Yet, based on history from policy innovation in other jurisdictions, industrialization is key for Africa's economic transformation.

Resource-driven development has its pros and cons. As always, the devil is in the detail; some questions are in order here. Is the resource curse a result of policy errors? Why is Malaysia able to diversify the productive base of its economy through foreign exchange earnings from natural resource exports? Botswana's diamond economy is improving the welfare of its citizens in the form of quality social services like education and healthcare, in addition to local job creation through PPPs. Some call it serendipity, but the theory of path dependence reviewed earlier under the theoretical framework challenges this. While there are qualifications, courtesy of prudent macroeconomic management and strong governance, Botswana – one of the poorest countries in the world at independence in 1966 – rapidly rose to become, by nearly all accounts, a success story. And despite the adverse impacts of commodity market volatility on Botswana's diamond-led development model, the economy remains shielded from exogenous shocks due to fiscal buffers and prudent stabilization policies (World Bank, 2021b).

The above discussion becomes particularly important in the context of the ongoing digital transformation in the global economy, and the regional integration agenda of the continent under the AfCFTA framework. As discussed under Africa's experience with economic rebasing, the significant and rising shares of services of economies across the continent have implications for the several low-wage and undocumented workers in the underground economy. Addressing market fragmentation, which continues to limit Africa's ability to operate in the mainstream of global commerce, is key. Yet, based on Arthur Lewis' surplus labor model, productivity gains from increased manufacturing economic activity, even in SMEs, can move the needle in critical ways.

Policies, actions, and institutions matter. And following Kingdon's MSF approach on the role of the policy entrepreneur, through agenda setting, in merging problems, policies, and politics, the time is ripe to embrace sifting through diverse perspectives to reimagine how Africa's vast and productive assets such as energy and natural resources, land, knowledge, and young labor force can be converted into the much-needed capital – under the appropriate property rights, collateral law, infrastructure, governance framework, trust, and other key institutional dimensions.

No doubt, the AfCFTA is a watershed for regional economic integration in Africa. The ongoing shift in the global economy's center of gravity is reinforcing the importance of the digital sector as the driver of future growth. Much like the economic reforms in the late 1970s transformed the Chinese economy and produced a period of spectacular growth – transforming it from a poor country to an upper-middle-income economy – the implementation of the AfCFTA must proceed simultaneously with other key political and institutional reforms across the continent to ensure high-quality, sustainable growth.

While digitization has a major role here, policy innovation can help optimize the state-markets relationship in a way that supports the market system, while also strengthening policy capacity. This will ensure governments and bureaucracies focus primarily on driving stable market expectations and a seamless business environment.

If real development is to take place, the people have to be involved.

— *Julius Nyerere*

REFERENCES

African Union. (2015). *Overview - Agenda 2063: The Africa We Want.* https://au.int/en/agenda2063/overview

Aubert, J. E. (2018). Rwanda's innovation challenges and policies – lessons for Africa. *Journal of Intellectual Capital, 19*(3), 550–561. doi:10.1108/JIC-01-2017-0018

Ayittey, G. (2009). An African Solution: Solving the Crisis of Failed States. *Harvard International Review, 31*(3), 24–27.

BlackRock. (n.d.). *China: The Essentials.* https://www.blackrock.com/uk/professionals/solutions/discover-the-china-opportunity/china-the-essentials

Collier, P. (2007). *The Bottom Billion: Why the Poorest Countries Are Failing and What Can Be Done About It.* Oxford University Press.

Congressional Research Service Report. (2019). *China's Economic Rise: History, Trends, Challenges, and Implications for the United States.* Congressional Research Service. https://crsreports.congress.gov

Ferguson, N. (2007). The Least Among Us. *New York Times.* https://www.nytimes.com/2007/07/01/books/review/Ferguson-t.html

Government of Rwanda. (2017). *7 years government programme: National Strategy for Transformation (NST1) 2017 – 2024*. https://www.nirda.gov.rw/uploads/tx_dce/National_Strategy_For_Trsansformation_-NST1-min.pdf

Guven, M., & Karlen, R. (2020). *Supporting Africa's urban informal sector: Coordinated policies with social protection at the core*. World Bank, Africa Can End Poverty blog. https://blogs.worldbank.org/africacan/supporting-africas-urban-informal-sector-coordinated-policies-social-protection-core

Hsu, S., Wu, Y., & Zhao, S. (Eds.). (2012). *In Search of China's Development Model: Beyond the Beijing Consensus*. Taylor & Francis. doi:10.4324/9780203834817

Kaufman, Z. (2019). *Lessons from Rwanda: Post-Genocide Law and Policy* (Vol. 31). Stanford Law and Policy Review Stanford.

Lewis, A. (1954). Economic Development with Unlimited Supplies of Labour. The Manchester School of Economic and Social. doi:10.1111/j.1467-9957.1954.tb00021.x

Moyo, D. (2009). *Dead Aid: Why Aid Is Not Working and How There Is a Better Way for Africa*. Farrar, Straus and Giroux.

Power, S. (2001). Bystanders to Genocide. *The Atlantic*. https://www.theatlantic.com/magazine/archive/2001/09/bystanders-to-genocide/304571/

World Bank. (2019). *Future drivers of growth in Rwanda: Innovation, integration, agglomeration, and competition*. World Bank Group.

World Bank. (2019). *Future drivers of growth in Rwanda: Innovation, integration, agglomeration, and competition*. World Bank Group. http://documents.worldbank.org/curated/en/522801541618364833/Future-Drivers-of-Growth-in-Rwanda-Innovation-Integration-Agglomeration-and-Competition

World Bank. (2021a). Rwanda: Overview. *Where We Work* https://www.worldbank.org/en/country/rwanda/overview

World Bank. (2021b). Botswana: Overview. *Where We Work* https://www.worldbank.org/en/country/botswana/overview

ENDNOTES

1 The phrase "African Solutions to African Problems" was coined in 1993 by Ghanaian political economist and author, George Ayittey, to reject imported and often contradictory foreign models in tackling many of the challenges in Africa.

2 The China Miracle has become part of the development lexicon for describing the spectacular achievements of China's economic reform over the past four decades.

About the Author

Fred Olayele's diverse career spans academia, government, finance, and international development. A distinguished economist and public policy expert, his research interests and practice areas cover trade policy, innovation, FDI, urban policy, political economy, and inclusive development. He has published and shared best practices in these areas at numerous conferences and institutions around the world. He has consulted widely and advised many public and private organizations in Canada, United States, and Africa.

Dr. Olayele brings executive leadership and all-round professional experience to technical economic advisory and public policy practice. He recently completed a three-year term as Chief Economist and Senior Vice President with the New York City Economic Development Corporation, where he oversaw a wide range of economic research and policy initiatives aimed at making New York the global model for inclusive growth and innovation – with collaborations across the public, private, philanthropic, and academic sectors. Prior to that, he held several economic policy positions and advised the Canadian provincial governments of British Columbia and Saskatchewan across the FDI, economic development, and energy policy domains. Earlier in his career, he was a global trade finance specialist with Citigroup.

Professor Olayele has held academic positions and taught graduate and undergraduate courses in economics, strategy, and public policy at the University of Regina and Carleton University. He has served as a visiting professor and guest speaker across universities and academic institutions abroad. He was a Visiting Scholar at the World Trade Institute in Bern, Switzerland, and a Visiting Professor of Trade and Development at the University of Las Palmas de Gran Canaria, Spain.

He serves as International Advisory Board Member with Washington, D.C.-based International Economic Development Council, and holds membership in the Economic Club of New York. He is the host of the podcast, Inclusive Economics for Impact.

A passionate teacher and public intellectual, he serves on various non-profit boards and supports many social causes. He is President, Economic Innovation Institute for Africa; Director-General, Pan-African School of Policy Innovation; Board Chair, Economic Club of Africa in New York; and Director, Sprott Centre for African Research and Business, Carleton University.

Among others, his research has appeared in *The International Trade Journal* and the *International Journal of Urban Sustainable Development*. His most recent books include *Regional Economic Systems after COVID-19: Actionable Insights for an Equitable and Resilient Recovery* (Edward Elgar Publishing) and *Sustainable Development in Post-Pandemic Africa: Effective Strategies for Resource Mobilization* (Routledge).

He earned his PhD in Economics from Lancaster University, United Kingdom; an MA in Economics from the University of Victoria in British Columbia, Canada; and a BSc (First Class Honors) in Economics from the University of Ado-Ekiti, Nigeria, where he was awarded the university prize for the overall best performance.

Index

2008 financial crisis 104, 209, 214
2030 Agenda for Sustainable Development 3

A

Addis Ababa Action Agenda (AAAA) 206
Advocacy Coalition Framework (ACF) 46-48
Africa 1-11, 13-14, 16-18, 24-25, 27-30, 32, 54-64, 71, 73-74, 91-99, 101, 104, 113-117, 119-134, 143-144, 146-147, 150-153, 155-157, 162-165, 168-177, 179, 184-185, 195-202, 205-208, 210-222, 224, 226-227, 229-237, 239-246, 248-257, 261-264, 267-272, 274, 279-289
Africa Clean Energy Corridor (ACEC) 171
Africa Continental Free Trade Area (AfCFTA) 3, 30, 60-61, 117, 124-125, 208, 239, 247-250, 256, 264, 274, 281-282, 284-287
Africa Growth Initiative 131, 195
Africa Union (AU) 65, 98, 262, 282, 287
African Development Bank 128, 169, 174, 195, 200, 251, 269
African Development Bank (AfDB) 128, 169-170, 174, 200, 206, 246, 251, 263, 269
African economy 1, 8, 16, 29, 234, 241
African Renaissance 2, 60, 73, 94-97
African socialism 4, 13
Agenda 2063 2-3, 30, 58, 60, 65, 94-98, 278, 282, 287
Agenda 2063: The Africa We Want 98, 282, 287
agglomeration economies 50, 61, 140-142, 255-256, 269
agriculture economies 5, 19, 57, 85, 93, 117-118, 123-125, 234, 239, 243-244, 260, 262-263, 268-269, 277-278, 281
Angola 4
apartheid 2, 266
Austrian economics 79, 82

B

bad governance in a small country 284
Botswana 24, 159, 266, 286, 288
Brookings Institute 6-7, 13, 93, 101, 129-131, 154, 175, 195, 201-202, 219, 237, 269-270
bureaucracy 1-2, 17, 36, 55, 89, 186, 287

C

Canada 30, 32, 100, 130, 137, 144-145, 151, 153, 165-168, 174-175, 177, 201, 249, 257-260, 270-271
capitalism 4, 23, 44, 70, 78, 83-84, 103-104, 106-112, 115, 128-132, 136, 149, 184, 276
central planning 4-5, 114, 285
China Miracle 116, 133, 280, 289
civil society 20, 26, 36-37, 45-47, 150, 193
civil war 60, 148, 277, 284
clean energy corridors 171
Cold War 5, 200, 207
colonization 2-3, 83-84, 100, 121
competitive advantage 20-21, 30, 154, 221, 234, 247, 270-271
complexity economics 79, 101

Comprehensive Africa Agriculture Development Programme (CAADP) 262
conflict trap 284
corporate innovation 20
COVID-19 10, 64, 78-81, 104-105, 110-111, 117, 147, 169, 172, 195-197, 202, 206-207, 230, 264, 277, 279, 282-283
cultural heritage 265

D

debt 5-6, 14, 62, 92, 123-124, 185, 198, 200, 207, 213-214, 222, 237
decarbonization 162-164, 168, 172-173, 217, 268
deforestation 216-217
democracy 37, 41, 44, 55, 70, 95, 110, 136, 145-146, 152, 185, 234, 266
dictatorship 37, 70
digital connectivity 245
digital economy 25-26, 28, 91, 94, 103, 107, 116, 145, 161, 168, 196, 199, 208, 230, 240, 243-244, 250, 257-258
digital finance 224, 226, 237, 243, 249-250, 253
digital revolution 14, 20, 28, 116, 157, 161, 172, 188, 195, 205, 218, 227, 239, 243-244, 250, 263
digital technologies 5, 27, 221-222, 235, 240, 244, 260, 278
digitization 19, 28, 82, 116, 191, 218, 222-224, 227, 264, 268, 274-275, 283-284, 287
diversification 6, 17-18, 32, 118, 122, 127, 135, 140, 151, 155, 157, 161, 164, 166-168, 175, 208, 213, 216-217, 226, 249, 256, 267
domestic economic policy 7
Dutch disease theory 158, 164

E

economic diversification 17, 127, 135, 140, 164, 168, 175
education 1-2, 5, 7, 19, 27, 60, 62, 65-66, 70, 74, 105, 138, 141, 181-182, 192-201, 203-204, 208, 210-211, 215, 222, 224, 244, 247, 249, 260, 266, 283, 286
efficiency 1-2, 11-12, 27-29, 54-55, 61, 87, 107, 116, 118, 122, 135-136, 139, 141-143, 151, 154, 157, 159, 164, 167, 169, 173, 180, 188, 192-193, 221-222, 238, 241, 245, 247, 249, 255-257, 264, 275-276
energy-intensive, trade-exposed (EITE) industries 161
environmental, social, and governance (ESG) 110-111, 177, 276
epistemology 11
Ethiopia 14, 85, 121, 134, 144, 146-151, 153, 155, 211, 224, 244
externalities 11, 20, 50, 54, 91, 112, 138, 140, 152, 181-182, 189, 211-212, 222-223, 240, 276
externalities, positive 20, 50, 138, 189, 212, 222, 240, 276
extraction (mining) economies 5, 159, 166, 216, 266-268

F

familyhood 9, 282
federalism 134, 137, 143-149, 151-155, 177, 257
Feed Africa Strategy 263
financial inclusion 106, 206, 221, 224-227, 236, 244-245, 250, 252
First Industrial Revolution 28, 45
fiscal decentralization 136, 143, 146
fiscal policy 26-27, 136, 154, 221-222, 226, 247, 283
foreign direct investment (FDI) 172, 217-218
Fourth Industrial Revolution 28, 45, 88, 119, 243
free riding 54

G

G7 countries 230
Gabon 216-218, 220
Ghana 4, 13, 24, 55, 65, 211, 264, 266, 270-271
GHG emissions 161-162, 165, 217
global economy 6, 20, 22, 44, 55, 82, 84,

88, 117-118, 161, 183, 213, 230, 267, 280, 286
global financial crisis (GFC) 10, 78, 80, 108, 209, 279
Global Innovation Index (GII) 24-25
global minimum tax 229-231, 234
Global North 105, 139
Global South 6, 61, 82, 135, 139, 231
global value chains 128, 206, 239, 249, 264
globalization 6, 17, 37, 49, 51, 88, 104, 109, 111, 119, 135-136, 141-142, 154, 191, 230, 244-245, 247, 253-254, 258, 282, 285
good governance 58, 95, 212-213
Great Depression 183
great trade collapse 243
Gulf Cooperation Council (GCC) countries 167-168, 175

H

Harambee 9, 282
healthcare 1-2, 10, 19, 27, 105, 145, 172, 182, 191, 211, 234, 279, 286
Helix Models of Innovation 44, 197, 256
horizontal fiscal imbalances 136-137
hydrogen (fuel) 166, 267-268, 270-271
hyperinflation 6

I

import substitution industrialization (ISI) 121-123, 258-260
incentive 11, 57, 86, 113, 127, 161, 165, 170-172, 213, 230
Income Share Agreements (ISA) 198-199
Incrementalism 7, 40-42, 54, 60-61, 63, 127, 144, 285
individualism 4, 9-10, 106, 124
industrial agglomeration 256
Industrial Revolution 18, 28-29, 45, 51, 83, 88, 91, 115, 118-119, 130, 243, 263
inequality 2, 6, 26, 36-37, 49, 61, 73-74, 78, 81, 83, 93, 97, 104, 106, 108-112, 126, 130-132, 135-136, 138-139, 142, 146, 151, 154, 162, 200, 203, 227, 247, 253, 266-267, 272, 276, 283
infrastructure 1-2, 10, 12, 18, 27, 62, 64, 74-75, 105-106, 115, 124, 135, 139, 164, 171, 180-182, 186-187, 191-192, 196, 198, 201, 205-208, 210-212, 219, 222-224, 227, 230, 246, 249-250, 262, 267-268, 278, 283, 286
innovation 1-3, 7-11, 16-33, 35-37, 39, 41, 43-44, 46, 49-52, 54, 56, 60, 64-68, 70, 79, 82, 84, 90-92, 103-104, 107-116, 118-119, 127, 132, 134-136, 140-145, 149-151, 153-154, 157, 161, 163-166, 168, 172-173, 179-181, 186, 188-189, 191-193, 196-198, 200-201, 204-206, 208-212, 214, 216-221, 224, 226-228, 231, 234-235, 237, 239-241, 243, 247-249, 251-253, 255-262, 264-265, 267-268, 270, 274-276, 278-279, 282-288
innovation economy 28-29, 43, 49, 142, 168, 180, 208-210, 218, 255-256, 258, 260, 268
innovation partnerships 55
innovation supercluster 258, 261
innovation, quadruple helix model 23
institutional idiosyncrasies 7
inter-jurisdictional spillover 136-137
International Monetary Fund (IMF) 6, 13, 24, 32, 128, 131, 154, 228-229, 235, 237
interpersonal relationships 9, 282

K

Kenya 24, 29, 92-93, 197, 211, 224-228, 236, 245-246, 264, 283
Keynesian economics 10, 74, 83, 180, 184
knowledge economy 17-18, 25, 28, 45, 66, 68-69, 71, 118, 240, 256, 268

L

labor markets 110-111, 279
Laffer curve model 223, 237-238
landlocked with bad neighbors 284
Leapfrog 5, 25, 28, 60, 120, 125, 168, 175, 201, 222, 224, 236, 242-244, 249-250, 253, 274, 283, 285
Leapfrogging 14, 28, 168, 169, 171, 281

limited government 6
local communities 2
local ownership 7

M

macroeconomics 6-7, 10, 14, 27, 62-63, 92, 121-122, 142-143, 172, 185, 227, 246, 257, 286
macroeconomy 17
Malabo Declaration on Accelerated Agricultural Growth 262
Mali 4, 211
manufacturing economies 5, 19, 21, 25, 33, 45, 80, 93, 117, 119-123, 125, 128-131, 157-158, 161, 209-210, 239, 243-244, 248, 250, 253, 259-261, 263, 268, 279-281, 284, 286
maritime economy 263
market failures 11, 27, 54, 85, 91, 182, 211
market-oriented economy 6
markets 5, 7, 17, 20, 24-25, 27, 29, 44, 71, 74, 80, 82-85, 89, 103-104, 106-111, 116, 121, 135, 142, 145, 160, 162, 166, 171, 183-185, 188, 191, 195, 208, 210, 239-242, 245, 247-249, 251-252, 256, 262-263, 266, 268, 275, 278-279, 284-285
Marshall Plan 183, 202, 256
marxism 82
Mauritius 24, 58, 234-235, 244, 246, 264
micro-, small, and medium enterprises (MSMEs) 170
microeconomics 63, 100, 179, 185, 257, 282
moral hazard 54
Morocco 14, 24, 29, 246, 263-264
Mozambique 4, 85
multilateralism 6, 63, 104, 221, 234, 281
Multiple Streams Framework (MSF) 42-44, 47, 56-57, 60, 98, 173, 284, 286
multi-stakeholder approach 22, 26, 29, 151, 277
multi-stakeholder development policy 2
municipal solid waste (MSW) management 187

N

National Strategies for Transformation (NST) 277-278, 288
nationalism 4-5, 282
natural resource trap 284
natural resources 108, 143, 157-162, 165, 167, 175, 216, 249, 255, 257, 263, 280, 286
neoclassical economics 9, 77, 79, 192, 247
neo-Keynesianism 184
neoliberalism 2, 6, 54, 108, 121, 123, 183-185, 194, 203
Net Zero 157, 167-168, 172, 177
New Deal for Energy in Africa (NDEA) 170
new institutional economics (NIE) 53-54, 278
New Public Management (NPM) 193-194
Nigeria 13, 24, 61, 92, 121, 123, 132, 134, 144, 146-152, 155, 170, 197, 208, 224-226, 236, 244-245, 264

O

oligopolies 103, 108
open data 20
open government 20

P

Pact for Skills 196, 201
Pan-Africanism 60, 94-95, 97, 100, 127, 284
Pareto Optimality 82, 87
Path Dependence Theory 48, 56, 59
policy capacity 8, 10, 25-26, 30, 32-33, 59, 191, 275-276, 278, 287
policy change 2, 7-8, 30, 35-37, 39-42, 46-48, 50, 52, 60, 63, 66-70, 98, 173, 187, 263, 285
policy diffusion 36-37, 67, 145, 149, 157, 164-165, 168, 173, 197, 205, 208-209, 261, 275-276, 278, 280-281, 284
policy failures 26, 52, 110, 275
policy innovation 1, 3, 7-11, 16, 19, 22-23, 25-27, 29-31, 35, 39, 41, 43-44, 51, 54-56, 60, 64-65, 84, 90-92, 108-111, 113, 116, 119, 127, 134, 136, 142,

144-145, 149-150, 161, 165, 168, 172-173, 179, 181, 188, 191-193, 196-198, 205, 209-212, 214, 216-217, 220-221, 227, 231, 234, 239-241, 247-248, 251, 258-260, 262, 265, 268, 274-276, 278, 282-287
policymaking 8, 22, 26, 31, 35-37, 39-41, 43, 46-48, 55-56, 61, 73, 75, 78, 81-82, 84, 86, 88, 90-94, 103, 127, 141, 163, 173, 247, 263, 275, 285
policy-market 1-2, 9, 17, 26, 198
political economy 1-5, 7-10, 13, 16-17, 27, 29-30, 35, 37-39, 53-54, 56-58, 60, 62, 67, 73-74, 76, 91, 96-97, 99-101, 103, 113-115, 117, 119, 121, 123, 127, 134, 137, 139, 143, 146, 149-150, 166, 173, 176, 180-181, 183, 191, 194, 212-213, 247, 257, 261, 266-267, 275, 282, 284
poverty 2, 6, 12, 18, 26, 28, 49, 57, 61, 63, 73-74, 89, 93, 97, 123-124, 126, 131, 136, 142, 146, 148, 162, 170, 176-177, 200, 218, 227, 231, 236, 238, 242, 247-248, 252, 254, 263, 266-267, 275, 280-281, 283, 288
private sector 1-3, 10, 20, 26, 36, 57, 62, 103, 108, 113-114, 124, 127, 148, 167-169, 172, 179-181, 185-186, 189, 191, 193, 198, 211-213, 215, 218, 226-227, 260, 265, 278
privatization 6, 10, 62-63, 71, 108, 119, 122-123, 162, 180, 185, 194, 203
productivity 17-20, 25, 28, 36, 55, 57-58, 74, 91, 93-94, 96, 108-109, 115-116, 118, 121, 124-127, 135, 141-142, 160-161, 167, 172, 184, 188, 199, 201, 215, 218, 224, 227, 240, 242, 244, 248-249, 255-258, 261-262, 267-268, 277, 280-281, 284, 286
programming framework 2
property rights 11, 13-14, 53-54, 84, 106, 185, 275-276, 286
public goods 5, 11, 27, 72, 113, 137-139, 179, 181-182, 191-192, 194, 211, 222, 275
Public Governance (PG) 193-194
public policy cycle 1, 3, 9
public policy life cycle 16, 23
public sector 3, 5, 12, 26-27, 47, 56, 68, 88, 90, 100, 108, 113, 135, 143, 146, 180, 182, 186, 188-189, 192, 194, 204, 211, 215
public-private partnerships (PPPs) 1, 8, 10, 12, 17, 117, 141, 179-181, 186-189, 191-194, 202-204, 206, 215-216, 256, 258, 275, 277-278, 286
Punctuated Equilibrium Theory (PET) 39-40, 54, 60, 285

R

rainforests 216
regulations 103, 107, 123, 137, 146, 161-162, 193, 212
Rentier Capitalism 104, 108-112, 128
rent-seeking 62, 114, 123, 159, 237, 284
Research and Development 18, 25, 28-29, 45, 50, 67-68, 166, 188-190, 201, 210, 256, 260
Ricardian model 240
risk allocation 11
risk taking 1-2
Rwanda 24, 55, 60, 211, 224, 246, 276-278, 287-288
Rwandan Civil War 60, 277

S

Second Industrial Revolution 45, 118, 130
sectoral dynamics 57
security 1-2, 27, 115, 126-127, 130, 146-147, 163, 177, 182-183, 191, 199, 208, 211-212, 222, 262-263, 269
Senegal 4, 211, 244
service economies 5, 81
service economy 93, 239, 243-244, 284
Seychelles 214-215, 219-220, 264
small and medium-sized enterprises (SME) 19, 142, 165, 167, 172, 201, 241, 249-250, 256, 258-260, 286
social disintegration 141
social institutions 11
Social Security Act 183
socialism 4-5, 82, 280
South Africa 14, 24, 29, 92, 121, 134, 144,

151, 156, 172, 197, 218, 232-233, 237, 246, 264, 267-268, 270-271
Sovereign Blue Bond 214
Soviet Union 5, 200
specialization 67, 140, 244
startup acts 205, 210-211, 220, 249
strategic innovation 20, 22
strategic resources 21, 31
Structural Adjustment Program (SAP) 6, 123-124
structural dynamics 7, 81
sub-Saharan Africa 6, 8, 13-14, 18, 24-25, 120, 124, 126, 128, 132, 163, 169, 175, 224, 254
sustainable development goals (SDG) 162, 175
sustainable energy systems 157, 164, 169

T

Tangier, Morocco 264
Tanzania 4, 24, 85, 92, 170
tax havens 230, 236
tax policy 221-222, 229
taxation 14, 28-29, 104, 136-137, 142, 185, 209-210, 221-223, 226-231, 233-238, 242, 283
technology 2, 10-11, 17, 19-21, 23, 28-33, 48-50, 70, 76, 82, 98, 104-106, 115-116, 118-119, 127, 135, 140-141, 162, 165-166, 168, 172, 189, 199, 203, 206, 208, 210-211, 220, 224, 226, 230, 239-240, 243-245, 247, 249, 252, 255-256, 258-261, 265, 268, 270, 277, 283
theory of convergence 104
Third Industrial Revolution 45, 118
three-sector model 5
tourism 11, 214, 235, 266, 271
trade 5, 7, 11, 14, 28, 33, 50, 53, 61-62, 74, 77, 83, 100, 106, 109, 116-119, 122-125, 128, 130, 132, 140-141, 148, 155, 157, 159, 161-162, 171, 174, 184-185, 200, 207, 213, 221, 230-232, 234, 239-240, 243-251, 254, 258, 263-264, 270, 278, 280-281, 284-285
tragedy of the commons 54
transaction costs 2, 10-11, 19-20, 27, 44, 53-54, 188, 240, 243, 275-276, 278
Transformation for Shared Prosperity and Improved Livelihoods 262

U

Ubuntu 2, 9-10, 124, 139, 282
Ujamaa 9, 282
unemployment 6, 75, 195, 202
United Nations 7, 14, 28, 33, 41, 92, 97, 105-106, 115, 117, 131-132, 140, 155, 161-162, 168, 175, 177, 184, 220, 222, 229, 237-238, 245, 251, 254, 262, 277
United Nations Economic Commission for Africa (UNECA) 132, 231, 246
United States 152-153, 167, 169, 177, 195, 224, 287
urbanization 19, 80, 105-106, 211, 216, 247, 249, 255, 262, 278, 283

V

venture capital 29, 60, 168, 196-197, 205, 208-211, 219, 240, 285
vertical fiscal imbalances 136-137

W

Wagner Act 183
Washington Consensus 5-6, 13-14, 54, 184-186, 202, 285
Washington Consensus framework 5-6, 13-14, 54, 184-186, 202, 285
welfare state 10, 180
World Bank 3, 6, 8, 13-14, 33, 104, 115-116, 123, 126, 128-130, 132, 146-147, 153-155, 160, 168, 175-177, 186-187, 192, 201-204, 213-217, 220, 236-237, 242, 248, 251-252, 254, 265-266, 271-272, 277-278, 280, 286, 288
World Intellectual Property Organization (WIPO) 24, 31
World War I 118, 183
World War II 10, 180, 183-184

Z

Zambia 4, 24, 92, 232

www.ingramcontent.com/pod-product-compliance
Lightning Source LLC
LaVergne TN
LVHW061542290926
849162LV00004B/880